D1329563

BETWEEN STAGE AND SCREEN
INGMAR BERGMAN DIRECTS

FILM CULTURE IN TRANSITION

Thomas Elsaesser: General Editor

Double Trouble
Chiem van Houweninge on Writing and Filming
> *Thomas Elsaesser, Robert Kievit and Jan Simons (eds.)*

Writing for the Medium
> *Thomas Elsaesser, Jan Simons and Lucette Bronk (eds.)*

The Film Spectator: From Sign to Mind
> *Warren Buckland (ed.)*

Film and the First World War
> *Karel Dibbets, Bert Hogenkamp (eds.)*

Fassbinder's Germany
> *Thomas Elsaesser*
> (summer 1995)

BETWEEN STAGE AND SCREEN
INGMAR BERGMAN DIRECTS

by

EGIL TÖRNQVIST

AMSTERDAM UNIVERSITY PRESS

Cover (front): Alexander, Ingmar Bergman's alter ego in *Fanny and Alexander*, behind his puppet theater, copied on the Royal Theater in Copenhagen. The Danish inscription above the proscenium opening means "not only for pleasure." Photo Arne Carlsson.
Cover (back): Ingmar Bergman directing his last feature film, *Fanny and Alexander*. Photo Arne Carlsson.

Cover design: Kok Korpershoek (KO), Amsterdam
Typesetting: A-zet, Leiden

ISBN 90 5356 137 4 (paperback)
ISBN 90 5356 171 4 (hardbound)

© Amsterdam University Press, Amsterdam, 1995

All rights reserved. Without limiting the rights under copyright reserved above, no part of this publication may be reproduced, stored in or introduced into a retrieval system, or transmitted, in any form or by any means (electronic, mechanical, photocopying, recording or otherwise), without the prior written permission of both the copyright owner and the auhor of this book.

CONTENTS

PREFACE

The present book is not an examination of how Bergman's stage, screen and radio productions have come into being, of the director's work in the rehearsal room, the sound studio, the cutting room. It is rather an examination of the results of this work. After all, Bergman's profile as a director is determined first and foremost by the completed productions, irrespective of how he has arrived at them. In my analysis of these end products, I combine more general aspects with close 'readings' of individual, often transcribed passages, since such a procedure in my view gives the reader optimal insights into Bergman's directorial distinction. The 15 production analyses are framed by a Prologue, in which Bergman's work as a director for different media and the problems involved are presented, and an Epilogue, where formal and thematic correspondences and differences between Bergman's stage, screen and radio productions are examined and where an evaluation of the stage/screen relationship is attempted.

Quotations from Ibsen, Strindberg and Bergman are rendered in American translation; whenever British translations are quoted, they have been adjusted to American norms. When the target text deviates so much from the source text that it no longer seems wholly adequate for my purpose, I have resorted to a variant of my own.

With regard to the use of tense, the principle followed is to use the present tense for durative (repeatable) presentational modes, while the past tense is used for non-durative modes (except in transcriptions). The existence of a durative recording of a stage presentation, in the form of video, cannot change the fundamental fact that it was intended as live performance, that is, as a non-repeatable theatrical event.

The typography of drama texts and film scripts varies somewhat. Since such variation seems both irrelevant and disturbing, I have deemed it wise to standardize the typography as follows:

(1) For stage and acting directions, I use italics throughout. The same principle is applied in my transcriptions of performance passages.

(2) Figure designations in the stage and acting directions as well as cue designations are capitalized and printed in roman.

Titles of non-English works are given in American translation; the original titles and, with regard to some Bergman films, British variants are added in the index. The dates of the films are those of first public screenings. Single quotation marks signify that a word or phrase is used figuratively.

A substantial part of this book has appeared earlier in various publications. The chapter on *The Ghost Sonata* is based on *Bergman och Strindberg: Spöksonaten – drama och iscensättning. Dramaten 1973*, Stockholm: Prisma, 1973. The section on *Miss Julie* relies on the discussion in *Strindberg's* Miss Julie: *A Play and Its Transpositions*, Norwich: Norvik Press, 1988. The examination of *Long Day's Journey into Night* appeared under the title "Ingmar Bergman Directs *Long Day's Journey into Night*" in *New Theatre Quarterly*, Vol. V, No. 20 (1989). The chapter on *A Doll's House* was first published as "Ingmar Bergman's *Doll's Houses*" in *Scandinavica*, Vol. 30, No. 1 (May, 1991). All of Part Two and sections of the Prologue and Epilogue were published in *Filmdiktaren Ingmar Bergman*, Stockholm: Arena, 1993. The chapter on *Stormy Weather* appeared under the title "Long Day's Journey into Night: Bergman's TV Version of 'Oväder' Compared to 'Smultronstället'" in Kela Kvam (ed.), *Strindberg's Post-Inferno Plays*, Copenhagen, 1994. The chapter on *Fanny and Alexander* first appeared in *Chaplin*, Vol. 25, No. 6 (1983), under the title "Den lilla världen och den stora: Kring Ingmar Bergmans *Fanny och Alexander*." All these publications have been thoroughly revised for the present book.

For invaluable assistance I wish to thank scenographer Gunilla Palmstierna-Weiss as well as the staff of the Royal Dramatic Theater, the National Archive of Recorded Sound and Moving Images, the Swedish Institute, and the Swedish Film Institute, all in Stockholm.

PROLOGUE

The Stage and the Screen

With his fifty feature films, around a hundred stage performances, some forty radio versions, about fifteen television transmissions, a few opera productions, and even a libretto contribution to a ballet – not to mention his work as a playwright, screenwriter, and adaptor – Ingmar Bergman has presumably proved more productive and versatile than any other director to date.

A Sunday child, born into a clerical Stockholm family on the French national holiday in the year ending the first World War, Bergman at an early age – as shown in *Fanny and Alexander* – was a 'director' already in the nursery. There he staged plays in his puppet theater and made up 'film' stories with the help of his *laterna magica*. When only 17 he wrote his first play; in the 1940s some twenty-three others were to follow, a few of which were published and staged.[1] His debut as a director, in the proper sense of the word, took place in 1938 when, at the age of 20, he staged Sutton Vane's *Outward Bound* with an amateur group at Mäster Olofsgården in Stockholm, himself playing one of the roles.[2] Still staging at least two plays a year, Bergman, soon 77, has declared that he will probably continue directing in the theater as long as he has the strength to do so.

For almost four decades Bergman has, in conformance with the Swedish system, divided his time between stage productions in the theater season and filming in the summertime, when the actors were available. To a great extent he has worked with the same actors in all three media under consideration here: Max von Sydow, Anders Ek, Allan Edwall, Bibi Andersson, Gunnel Lindblom, Gertrud Fridh, to mention but a few. In several cases – Birger Malmsten, Gunnar Björnstrand, Eva Dahlbeck, Maj-Britt Nilsson, Harriet Andersson, and Ingrid Thulin come to mind – there are actors who have largely appeared in his films, while the opposite (Benkt-Åke Benktsson, Karin Kavli, Toivo Pawlo) also, though more rarely, holds true. It has become a truism to say that Bergman's achievements on stage and screen are inseparably related to his long-standing close connections with a group of outstanding actors and actresses and the inspiration he receives from and gives to them.[3]

After his first screenplay, *Torment*, had been filmed by Alf Sjöberg, Bergman's career as a film director began in 1946 with *Crisis*, based on his own adaptation of a Danish play. This part of his career ended in 1982, with *Fanny and Alexander*, when he decided to stop filming because of the physical strain it involved. Most of Bergman's radio productions were done in the late 1940s and in the 1950s. His debut as a TV director came in 1954, with Hjalmar Bergman's *Mr. Sleeman Is Coming*.

Unlike novels or poems, plays lead a double life. Having two kinds of recipients – readers and spectators – drama is a hybrid genre. With an increasing number of film scripts being published, film is gradually moving in the same direction. It has not always been like that. For a rather long time, films had only one kind of recipient: the spectator. The script on which the film was based was rarely published. While you could choose between reading or watching Shakespeare, Ibsen, or Strindberg, you had to be content with watching Griffith, Eisenstein, or Sjöström. Only when a director based his film on a published novel or play, could you as reader acquaint yourself with a text that had some connection with the film in question. Even now the publication of a film script is a sign that we are dealing with an artistic product.

Film is an international medium, theater a national one. As a film director Bergman is world-famous; as a stage director he is little known outside his own country. Even if a production by the Royal Dramatic Theater in Stockholm, directed by Ingmar Bergman, may be seen nowadays in London, Paris, New York, Amsterdam, Madrid and Rome, the audience attending it will be very limited compared with the audience attending his films. Besides, unlike the film audience, the theater audience will either listen to a language they do not understand, or will be provided with simultaneous interpretation via earphones, which is an unsatisfactory solution of the language problem, since it prevents a proper reception of the paralinguistics of the performance, the *way* in which the speeches are enunciated.

As Bergman himself has pointed out, there is a close connection between his work for the stage and for the screen. In 1963 he declared:

> My films are only a distillation of what I do in the theater. Theater work is sixty percent.... Not even considering the connection between *The Seventh Seal* and my production of *Ur-Faust* (although they came about in the reverse order). Not even considering the connection between *The Face* [*The Magician* in the U.S.] and my production of *Six Characters in Search of an Author* in Malmö.[4]

Bergman here seems to indicate that his work in the theater – the contact with outstanding drama texts – has inspired him to pursue certain ideological, thematic, and formal patterns within the film medium.

In a statement made seven years later, he says: "Between my job at the theater and my job in the film studio it has always been a very short step indeed. Sometimes it has paid off, and sometimes it has been a drawback. But it has always been a short step between."[5] Some of the films, he points out, have even been "surreptitious plays."[6] Even in the mid-1950s, he remarks, "there was a frustrated dramatist in me. I wrote stage plays for the screen in those days, because the theater seemed closed to me."[7] It is noteworthy in this connection that the film *The Seventh Seal* grew out of the play *Wood Painting*; that, conversely, the film *Torment* and the TV series *Scenes from a Marriage* were transposed for the stage; and that films like *Smiles of a Summer Night*, *Brink of Life*, *The Silence* and *Autumn Sonata* without any drastic changes could be turned into stage plays.

Bergman's films deal with themes that have sometimes been regarded as typically Swedish: loneliness, lack of communication, somberness.[8] Although there may be some truth in this, "the question is not so much how 'Swedish' Bergman's movies are, but to what extent they have colored our perception of what is Swedish."[9] Besides, the characteristics just mentioned are not unequivocally Swedish. The international aspect of Bergman's films has certainly less to do with northern exoticism than with the universality of his pervading themes: the relationship between good and evil, dream and reality, art and life, mask and face, men and women, adults and children, conscious and unconscious. And though some of them – the recurrent theme of humiliation, the 'ideological' significance of music – carry a more individual signature, there is nothing Swedish about them. In fact, Bergman's metaphysical and psychological rather than political and social concerns seem fairly removed from what one might see as characteristic Swedish qualities. It is, then, not surprising that many of his films have had a greater success abroad than in his native country. This is not saying, of course, that Swedish nature and culture have not been of enormous importance to Bergman, who has often declared that he constantly revisits his childhood.

Of particular interest in our context, considering Bergman's profession, is his depiction of the relationship between theater and life. In his work, the theater – this protected home of dreams – frequently becomes a metaphor for this world of illusions. The theater family in *Fanny and Alexander* is named Ekdahl in recognition of the fact that, like Ibsen's Ekdal family in *The Wild Duck*, they live by illusions. The illusion is loved and hated simultaneously or alternately. Emilie Ekdahl's exit from the theater and return to it (she has a predecessor in Elisabet Vogler in *Persona*) is paradigmatic for the ambivalent attitude to the house of dreams – to illusion – characteristic of many Bergman figures as well as of their originator.[10]

Bergman's continuous work as a stage director means that for long periods he has been living almost daily with a particular play in heart and mind. Many of these plays have left traces in the films. This is, of course, especially true of the plays that have meant the most to him, ones that he has staged several times: Shakespeare's *Macbeth*, Molière's *Don Juan* and *The Misanthrope*, Ibsen's *Peer Gynt*, *A Doll's House*, and *Hedda Gabler*, Strindberg's *Miss Julie*, *A Dream Play*, and *The Ghost Sonata*, Pirandello's *Six Charac-*

ters in Search of an Author. There is much to be said for the view that "no other film director after the breakthrough of the sound film has been so influenced by the theater."[11]

Molière, Ibsen, Strindberg and, later, Shakespeare are dramatists he has frequently returned to. Of these, Strindberg holds a special place. "My household gods," Bergman points out, "were Strindberg, whom I began to consume already when I was twelve, and Hjalmar Bergman, whom I discovered a few years later."[12] Strindberg "expressed things which I'd experienced and which I couldn't find words for."[13] This statement seems to imply that a major reason why Bergman turned to directing fairly early on was that as a director he could express audiovisually what he was unable to express verbally.

Characteristic of Strindberg as a playwright is his endeavor to engage his audience emotionally. Bergman likewise admonishes his theater audience: "It is in your hearts, in your imagination that this performance is to take place."[14] He expresses the same view when speaking, in connection with his films, of the importance to "faire communiquer le public, de le faire participer," and when he praises black-and-white film because it gives the spectator the opportunity to "voir les couleurs" in his or her own imagination.[15] In his plays Strindberg functions as a hypnotizer. The theater becomes a weapon directed towards our emotional life. The same is true of Bergman, whose stage and screen productions in this respect belong to Strindberg's extreme form of Aristotelian theater. The film medium is here supportive, for "no form of art goes beyond ordinary consciousness as film does, straight to our emotions, deep into the twilight room of the soul."[16] As a film director, via his magic lantern, Bergman has had better possibilities to hypnotize his audience than as a theater director – or as a playwright.

With the first part of his trilogy *To Damascus*, Strindberg in 1898 created the first subjective drama in world literature. An overwhelming part of this play is a projection of the protagonist's, the Stranger's, thoughts and emotions. *His* experience of the surrounding world becomes *our* experience. The border between objective and subjective is blotted out. The varying locations and weather conditions represent above all inner realities. The same is true of many Bergman films. The barren island in *Through a Glass Darkly* stands for a feeling of isolation, the frosty, gray November landscape in *Winter Light* for emotional chill, and so on. In *To Damascus*, as in Strindberg's dream plays generally, there is a diffuse borderline between dream and reality, resulting in a feeling that life is a dream. This diffuseness is characteristic also of Bergman's work, which is in other respects very lucid. It is in fact a key to it.

Scenes of unmasking often appear in Strindberg's work. The most explicit one is found in the second act of *The Ghost Sonata*, where the Old Man, Hummel, unmasks the Colonel; later, when the guests begin to arrive for the ghost supper, he declares: "You keep calm and we'll continue to play our old roles a while longer." The focal scene in a Bergman production is often one of unmasking. After this scene, the characters resume their roles and hide behind their social masks. Vampirism is another frequent theme with Strindberg, appearing in several Bergman films, notably in *Persona* and *The Hour of the Wolf*.

In the literature, drama and film of the twentieth century, man's inability to communicate with his fellows in any deeper sense is a constantly recurring theme. One of the possible means of communication is language. As a stage and screen director, Bergman distrusts language as a means of establishing contact. On the contrary, he maintains, language is normally used to build walls between people behind which they may hide.[17] This idea, which echoes the Old Man's claim in *The Ghost Sonata* that the different languages have been invented in order to hide the secrets of the tribe, seems to underlie the enigmatic words on the blackboard in the exam scene of *Wild Strawberries*, later developed in *The Silence*, where the three main characters are confronted with a language, created by Bergman and unintelligible both to them and to us. The inability to understand each other's language becomes a metaphor for the inability to understand one another generally. While Anna in *The Silence* tries to communicate by means of her senses, the unintelligible language becomes an admonition to Ester. Her job as a translator is an adequate symbol of her search for verbal communication. She is akin to the Student in *The Ghost Sonata*. Like him, Ester is a seeker who tries to decipher the meaning of life. But in contrast to her, the Student is clairvoyant. His true counterparts in Bergman's films are the young ones, the children. Their purity and openness contrast with the constant role-playing of the adults. This is true of Minus in *Through a Glass Darkly*, of Johan in *The Silence* and of Fanny and Alexander in the film of that name.

The search of Bergman's protagonists is often expressed in the form of a journey. Just as in Strindberg's post-Inferno plays, the journey here plays an important thematic and structural role, functioning as "a catalyst for the conflict between the present and the past, between imagined and real values."[18] It can be a train journey, returning the characters to an environment they have left behind them, as in *Three Strange Loves*, or a voyage in remembrance of things past, as in *Illicit Interlude*. In *The Seventh Seal* we accompany Antonius Block on his way to his waiting wife – and to death. Similarly, we accompany Isak Borg in *Wild Strawberries* on his presumably last journey, from Stockholm to Lund. In *Winter Light* we journey with Tomas, the doubting clergyman, from one church to another. When Bergman once, speaking of this film, declared that "everything became stations on the road for the priest," he indicated not only the connection with Christ's way to Calvary but also the connection with Strindberg's dramas of penance.

Bergman has rightly been called the most energetic pursuer of the Strindbergian chamber play.[19] Although the term 'chamber play' in the first place has a spatial meaning, Strindberg gave it a generic status. In his *Memorandum to the Members of the Intimate Theater* he writes:

> ... in drama we seek the strong, highly significant motif, but with limitations. We try to avoid in the treatment all frivolity, all calculated effects, places for applause, star roles, solo numbers. No predetermined form is to limit the author, because the motif determines the form. Consequently: freedom in treatment, which is limited only by the unity of the concept and the feeling for style.[20]

But the term 'chamber play' relates also to music. In his *Memorandum* Strindberg speaks of "the concept of chamber music transferred to drama. The intimate action, the highly significant motif, the sophisticated treatment."[21]

Bergman has borrowed the term from Strindberg:

> *Through a Glass Darkly* and *Winter Light* and *The Silence* and *Persona* I've called chamber plays. They are chamber music – music in which, with an extremely limited number of voices and figures, one explores the essence of a number of motifs. The backgrounds are extrapolated, put into a sort of fog. The rest is a distillation.[22]

The Ghost Sonata ends with a 'coda,' a swift recapitulation of earlier themes and an execution: the faith in a benevolent God which is the prerequisite for the Student's intercession for the Young Lady. In the same way, *Through a Glass Darkly* ends with a 'divine proof' – the idea that God is love – and this forms, says Bergman, "the actual *coda* in the last movement."[23] Just as Strindberg calls *Master Olof* and *A Dream Play* symphonies, so Bergman calls *The Seventh Seal* "an oratorio."[24] And just as *The Ghost Sonata* by its very title implies a relationship with the sonata form, so the title *Autumn Sonata* has the same implication. With his chamber plays, Strindberg has renewed drama. By applying Strindberg's idea to film, Bergman has renewed film art.

Olof Molander, the leading Swedish stage director in the 1930s and 1940s, especially renowned for his Strindberg productions, has acted as an important mediator between Strindberg and Bergman. In the program for his 1945 performance of Strindberg's *The Pelican*, Bergman clearly stated his indebtedness to Molander, who has made us see the magic in Strindberg's dramaturgy. ... [He] gives us Strindberg without embellishments or directorial visions, tunes in to the text, and leaves it at that. He makes us hear the poet's anxiety-driven fever pulse. ... We listen to a strange, muted chamber music. ...

First it was *A Dream Play*. Night after night I stood in the wings and sobbed and never really knew why. After that came *To Damascus*, *Saga of the Folkungs*, and *The Ghost Sonata*. It is the sort of thing you never forget and never leave behind, especially [not] if you happen to be a director....[25]

Opposing the idea of a director's theater, Bergman here implicitly characterizes his own ambition to be a humble elucidator of the play text, loyal to the spirit, if not to the letter, of it. Since the demarcation line between letter and spirit is unclear, it is often difficult to determine to what extent Bergman's stage adaptations of drama texts have affected one or the other. Unwilling to compromise with his own vision, he changed the opening and ending of Tennessee Williams' *The Rose Tattoo*, minor parts were cut, and the collective scenes were omitted. In Strindberg's *The Crown Bride*, he left out most of the folkloristic passages and the ghostly ingredients, while in *Erik XIV*, by the same author, he added a court jester, appearing in the history books but not in the play text.[26] Bergman's versions of Strindberg's so-called post-Inferno plays have proved especially controversial in this respect. Strindberg's faith in a life hereafter that would justify the misery of this life is not shared by Bergman, who from the early 1960s has stressed his belief in human love as the only salvation for the single life granted us. While Bergman's productions of these plays have nevertheless been convincing, it is not because he has been true to their spirit but because he has been able to transubstantiate the texts in such a way that his own vision has come to penetrate them. The subtitle given to the published version of his 1970 production of Strindberg's *Dream Play* – "an interpretation by Ingmar Bergman" – adequately summarizes his own very distinctive contribution to the plays he is directing.

If the relationship between drama text and performance is complicated, the one between script and film is hardly less so.[27] While many of Bergman's early film scripts are unpublished, nearly all scripts beginning with *Through a Glass Darkly* (1961) have been published both in Swedish and in English translation. Owing to Bergman's dissatisfaction with the Swedish critics in the 1950s, who often complained about his clumsy language, some of the early scripts have been published only in translation; this concerns such significant films as *Smiles of a Summer Night*, *The Seventh Seal*, *Wild Strawberries* and *The Magician*.

Other circumstances further complicate the matter. Thus scripts for some of Bergman's early films have been written by others. Moreover, Bergman has changed his attitude to the relationship between script and film. In 1961 he could still embrace the principle of faithfulness:

> Don't leave your script in the lurch in the middle of shooting. Be faithful to what you wrote, even if now, here in the studio, you think it represents a bygone phase. Don't meddle with the unity it had *then*. That sort of thing is dangerous from both an artistic and a practical production point of view. If you want to record new results, then wait until the next film.[28]

Five years later he took a very different view, seeing now the script as "a very imperfect *technical* basis for a film."[29] And in 1969 he declared that

> The script is nothing but a collection of motifs which I work over with my actors as the filming proceeds. The final decisions I make in the cutting room, where I cut away all obtrusive elements.[30]

In 1976 he was so negative about film scripts that we may wonder why he chose to publish the scripts at all:

> It is hard to write a screenplay.... The words can never express what the finished film wants to convey. ... a filmscript is always a half-finished product, a pale and uncertain reflection.[31]

In 1987 his faith in the script seemed somewhat restored:

> The rhythm in my films is conceived in the script, at the desk, and is then given birth in front of the camera. All forms of improvisation are alien to me.[32]

It is hard to see how the rhythm of an audiovisual medium could to any significant degree be caught in a textual medium. On the contrary, the cutting continuity of an average film, containing hundreds of shots, would reveal that the rhythm is necessarily very different from that indicated by the script. In Bergman's case rhythmical discrepancies may also arise from monologues in the script being turned into dialogues in the film or subsequent sequences in the script being turned into simultaneous, cross-cut episodes in the film.

As a matter of fact, by his own admission Bergman's scripts have often lacked a clear orientation toward a specific medium. The dialogues in his most recent book, *The Fifth Act*, were written, he says, "the way I have written for the last fifty years – it looks like theater but might as well be film, television or merely reading matter."[33]

As Bergman himself indicates, the discrepancy between script and film tends to be greater in the late films than in the early ones. In these films, many situations in the scripts are omitted, while, conversely, they contain much that does not appear in the scripts. In this respect the scripts of these films are comparable to drama texts, where the stage directions merely register a fraction of the audiovisual elements of a performance. The appearance of ingredients in the scripts that cannot be realized in films (smells, colors in relation to black-and-white film, etc.) also demonstrates that such ingredients are more indicative than prescriptive.[34] Well aware of this, Bergman refers to his published scripts as "film stories." The label suggests that we deal with something that can be read by itself, something that has deliberately been made friendly to the reader. Another complicating factor is that even one and the same film will show national differences. A Bergman film without subtitles differs from a subtitled version, and this again from a dubbed version. It can even differ in width and length, whether because Bergman himself has produced two different versions – as in the case of *Face to Face* and *Fanny and Alexander* – or because film censorship has demanded certain cuts, cuts which may differ from one country to another. The situation of reception, finally, may vary considerably. A Bergman film in a large cinema with perfect audiovisual equipment is rather different from a Bergman film on television.

As a result of these complicated circumstances (with regard to production, distribution and reception), the literature about Bergman's films – there are still very few works devoted to his work in the theater – has become rather heterogeneous. While most analyses seem founded primarily on a reading of the published scripts, some of them are based – as are the film reviews – mainly or exclusively on a viewing of the films. (The intermediate stage – Bergman's own director's copies – are still, if at all preserved, a missing link.) As a result, different presentational modes (one textual, the other audiovisual) and different stages in the creative process (a semi-product as compared with a finished product) are indiscriminately brought together under the same common label: the name of the film. There is, after all, a considerable distance between, say, an analysis of an original Bergman film and an analysis of a translation of a Bergman script. It is still an open question what influence defective translations and subtitles/dubbing have had on the international Bergman criticism.

The differences between script and film may concern the characters' actions: in the script of *Through a Glass Darkly*, David burns the manuscript of his novel; in the film he does not. They may involve the place of action: in the script of *Autumn Sonata* Eva is seen in the churchyard, where her little son Erik is buried, together with her mother Charlotte, while at the end she is alone, somewhere out of doors; in the film their conversation takes place in Erik's room, while the location at the end is the churchyard. The differences may concern the time when a piece of information is given: the spectator of *Winter Light* immediately sees that Märta Lundberg, the Christ figure in the film, wears a furcoat made of sheepskin; the reader of the script learns this much later. The textual medium is often more explicit than the audiovisual one. When it says in the script of *Cries and Whispers* that *"the sun breaks out like shimmering horizontal spear points,"* the enmity of the sunlight is more obvious to the reader than to the spectator.

Why then bother with the scripts? Is it not the finished product that matters? In the choice between script and film, the latter must obviously have priority. But just as it is natural to analyze a stage performance with a certain consideration for the drama text on which it is based, it is legitimate to analyze a film with regard to the script functioning as a blueprint for it. In both cases there are ingredients which in one form or another – by elucidations or divergences – illuminate the final product.

What distinguishes the significant stage and/or screen director is his or her ability to create images which communicate something that is difficult or even impossible to express in words. This something is frequently of a metaphoric nature. Naturally, some images in a Bergman stage or screen performance are more complex than others. Also, some passages are richer in metaphors than others. The borders are fluid and highly dependent on the interpretative imagination of the recipient. Thus, a grouping may become expressive when combined with what is, has been or will be said, a costume when combined with another one. A face may take on a new meaning when lit in a different way or, in screen versions, when seen at a different distance or angle. A dissolve may seem significant when regarded in its thematic context. In all these cases we deal with visual imagery. The same is true of acoustics. A sound may become significant through striking changes, through repetition, or even through sudden absence. Or it may become so because of a suggestive concurrence or contrast between sound and image.

Since both theater and film make use of words, sounds, and visual images, it is possible to distinguish between verbal, acoustic, and visual imagery. In combination, the three types create – in the imagination of the spectator – a metaphoric network of considerable complexity and power. (In radio drama, the visual component is relegated to the recipient's imagination, which in fact makes it very powerful.)[35] In the following chapters we shall see how this is done in some of Bergman's most successful stage, screen, and radio presentations.

PART 1

THE STAGE DIRECTOR

Strindberg, *The Dream Play* (1970)

With his pioneering *Dream Play* (1902),[1] Strindberg set the tone for the non-Aristotelian drama to come. Loosely imitating the form of a dream to evoke the feeling that life is a dream, the traditional division of acts and scenes is lacking. For the same reason, there is no list of *dramatis personae*.

The play describes how Indra's Daughter descends to the Castle of Earth, where she is reincarnated as Agnes. Gradually, she is made aware of human misery. The nadir is reached in the middle of the play, where she experiences the most intimate kind of human relationship – marriage – as imprisonment. She now longs for freedom. At the end she returns to heaven.

Reputedly the daughter of an Indian god, Agnes is an *agnus dei*, a female Jesus. Being a divine creature, she is by definition different from all the other characters in the play. This is indicated not least by the alienating third-person form of her recurrent "Det är synd om människorna," a phrase meaning not only "Human beings are to be pitied" but also "Human beings are rooted in sin." In the early part of the play the former meaning prevails, but gradually the latter gains ground.

Together with the Mother and the Doorkeeper, the Daughter forms a female trio advocating acceptance of life, while the three prominent men in the play (the Officer, the Lawyer and the Poet) refuse to accept life as an inexplicable vale of tears. Everyone wonders what is behind the mysterious door, that is, what the meaning of life may be. The conflict between (Oriental) acceptance and (Occidental) rejection is never completely resolved. Yet the notion that mankind suffers meaninglessly is gradually overruled by the Schopenhauerian idea that there is a higher meaning in suffering.

Strindberg indicates the fluid, dreamy nature of the play by letting various properties take on a new look when they become part of a new setting. Apart from being dreamy 'dissolves,' these transformations serve to evoke a feeling that we cannot trust our senses and that human understanding is limited. This is explicitly demonstrated in the three visions of the second cave scene, where the Poet imagines that he sees a ship, then decides that it is a house or a tower until, finally, he discovers that it is a church. Gradually, his eyesight improves. Similarly, Strindberg's arrangement of scenery and properties time and again remind us that *our* imperfect eyesight gradually improves, as when we discover that the earthly paradise called Fairhaven is not Paradise, or that the four-leaf clover (representing luck, worldly success) found in the door in the theater corridor, when appearing in the door leading to the sacristy is actually a (Greek) cross, that is, the symbol of suffering and altruistic love. Similarly, the Officer's bouquet of red roses gradually turns into the Lawyer's *"crown of thorns."* Vicarious suffering is the meaning of life.

Bergman's first production of *A Dream Play* – he has by now produced it four times – was transmitted on May 2, 1963. With its 28 scenes and 36 actors and actresses, it was the largest production undertaken so far by Swedish television.[2] Although on the whole it was well received, Bergman found it in retrospect a bit of a failure. "The Swedish TV version had come to grief owing to technical disasters (video tapes couldn't even be edited in those days)."[3] When compared to his second, stage production seven years later, most critics found that

> the dreamy nature [of the play] was managed better on the stage. Why? Was it because color television had not yet started in Sweden? Or because the many close-ups of faces reduced the possibilities for suggestion via the scenography? Because the electronic cameras needed so much light that it was difficult to bring about chiaroscuro?[4]

Bergman's TV version, in black-and-white, opens with a quotation from Strindberg's Explanatory Note to the play superimposed on the face of the author. The face dissolves into a cloud. In the next shot Indra's Daughter is seen approaching a barred gate. She opens it and enters the Prison – rather than the Castle – of Life. Substituting Strindberg, as it were, for Indra and abstaining from the author's *Prolog im Himmel*, Bergman immediately clarifies that his performance is not an 'objective,' divine report about the sad state of mankind but a subjective dream on the part of the author, whose alter ego is the Poet in the play – as indicated especially at the end where the opening is reversed. The Poet here enters a cloud which dissolves into an extreme close-up of Strindberg's face.

Who is the dreamer of the play?[5] The most natural answer to this question would be: the recipient. Bergman preferred to make the author the dreamer – disregarding the fact that his production deviates from Strindberg's text in other ways than in just this respect. To put it differently: in his TV performance Bergman indicated that Strindberg is the dreamer of a version that he himself, as director, had fashioned to a great extent. The idea of the author as the dreamer of the play was to return in Bergman's first stage production of the play but this time with the Poet in the play as the dreamer and creator of it.

The scene shifts, which have contributed to the view that *A Dream Play* is more cinematic than theatrical, have always proved a problem to stage directors. Characteristically, it took an outstanding film director like Bergman to overcome this problem.

In his second production of the play, opening on March 14, 1970, at the Small Stage, seating 350, of the Royal Dramatic Theater in Stockholm (usually called Dramaten) Bergman settled for an extremely simple permanent setting with a minimum of properties – as he had done in his TV performance. In this way very swift and smooth scene changes could be brought about.

Advertized as *The Dream Play*, Bergman's "interpretation," published three years after the performance,[6] retained the number of scenes (15) that can be distilled out of Strindberg's play.[7] The dialogue was condensed; a number of references to Oriental religion, considered of little relevance to a modern Western audience, were omitted. The dialogue was somewhat rearranged; thus the opening and the closing speeches were given to the Poet rather than to Indra's Daughter. The omissions and the swift scene changes resulted in a performance lasting about 45 minutes less than what is normally the case.

During the whole performance a table (the Poet's writing-desk) was seen in the same fixed position. For the various scenes temporary screens and a few pieces of furniture were added. An evenly distributed, grayish light fell across the stage most of the time, indicative of the somber everyday mood pertaining to this shadowy world.

Remaining on the stage throughout, Bergman's Poet (Georg Årlin), in black, replaced Strindberg's Indra's Daughter as the character witnessing the various scenes, like her more of an observer than someone involved in the action, sometimes sitting at his desk, sometimes hiding himself under it, constantly eavesdropping on his characters, occasionally reading from his own script. At the same time, Bergman's Poet, being the dreamer of the play, was the shaper of the action and the characters. In this capacity he could be seen not only as the author but also as the director of the play, a Strindbergman. In the figure of the Poet, Strindberg's collocation of reality, dreams, and poetry were made one flesh.

By contrast, Indra's Daughter was split in two: the divine Daughter (Kristina Adolphson) and the earthly Agnes (Malin Ek). The Daughter appeared in a long white robe with a mantle attached to it, whereas Agnes wore a simple blue or gray dress with a white collar, completely unadorned, a weak – and representative – member of mankind, deprived of the possibility to return to a consoling celestial origin.

The performance opened not up in Heaven, as with Strindberg, but down on Earth, with a symbolic situation. In the gray light the characters gathered on the empty stage like shadows, then began a treadmill walk to the sound of a barrel organ – a period instrument favored by Bergman. The opening scene, a critic said, was "a metaphysical image of mankind's shadowy wandering in the wilderness."[8] Suddenly the movement was frozen in the middle of a step – as in a film – and the play proper began.

From the very beginning the meta-aspect of the production was made clear. Sitting at his writing-desk, the Poet whispered the first lines to Agnes and the Glazier, which they then repeated aloud – a very concrete way of illustrating the transference of written into spoken words, of drama text into live performance.

In Bergman's 1970 *Dream Play* production, the Poet and Agnes, in the foreground, were separated from their ideal counterparts, the Scald and the Daughter, who appeared on a raised stage in the background in front of Lennart Mörk's nonfigurative design.

The Prologue was partly included, but it did not open the play. Instead, it was placed at the beginning of Scene 4, labeled "The Theater." Moreover, Indra (here called the Scald) and his Daughter, far from appearing alone in Heaven, appeared on a small elevated platform at the back of the stage, where they were observed by a stage audience (humanity), including the Poet and Agnes. Instead of Strindberg's celestial reality, the audience was confronted with the world of theatrical illusion, indicated also by the fact that the Scald and his Daughter were applauded for their 'theatrical performance.' Strindberg's independent divinities were transformed into products of the human brain, theatrical inventions, poetic fantasies.

In Bergman's version of the degree ceremony (in the church scene), three extras incarnated an altar piece visualizing the Crucifixion. The pretentious immaturity of the academic world was indicated by having children dressed up in tails and Swedish student caps. Accompanied by Chopin's Funeral March – borrowed from Olof Molander's *Dream Play* productions – the Officer (Holger Löwenadler) and the Lawyer (Allan Edwall) entered to receive the symbols of their doctor's degrees:

> Entering this bizarre scene, the Lawyer ... found himself literally trapped in a nightmarishly logical Chaplinade from which he could not extricate himself. This "terribly ugly, unsuccessful, embittered character in an old tailcoat, whiny with use, that hangs around his shoulders," (Zern) stumbled onto the stage, bowed to the assembly – and then discovered that he was still wearing his galoshes. Desperately, he tried to unbuckle and remove them – only to be assaulted by the foul smell of his wretched old coat, heavy as all his clothes are with "the stink of other men's crimes." Quickly the sniffing spread; soon everyone present was holding his nose. In his mortification the Lawyer then tried to remove the offending coat – with the result that his trousers fell down, and he was reduced to the ultimate indignity of hopping about, unable to pull them up again.[9]

In this nightmarish "Chaplinade," possibly inspired by Reinhardt's similar treatment of the School scene,[10] Bergman, by his own admission,[11] set himself in contrast to Molander.

In conformance with Swedish academic tradition, the Officer was laureated, while in Bergman's amplification of Strindberg's idea, Agnes took the crown of thorns from the crucified Christ and placed it upon the Lawyer's head. Suffering vicariously, the Lawyer nevertheless found himself unworthy of the crown of thorns. When he put it aside, the Poet picked it up and coquettishly tried it on before an imaginary mirror (the audience in the auditorium). "*Satisfactio vicaria* [was] transformed into literary coquetry."[12]

The Coalcarriers' scene, where class differences are especially emphasized, was drastically – and successfully – integrated into the Fairhaven scene, that is, transposed from Italy to Everywhere. As the blackened coalcarriers entered, the movements of the white-dressed vacation celebrators at Fairhaven (tennis players, dancing couples) were frozen. In this manner Bergman could retain, in condensed fashion, Strindberg's black-and-white pattern.

The Fairhaven scene in the 1970 *Dream Play* production. The Poet, in dark clothes, was visibly kept apart from the white-clad holiday makers.

In Bergman's reduced version there was no burning castle to be seen at the end. Instead, there was a purely symbolic fire: a large, nonfigurative, red design on a screen. No doubt meant to activate the spectators by presenting them with an enigma, this design by scenographer Lennart Mörk was variously interpreted as "the burning castle of the dream," "the human circulatory system," "flickering flames from the earth's interior," and "the inside of the eyelid as we see it when we doze off."[13]

Instead of the altar, not prescribed by Strindberg but usually figuring in stage productions of the play, there was the Poet's table, where the characters sacrificed their attributes, that is, took leave of their roles in token of the fact that these were merely products of the Poet's imagination.

Finally, the Poet stepped forward and all the other characters, facing the audience, gathered around him – Bergman's counterpart of Strindberg's *"wall of human faces, asking, sorrowing, despairing"* – while he, rather than the Daughter, spoke the final lines about the schizophrenic predicament of humanity: the desire to leave and to stay. Then the stage was left almost empty.

> The spotlight on the Poet's table was extinguished. The final image was ... no depiction of a flowering castle of redemption and deliverance, but simply a glimpse of Agnes, the woman who has taken upon herself all mankind's suffering in her heavy gray shawl, still seated alone on the empty stage, her hand pressed convulsively to her face in speechless anxiety.[14]

Bergman's second production of *A Dream Play* was reductive in more than one respect. Apart from effectively condensing Strindberg's dialogue and largely ignoring his stage directions in favor of a 'Shakespearean' empty stage, the director transformed the author's metaphysical perspective, in which the existence of divine creatures and a divine plan is still assumed, into an immanent, meta-theatrical, Pirandelloan conception,[15] in which the divinities were revealed as actors posing to a stage audience – much as the Poet posed as a divinity in the church scene. Metonymically representing humanity at large, this stage audience was linked with the real audience. As a result a sense of *theatrum mundi* was created.

Rarely has Bergman been so Shakespearean as in his 1970 production of *A Dream Play*, where literally all the world was a stage and where the characters were not only walking shadows who strutted and fretted their hour upon the stage but also "such stuff as dreams are made on."

Yet since the whole play, in Bergman's version, was presented as a dream by the Poet, Shakespeare's 'objective' conception of the world was overruled by his subjective view of it. As Strindberg puts it in his Explanatory Note for the play: "one consciousness is superior to them all [the characters]: that of the dreamer."

Strindberg, *The Ghost Sonata* (1973)

In a Prologue written for the opening of his own Intimate Theater in Stockholm, where *The Ghost Sonata* (1907) was first performed, Strindberg speaks of the journey that mankind must undertake "from the Isle of the Living to the Isle of the Dead." He was alluding to Arnold Böcklin's well-known paintings of these subjects; at his request copies of these were placed at either side of the stage in the Intimate Theater.[1] In *The Ghost Sonata* we witness a similar journey. The house we see on the stage represents the House of Life, which at the end vanishes and is replaced by the Isle of the Dead. Without actually realizing it, we have been on our way to another reality. Along with the Student, we gradually discover that the house which on the outside looks so attractive (Act I) is far less attractive inside (Act II). Life may not be what we had expected but *amor vincit omnia* (Act III). Yet even this proves to be an illusion: like everyone else, the Young Lady is tainted by Original Sin ("sick at the core of life"). The stable, attractive house has proved to be a mirage. The true reality – this is what Strindberg wants us to experience – is to be found in the life hereafter.

The fundamental idea of the play, then, is that life on earth is painful and illusory and that when we die we are saved, returning from this pseudo-existence to the original one. Only by hoping for this can we endure our earthly life. This ties in with the idea that the living are actually ghosts – as indicated by the cue designation "The Mummy" and the reference to the "ghost supper" in Act II.

The Student is "a Sunday child," who "can see what others cannot see"; he is a student of languages trying to find the unity behind and beyond the linguistic Tower of Babel that mankind has erected "to keep the secrets of the tribe." He is the only one in the play who sings, "matching human language with the 'universal language' of Music."[2] At the same time, he is Everyman, starting out in life enthusiastically but ending it in disillusion. His hope for a better existence hereafter, justifying the pain of this life, is not an individual hope but a representative one, the hope of mankind.

The play loosely adheres to the unities of time and place. Act I opens on a Sunday morning; Act II happens in the afternoon and evening of the same day; Act III is set a few days after the Old Man's (Hummel's) funeral, about a week later.

The acts are linked spatially. Along with the Student we move from the street (Act I) through the round parlor (Act II) to the hyacinth room (Act III), from wider to narrower space, a Dantean journey in reverse. By synchronizing this inward movement with the Student's increasingly negative view of life, Strindberg indicates a connection between life experience and denial of life.

Strindberg's use of space in *The Ghost Sonata* is quite cinematic. "The gradual revelation of the rotten foundations of the house...is presented visually by a zoom from act to act towards the center of the house." The spatial "turnaround" in Act III has its counterpart in a reversed point of view: that of the young couple, now in the foreground, replaces that of the old people, now in the background.[3]

The duplicity characteristic of mankind – the attractive social mask hiding the ugly face – is represented by the *"façade"* of the House of Life. In a fairly literal translation the initial stage directions read:

> *The ground floor and the first floor of the façade of a modern house; only the corner of the house is visible, ending on the ground floor in a round parlor, on the first floor in a balcony and a flagstaff.*
> *Through the open windows of the round parlor, when the blinds are raised, a white marble statue of a young woman is seen, surrounded by palms and brightly lit by rays of sunshine. In the window to the left pots of hyacinths (blue, white, pink) can be seen.*
> *On the balcony rail at the corner of the second floor can be seen a blue silk quilt and two white pillows. The windows to the left are hung with white sheets. It is a bright Sunday morning.*
> *In the foreground in front of the façade is a green bench.*
> *To the right in the foreground is a street drinking-fountain, to the left an advertisement pillar.*
> *To the left at the back is the entrance, which reveals the staircase, the stairs of white marble and the banister of mahogany and brass; on both sides of the entrance on the pavement are laurel bushes in tubs.*
> *The corner with the round parlor faces also a side street, which is thought to lead inwards towards the backdrop.*
> *To the left of the entrance, on the first floor, is a window with a gossip mirror.[4]*

The play opens as follows (figures indicating sequences[5] added):

> 1 *When the curtain rises the bells of several churches in the distance are ringing.*
> *The doors of the façade are open; a woman in dark clothes is standing motionless on the stairs.*

The CARETAKER'S WIFE *sweeps the entrance hall; she then polishes the brass on the front door; finally she waters the laurels.*
The OLD MAN *is sitting in a wheelchair by the advertisement pillar reading a newspaper; he has white hair and beard and wears glasses.*

2   *The* MILKMAID *comes in from the corner with milk bottles in a wire basket; she is in summer clothes, with brown shoes, black stockings, and a white beret; she takes off the beret and hangs it on the fountain; wipes the sweat from her forehead; drinks from the cup; washes her hands; arranges her hair, using the water as a mirror.*
A steamship bell can be heard ringing, and the bass notes of an organ in a nearby church now and then break the silence.

3   *After a couple of minutes of silence, when the* GIRL *has finished her toilet, the* STUDENT *comes in from the left, unshaven and showing he has not slept. He goes right up to the fountain. Pause.*
STUDENT. May I have the cup? *The* GIRL *pulls the cup toward herself.* Haven't you finished yet? *The* GIRL *looks at him with horror.*
OLD MAN *to himself.* Who's he talking to? – I don't see anyone! – Is he crazy? *Continues to watch them in great amazement.*

Compare this to the ending of the play:

The YOUNG LADY *has drooped, seems to be dying, rings.* BENGTSSON *enters.* Bring the screen! Quickly – I'm dying!
BENGTSSON *returns with the screen, which he opens up and puts in front of the* YOUNG LADY.
STUDENT. The liberator is coming! Welcome, pale and gentle one. Sleep, you lovely, innocent, doomed creature, suffering for no fault of your own. Sleep without dreaming, and when you wake again ... may you be greeted by a sun that does not burn, in a home without dust, by friends without stain, by a love without flaw. You wise and gentle Buddha, sitting there waiting for a heaven to grow out of the earth, grant us patience in our ordeal and purity of will, that the hope may not come to nought!
The strings of the harp hum softly; the room is filled with a white light.

    I saw the sun. To me it seemed
    that I beheld the Hidden.
    Men must reap what they have sown,

blest is he whose deeds are good.
Deeds which you have wrought in fury,
cannot in evil find redress.
Comfort him you have distressed
with loving-kindness – this will heal.
No fear has he who does no ill.
Sweet is innocence.

A moaning is heard behind the screen.

You poor little child, child of this world of illusion, guilt, suffering and death, this world of endless change, disappointment, and pain. May the Lord of Heaven have mercy on you as you journey forth...

The room vanishes; Böcklin's Toten-Insel *becomes the backdrop; faint, quiet, pleasantly sad music is heard from the isle.*

Böcklin's monumental painting *Toten-Insel* shows an isle with high, crater-like rocks surrounding a group of tall cypresses. In the walls of the rocks, there are openings like those of sepulchral chambers. On the shore below, in the centre, there are stairs of white marble; here the recently dead are received. *"A black boat with a black oarsman, carrying a white coffin with a white figure standing next to it"* – Strindberg's stage directions for his unfinished sequel of *The Ghost Sonata*, entitled *Toten-Insel* – approaches the stairs across the still water.

In *The Ghost Sonata* the final projection of this painting forms an antithetic counterpart to the solid house façade of the play's opening. The marble stairs of the house – the entrance to Life – correspond to those of the isle, the entrance to Death. The windows have their counterparts in the sepulchral openings. The white marble statue inside the house, *"surrounded by palms,"* resembles the erect white figure in the boat, surrounded by the cypresses of the isle – evergreen like the laurels outside the house but with a more aspiring shape. The mournful Dark Lady *"standing motionless on the stairs"* corresponds to the black oarsman in the boat. Even the fresh water of the street drinking-fountain, which the Milkmaid *"in summer clothes"* uses as a mirror, has its counterpart in the still water around the isle in which the white figure in the boat is reflected.

It is from this isle of the blessed that the ghostly Milkmaid emanates. This explains why she wears summer clothes even though she was drowned in the winter. And it is to this isle that the Young Lady journeys forth in the final tableau. The house of earthly existence – the Old Man's realm – has collapsed and in its place we see its spiritual counterpart, "a home without dust," the Isle of the Dead, "the station of rest or the first summer vacation" as Strindberg calls it in one of his *Blue Books*.

The connection between the beginning and the end of the play is also emphasized by the sound effects.[6] When the curtain rises on Act I, we hear the ringing of bells of "*several churches at a distance.*" While the Milkmaid washes her hands – an act of purification – and looks at herself in the "fresh water" of the street drinking-fountain, "*a steamship bell can be heard ringing, and the bass notes of an organ in a nearby church now and then break the silence.*" By this puzzling combination of sound-effects Strindberg from the very beginning creates a strange and solemn mood. Only in retrospect, when we have witnessed the ending, do we realize their metaphoric significance, do we understand that the ringing of the steamship bell signifies a leave-taking of the shore of life and that the organ music is there to help on the last journey.

"The first great absurdist drama and the greatest play ever written in Swedish."[7] Bergman's high evaluation of *The Ghost Sonata* explains partly why he was willing to stage this play for the third time. Other reasons were that the right actors were available for the main parts and that he had new ideas about how to stage the play, especially the problematic third act. Despite its chamber play format, the play, opening on January 13, 1973, was performed at the Big Stage of Dramaten. Bergman chose to place the modern house façade of Act I not upstage, as Strindberg has it, but in the auditorium. A few years earlier he had done the same thing with the attic in Ibsen's *The Wild Duck*. A major reason in both cases was that with this arrangement the characters would no longer turn away from the audience. To Bergman this was of paramount importance. As he stressed during rehearsals, what the characters witness is less important than their reaction to it.

In *The Ghost Sonata*, where the house represents Life and its inhabitants stand for humanity, the spatial reversal was meaningful also in the sense that it linked the audience with the characters on the stage. Appearing on either side of the proscenium frame, the inhabitants of the house came to function as mediators between the audience inside the House of Life and the characters out in the street.

At the same time, Strindberg's idea was partly retained. A beautiful *art nouveau* building was projected on the black screens in the rear. As the Old Man (Toivo Pawlo) and the Student (Mathias Henrikson) watched the house in the auditorium, the spectators watched the house they were describing on the screens. The result was a dreamlike mirror effect, inducing a feeling of being strangely "face to face," seeing something "through a glass darkly" – to quote two Bergman film titles. This state was further heightened by the similarity between the stage, enclosed by concave screens, and the horseshoe shape of the auditorium, turning the whole locale into a global "wooden O" or *theatrum mundi*.

At the start of the play, the Student relates how he has witnessed the collapse of a house in a neighboring street the day before; at the end, the house on the stage collapses. The implication is that the houses are one and the same: the House of Life. Bergman's scenographic solution meant that Strindberg's partly verbal and partly visual metaphor of the dreamlike, illusory nature of life was retained purely visually.

What I have called the Student's Dantean journey in reverse was necessarily obscured by placing the house in the auditorium. Instead, the generation motif was emphasized in the scenery of the last two acts, where the old, experienced, guilt-laden people occupy the round parlor and the young, innocent, hopeful ones, the hyacinth room. In the two rooms two phases of life and two contrasting views of it were exposed. The contrast appeared not least in the interior decoration. In the round parlor, out-of-focus projection showed a typical turn-of-the-century wealthy bourgeois interior – overloaded, dark; five sturdy black and red chairs completed the impression of somberness. In the much loftier hyacinth room, by contrast, two slender white chairs and a white-and-gold harp dominated the picture; only gradually did the spectators become aware of a contrasting property: the black death screen.

Three times (once in each act) the projected exterior/interior scenery was momentarily replaced by a projected high stone wall. Whenever this occurred, there was a sound reminiscent of thunder. The projections appeared in moments of intense anguish on the part of the Old Man (Act I), the guests at the ghost supper (Act II), and the Student and the Young Lady (Act III). By these audiovisual effects the director wished to communicate a sense of claustrophobia, a feeling of being imprisoned in "this madhouse, this reformatory, this charnel house the earth," as the Student puts it, and the concomitant longing for "the liberator," death.

The contrast between house façade/decorated interiors on the one hand and bare wall, on the other, also served to stress the mask-face dichotomy that is so pronounced in the play: the projection of the bare wall signified an unmasking, a laying bare of hidden ugliness.

The dreamy note struck in the opening was not only maintained but augmented in the course of the performance. Twice, for a minute or so, the curtain dropped to allow for necessary changes of scenery and costume. But even during these short intervals the audience was kept in a dreamlike mood through a strange 'snowfall' – rising and falling dots of light projected on the curtain – creating a sense of dizziness. The second time the snowfall appeared, the face of the aged Strindberg could be vaguely divined in it, indicating that the audience was sharing the playwright's experience of life – a surprisingly subjective touch.

With regard to the stage lighting, we may distinguish between functional, realistic, symbolic, and atmospheric lighting. Functional lighting was provided when the Student started to tell the story about the house that collapsed the preceding day; at this point, the lighting on the stage was dimmed, while the Student was strongly lit. As a result, attention was focused on him and the story he had to tell. The lighting here helped to emphasize a thematically important passage in the play.

Seemingly more realistic was the strong white light directed toward that part of the stage to which the Student was wheeling the Old Man in response to his request to sit "in the sun." On closer inspection, however, the sunlight here had above all a symbolic significance: sensing that he is soon to die, the old sinner, hoping for divine Grace, is drawn to the warm sunlight.

Especially in Act III, atmospheric light was important. Here there was a change from warm to cold and back to warm light, corresponding to the three "notes" the director sensed in this act: tenderness – bitterness – tenderness. The hyacinths mentioned in the play text never materialized in the production. They were merely indicated in the Young Lady's hyacinth-blue dress and in the lighting: mixed blue and white light. As the Young Lady, kneeling on the floor, stretched out her hands, the bluish-white light colored her dress to indicate that "she surrounded herself with a barrier of color and warmth and fragrance."[8] By contrast, an uncharitable cold light accompanied the Student's unmasking of the Young Lady, which directly led to her death.

In his acting directions, Strindberg gives rather sparse and somewhat capricious information about his characters' outward appearance. We lack information about how the Old Man is dressed in Act I and what the Young Lady wears in Act III. On her second appearance, we learn that she *has changed her clothes* but we are not told in what way. In Act I, the Colonel appears *in civilian clothes.* How he is dressed in the following acts Strindberg does not tell us, but assuming that he wears his uniform in Act II, the author could rely on widespread knowledge of Swedish military fashion around the turn of the century.

In Bergman's production, the costumes were meticulously designed, sometimes with regard to factual circumstances but more often with an eye to their symbolic significance. In addition, there was an overall color pattern. Thus, Act I was dominated by grayish tints. In Act II, the characters appeared in costumes which were realistic in cut but so glaring that they looked like dresses for a fancy-dress ball; here "the world of illusions" was at its strongest. In the final act, by contrast, the costumes were pale. The masquerade was over, and the characters seemed to incarnate the Mummy's contrite recognition that "we are poor human beings."

One of the innovative traits in the production was Bergman's emphasis on the relationship between the Colonel (Anders Ek) and the Mummy (Gertrud Fridh). Strindberg's Colonel incarnates duplicity. Behind an aristocratic mask – moustache, false teeth, wig and corset, a dubious title and a false noble name – he disguises the fact that he is a former servant and sponger.

In Bergman's production, the Colonel first wore a long, black silk dressing-gown, announcing his aristocratic pretensions. In Act II, he had dressed up for the ghost supper in uniform. Although he claims to have been "an acting colonel in the American voluntary service," his gold-braided, scarlet uniform did not seem to fit the claim at all. Instead the glaring color served to bring out the fact that the Colonel was disguising himself behind a socially impressive persona. In addition, the red color linked him with his wife, the Mummy, and his servant, Bengtsson.

In Act III, however, his red uniform was replaced by an old, worn, gray velvet dressing-gown, strongly contrasting both with the uniform and with the elegant silk gown he wore in Act I; the boots had been replaced by slippers; the wig and the monocle were gone; so was the iron corset, and as a result he had lost his artificial erectness. The stiff gait had been replaced by a tired man's bent shuffling along. At the end he had arrived at a resigned acceptance of suffering and compassion for all human beings reminiscent of a Buddhist outlook.

The explicit references to Buddha in the play text were all omitted in the production, partly because these ingredients would be alien to a Western audience, partly because Bergman's version did not allow for any divine superstructure. Instead the Colonel in the final act was turned into a 'Buddhist monk' with shorn head, simple gown, mild voice and radiant face. Sitting next to the death screen in a humble, harmonious position, he incarnated the attitude to life which the Student in the play text prays to Buddha for: "patience in the trials, purity of will."

The change in the Mummy's costume from Act II to III was similar in kind. Her ghostly parrot-costume, intensely red below in Act II, became almost colorless in the final act. Sapped of her lifeblood, in her long gray-yellow-white dress she was now proclaimed a living corpse.

Corresponding to the Mummy's dress in Act II was the Young Lady's petticoat in Act III: dirty, blood-stained around the womb, a visual confirmation of the Student's suspicion that the most beautiful flowers – the smeary petticoat was disguised by an ethereal hyacinth-blue dress – are the most poisonous and that the Young Lady is "sick at the core of life."

According to Bergman himself, a fundamental idea behind his production was "the fact that the Young Lady is slowly turning into another Mummy."[9] To convey this idea to the audience the director had the same actress, Gertrud Fridh, play the roles of both mother and daughter, assisted by a mute stand-in when necessary. The idea that the Mummy has once been what the Young Lady is now and, conversely, that the Young Lady is an embryonic Mummy was indicated in various ways. By position: the Young Lady in Act I and the Mummy in Act II were placed in the same position next to the marble statue representing the Mummy as young; moreover, the Young Lady's coiffure was strikingly similar to that of the marble woman. By gesture: at times the Young Lady would flutter her hands in a manner reminiscent of the Mummy's parrot gestures. By costume: the Mummy's dirty and tattered gray-yellow dress turning red from the womb downwards resembled the dirty and bloodstained petticoat in which the Young Lady was finally revealed. By movement: notably in the following passage in Act III (the acting directions refer to Bergman's version):

> YOUNG LADY. ... *Turning to the* STUDENT, *thumb in mouth, whispers.* What's the worst thing you know?
> STUDENT *whispers.* Counting laundry. Ugh!
> YOUNG LADY. That's my job. Ugh!
> STUDENT. What else?
> YOUNG LADY. To be awakened at night and have to get up to fasten the window-catch...because the maid has forgotten to.
> STUDENT. What else?
> YOUNG LADY. To climb up a ladder and mend the cord of the damper when she has torn it off.
> STUDENT. What else?
> YOUNG LADY *with a shrill voice, increasingly faster.* To sweep after her, to dust after her, to make a fire in the tile stove after her – she just puts in the wood! *Starts slowly turning around.* To watch the dampers, to dry the glasses, re-lay the table, uncork the bottles, open the windows to air the rooms, re-make my bed, rinse the water decanter *Slowing down, increasingly adopting the* MUMMY'S *tone of voice.* when it gets green with slime, buy matches and soap that we're always out of, dry lamps and trim wicks, so the lamps won't smoke and so that the lamps won't go out, when we have company I have to fill them myself...

This passage has long been considered a sad example of how Strindberg could not always keep his own household problems outside his work. We know from his *Occult Diary* that many of the everyday chores mentioned in this passage tormented him.

However, in Bergman's production it was made clear that the catalogue of unpleasant chores should be understood not literally but figuratively, as so many examples of the obligatory "drudgery of keeping the dirt of life at a distance." In addition to this, the passage became the most telling instance of the thematic connection between the Young Lady and the Mummy, of how the former is destined to turn into the latter. In the Young Lady's speech, as quoted above, the development from childhood (thumb in mouth) to old age (mummification), the gradual 'dying' to which we are all condemned in the course of life, was demonstrated by tone of voice and body language.

Just as the outward similarity between the Mummy and the Young Lady, between mother and daughter, suggested the frightening destiny of human development, so did the outward resemblance between the Old Man and the Student. Like Strindberg's Old Man, Bergman's was provided with a beard (plus a moustache) and glasses. So was his Student. In this way the idea was conveyed that the Student incarnates an earlier stage in the Old Man's life and that, conversely, the Student is destined eventually to turn into another Old Man – an idea that Strindberg hints at, not least through his age-oriented cue designations. Taken together, the male and the female couples thus presented a picture of the fate of humanity.

In providing the Old Man also with a skullcap and a diamond ring, indicative of his Jewish origin, Bergman took a risk. Turning the most dislikeable character into a Jew would inevitably be seen as an anti-Semitic statement by some spectators. Actually, the reason was quite the opposite. The Old Man was meant to appear as a pariah revenging himself on the society which oppresses him. His usurping mentality, his desire to unmask people of higher station could in this way be socially justified or at least motivated.

The theme of food has a prominent place in Strindberg's writings. In *The Ghost Sonata*, the antithesis of the blood-sucking vampire is the suckling mother. The Old Man and the Cook are the vampires of the play. The opposite, nourishing role we find in the character who is but an apparition: the Milkmaid. It is she who represents the nurturing, loving force in life. When Strindberg provides the Cook with "a coloring-bottle with scorpion letters on it," he gives her an attribute which blatantly contrasts with the Milkmaid's white milk bottles.

Thematically important are also the biblical allusions. When, in the opening, the Student tells the Milkmaid that he has "bandaged up injured people and kept watch over the sick all night," we associate him with both Jesus and the good Samaritan. Strindberg's allusion to John 4.7-14, where Jesus meets a woman of Samaria at Jacob's well, provides a key to the whole scene.[10] "Give me to drink," Jesus asks her. "Give me a drink of water," the Student asks the Milkmaid. The contrast in the biblical text between Jacob's earthly water, which only temporarily quenches the thirst, and Jesus' "living water" which does so eternally is latently present in the contrast between the earthly existence on which Jacob (!) Hummel's power rests and the heavenly one to which the Milkmaid belongs and for which the Student finally hopes.

Let us now see, more closely, how the opening passage has been rendered by Bergman (the position numbers correspond to those on the ground plan on p. 42):

1   *Projection on the screens of a beautiful white* art nouveau *apartment house and on the cyclorama of part of a church. Left and right (at 3 and 6, respectively) a banister of silvered brass. Right (at 11) a gray street drinking-fountain with pump and cup. Left downstage (at 1) a grandfather clock and a black chair. Right (at 7) a white marble statue of a beautiful semi-nude young woman. Projections of palm twigs on clock and statue. All projections, in black-and-white, are slightly out of focus. White light, chiming of church bells.*

The OLD MAN *sits in a black wheelchair at 10, reading a paper. His hair, moustache and beard are white. He wears glasses. He is dressed in a black overcoat with a velvet collar, black striped trousers, black boots, black-green neckerchief with a diamond tie-pin, a diamond ring on his pink, a black skull-cap on his head, on his knees a gray blanket.*

2   *The* MILKMAID *enters at 5 with milk bottles in wire baskets, which she puts down next to the drinking-fountain. She wears a simple, light-gray cotton dress, a peaked cap of the same material, a white apron, gray stockings, black boots, a black purse hanging at the sash. Her hair is braided into a plait.*

The OLD MAN *looks worriedly around, tucks the blanket around himself.*

3   *The* COLONEL *enters at 7 with his back to the audience. He wears a black wig and a long black-silk dressing-gown. He pats the statue on the bottom and starts observing it.*

The MILKMAID *wipes sweat from her forehead, washes her hands, arranges her hair, mirroring her face in the water; then puts the cap back on her head.*

4   *The* DARK LADY *enters at 5, walks back and forth in the opening upstage, looking around. She wears a dark-gray silk coat, a big hat with roses and gauze, dark-gray gloves, and carries a black parasol. Her hair is chestnut red. When she moves, the hem of a bright red petticoat can be seen.*

5   *The* CARETAKER'S WIFE *enters at 3 with a laurel tree. She is poorly dressed in a gray skirt, gray blouse, black-and-gray knitted vest, a black kerchief on her head, slippers. She stops, looks at the* DARK LADY, *exits at 5.*

6   *The* MILKMAID *works the pump and drinks from the cup.*

7   *The* FIANCÉE *enters at 1, sits down on the chair, looks at the (imaginary) gossip mirror, starts to crochet. She wears a black-violet silk dress from the 1880s, a black laced shawl, and a black laced cap. Her hair is gray.*

8   *The* STUDENT *enters at 5. He has a reddish-blond moustache and beard. He wears glasses, a light-gray linen jacket, gray striped waistcoat, unbuttoned white shirt, gray shoes, everything a bit torn and dirty. Around his left hand he has a bandage. His head is bare. He walks right up to the fountain.*

STUDENT. May I have the cup?
OLD MAN *shudders, looks to the right.*
MILKMAID *pulls cup toward herself.*
STUDENT. Haven't you finished yet?
MILKMAID *looks at him with horror.*
OLD MAN *to himself.* Who's he talking to?
STUDENT. What are you staring at? Do I look so terrible?
OLD MAN *to himself.* Is he crazy?

A comparison with Strindberg's text reveals that the number of sequences there (3) was increased to 8 in Bergman's production; 7 of these occurred before a word had been uttered. (For the whole play, the total is 49 sequences in the play text as against 94 in the production.) The difference indicates the cinematic swiftness with which Bergman opened his production. Unlike Strindberg, he began the play with the Old Man alone on the stage. When the Milkmaid entered, he sensed her presence, looked around worriedly and tucked the blanket around himself – as though he suddenly felt cold. The Milkmaid, Bergman thereby suggested, had been evoked by the Old Man's guilt-feelings.

While Strindberg opens the play with several sound effects, Bergman limited himself to one: the chiming of the church bells – a very natural sound since it is Sunday morning and, moreover, time for the dead Consul's funeral. The mournful sound faded away as the Milkmaid left, returned briefly when the dead Consul appeared, and was heard for the last time when the Milkmaid was represented as drowning. Since the Old Man has 'murdered' both of them, the mournful chiming of the bells was actually not so much a realistic sound as an expression of his pangs of conscience. The handling of this sound-effect seemed well attuned to Strindberg's drama of "half-reality."

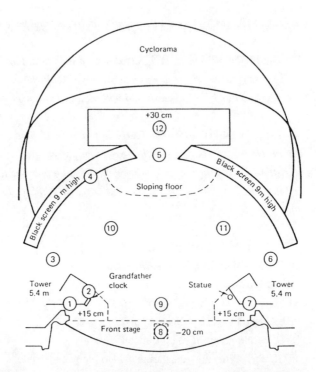

Bergman's and Marik Vos' setting for Act I in the 1973 production of *The Ghost Sonata*. (When the play opened the Old Man was sitting in the wheelchair left.) On the black screens diffuse projections of an *art nouveau* building and, on the cyclorama, of part of a church. The clock, left, and the marble statue, right, were not projections but three-dimensional properties. Cf. the ground plan.

Bergman rearranged the end even more than the opening:

The COLONEL *goes up to the* YOUNG LADY, *puts one arm around her shoulder, tenderly.* The liberator is coming. Welcome, pale and gentle one. *He moves the* YOUNG LADY *behind the screen. A little later her hand is seen falling on the floor to the right of the screen. The* COLONEL *sits down on the floor, takes her hand.*

COLONEL. Sleep, you lovely, innocent, doomed creature, suffering for no fault of your own. Sleep without dreaming, and when you wake again ... may you be greeted by a sun that does not burn, in a home without dust, by friends without stain, by a love without flaw.

The STUDENT, *standing by the harp, recites in a toneless voice.*

I saw the sun. To me it seemed

that I beheld the Hidden ... seemed?

Men must reap what they have sown,

blest is he whose deeds are good ... Good?

Deeds which you have wrought in fury,

cannot in evil find redress.

Comfort him you have distressed

with ... with loving-kindness – this will heal.

No fear has he who does no ill. *Looks at the* COLONEL. No fear has he who does no ill ...

Sweet is innocence ... Innocence? *Shakes his head, exits right.*

The MUMMY *comes in from the rear, pushes the screen gently away, sits down on the chair next to it, looks at the* YOUNG LADY *(who is lying on the floor, her back to the audience), puts one hand on the* COLONEL'S *shoulder.* You poor little child ... *Light in rays from above. Occasional harp notes during the final speech.* ... child of this world of illusion, guilt, suffering and death, this world of endless change, disappointment, and pain. May the Lord of Heaven have mercy on you as you journey forth...

A final harp-note. Slow black-out. Curtain.

The conception of life underlying Bergman's production was almost the opposite of Strindberg's; in the director's own words, "the only thing that can give man any salvation – a secular one – is the grace and compassion that come out of himself."[11] In line with this view, the projection of *Toten-Insel* had to be omitted. The Old Icelandic poem called "The Song of the Sun," which the Student had recited in a romantic-idealistic way, to the

The final 'holy trinity' grouping in the 1973 *Ghost Sonata*. From left to right: the dead Young Lady, the Mummy, and the Colonel.

accompaniment of occasional harp notes, at the end of Act II was now recited tonelessly, without any accompanying music, the harp having turned "deaf and dumb" to him. Bergman: "If the Student reads the poem with a sceptical tone the second time he recites it and recognizes that it turns to dust, then it seems to me meaningful.... Every sentence in that stanza seems dubious."[12]

The final speeches of the play express compassion for the dead Young Lady and faith in a better life hereafter. Strindberg, who has the Student deliver these speeches, stresses the latter; Bergman, who gave them to the Colonel and the Mummy, the former. In the performance, the divine aspect was constantly toned down in favor of human love and compassion. In the text the Colonel and the Mummy seem to share a mummified matrimonial existence. In the production, they were turned into two people who despite their crimes – or because of them – were tied to one another in a feeling of mutual loyalty. When the Old Man during the ghost supper revealed that the Young Lady was *his* daughter, not the Colonel's, the Mummy grasped the Colonel's hand. A little later, when she testified to the misery of mankind, she stood behind the Colonel with a protecting gesture, while he in turn grasped her hand.

In the final act of the play text, the Colonel and the Mummy are seen in positions illustrating that they have drifted away from each other: they are sitting close to the death screen in the round parlor, *"inactive and silent"* – a pre-Beckettian couple waiting for death, "the liberator." In Bergman's version, by contrast, they were reunited at the end. By giving the Student's concluding prayer for the dead woman to *both of them*, the director was able to stress their unanimity. This was strengthened by the choreographic pattern in the final tableau. The Mummy's hand rested tenderly on the Colonel's shoulder. He in turn lovingly held the hand of the Young Lady. Both of them regarded their dead 'daughter' – a secular holy trinity harking back to Jof, Mia, and their little son Michael in *The Seventh Seal*, the loving trinity that is saved from the Black Death.

"We have broken up and left each other infinitely many times, but then we're drawn together again," the Mummy states in Act II, referring to her marriage to the Colonel. Bergman demonstrated how the two were "drawn together" first when the Old Man threatened them, then when the Young Lady was taken from them. Her death was not in vain.

In the closing moments of Bergman's performance, the harp that was "deaf and dumb" to the Student began to play, when the Mummy prayed for her dead daughter. In addition, there was a combination of soft light, representing the love and compassion experienced at this moment by the Colonel and the Mummy, and strong light from above, indicating the spiritual nature of their state of mind and their hope – Bergman did not cut this religious reference – that "the Lord of Heaven" would show the Young Lady the same compassion as they did. Yet the separate harp notes, composed for the occasion, ended on a dissonance, undermining the hope expressed in the Mummy's prayer.

Strindberg, *Miss Julie* (1985)

Bergman's *Miss Julie*, opening at Dramaten on December 7, 1985, was his second stage production of the play and the first one in Swedish. Four years earlier he had staged it at the Residenztheater in Munich with German actors, a production which has been thoroughly documented.[1]

Central to Bergman's Munich production was the idea that Julie, the daughter of a count, "is a big helpless animal who is done to death by smoothly functioning beasts of prey. ... Defeated by her own kind, destroyed by the others."[2] By "the others" Bergman apparently meant not only Jean, the Count's servant, and his 'fiancée' Kristin, the cook, but also the people who figured more prominently in both stage versions than in the play text. It is possible that Alf Sjöberg's well-known film version of the play provided an inspiration.

In Bergman's view Julie is a woman "who is already wounded and who fights for her life in a ... hopeless kind of way – hopeless because she wants only to die." She is a "loser," while Jean is a "winner." This does not mean that she is weak. On the contrary, "when Julie makes up her mind to die, ... she becomes the stronger of the two. And Jean collapses."[3]

Bergman thus pitted the life-denying Julie against the life-affirming Jean – much as he had earlier, in *The Seventh Seal*, contrasted the Knight with his servant Jöns. In that respect, his stage interpretation meant a very loyal reading of the text. But in his interpretation of the third character, the cook Kristin, he differed with almost all earlier directors of the play. Kristin was depicted not as "a female slave ... conventional and lethargic; instinctively hypocritical" – Strindberg's characterization of her in the preface to the play – but as a young, sensual, forceful woman, who "rules not only her kitchen, but also Jean. *She* is the reason why Jean is a winner – because [she] is the strongest of them all. She knows that one day ... [she and Jean] will rule this house together."[4]

By and large, the conception of the play and characters underlying the Munich production was carried over to the one in Stockholm. Again the audience was confronted with a young, attractive, powerful Kristin (Gerti Kulle). Jean (Peter Stormare) combined a boyish vitality with a desire to embellish his life with made-up stories. Julie (Marie Göranzon) was visibly marked by the past. Brought up as a boy, she was pronouncedly masculine with her short, straight hair and her authoritarian manners. Her attitude to Jean was contemptuous rather than inciting – as though she was suffering from a sexually grounded fear of being dominated by a man.

Scenographically, too, the two productions, both designed by Gunilla Palmstierna-Weiss, were very similar. But there was one notable difference. In the German version, done on a big stage, the spectators could see not only the kitchen but also part of Julie's and the Count's domain above it: the lower part of three big French windows, family portraits, a coat of arms. In the beginning, they could even see the legs of some shadowy figures, while at the end, one such figure (the Count) could be divined. The spirit of the Count hovered literally above the whole performance.

In Stockholm, where the play opened at the Small Stage of Dramaten, this superstructure could not be retained. But a remnant of it was kept in the form of a huge beam running from left to right at the front of the stage, indicating a strongly supported superstructure and a suppressed kitchen level.

The midsummer atmosphere was more explicit in the German version than in the Swedish one, necessarily so, since the German audience would not be familiar with this piece of Swedish folklore.

Unlike Strindberg's kitchen, which is oblique in relation to the footlights, thereby including the audience, as it were, in the kitchen, that of Ms. Palmstierna-Weiss ran parallel with them. The coloring was sparse: green (the birches), brown (the copper pans), violet (lilacs and, partly, windows), and gray. Gray was the dominant color. The scenery was like a graphic sheet, containing no fewer than ten different shades of gray. The reason for this was not so much that this color would fit a proletarian environment; more important was the fact that gray

is a neutral color, showing the rhythm of day and night from afternoon light to evening light to nocturnal darkness – it is never truly dark since it is midsummer – to warm sunrise to a terribly ice-cold bluish-white light which you can only experience in the North. The gray nuances absorb and transform the light. A cold shade results in a very cold, colorless room, while a warm light on the gray makes the room come alive, lightens it up. These are effects which you cannot achieve with other colors.[5]

The violet of the lilacs had its counterpart in Julie's violet-colored costume, cut like a young girl's summer dress. Traditionally, violet stands for mourning; as such it was a color used only by ageing women. In this respect, Julie's dress was more symbolic than realistic, connoting her presentiments of death; and the contrast between the negative color and the vital design of the costume was indicative of her split mind.

Jean wore in the beginning his black servant's livery, a very explicit social costume, while Kristin, unlike Strindberg's cook but in agreement with nineteenth century reality, appeared in a dark dress, somewhat shorter than Julie's and with shorter sleeves than hers, as an indication that Kristin's costume is a working dress. Similarly, Julie's white linen, which could be glimpsed, contrasted with Kristin's beige one, made of much coarser material.

A transcription of the opening of the performance might read as follows:

A large, light-gray souterrain kitchen. In the rear wall three small, violet-tinted windows, partly opaque, through which tree-tops can be seen. In the middle of the wall two swinging glass doors, reached by a short flight of stairs. A gray-white cast-iron stove, with an exhaust hood, by the left wall, a kitchen sink behind it, a chair in front of it. To the right a simple table, of light-gray pine, with three chairs and three backless stools, all gray. In the right wall a door leading to JEAN'S *room. The kitchen is decorated with birch branches. On the table a bowl with violet lilacs. A water barrel with a ladle, an ice-box, and a washstand concealed by a folding screen in the back-ground. A large cupboard with porcelain and glassware around the corner to the left. A large bell above the glass-doors. To the left of it a speaking-tube. A coffee pot on the stove.*

Empty stage. Fiddle music in the distance. KRISTIN, *in dark dress with an apron, enters from left. She puts some logs in the stove, exits left, enters again with a plate.* JEAN *enters quickly from rear. He wears black livery, gray-and-black striped waistcoat, a black cap and black low boots and carries a pair of high, black riding boots, which he puts down in front of the stove. He removes his cap and wipes the sweat from his forehead.*

JEAN. Miss Julie's crazy again tonight – absolutely crazy!

KRISTIN. Well, so here you are at last.

JEAN *up to the water barrel.* I took the Count to the station. And as I was passing the barn on my way back, I went in for a dance. Who do I see but Miss Julie leading the dance with the gamekeeper. But the minute she sees me, she rushes straight into my arms *Drinks from the ladle.* and invites me for the ladies' waltz. *Takes a few waltz steps.* And she's been waltzing ever since – I've never seen anything like it. She is crazy!

KRISTIN *laying the table.* Always has been. But never so bad as during the last two weeks, since her engagement was broken off. *Returning to the stove.*

JEAN *glancing in the newspaper he has picked up from the table.* Yes, what was all that about? He was a gentleman, even if he wasn't rich. Ah! Aren't they fussy! *Folds the paper and throws it on the table.* Strange, though, a lady like her, hmm, that she'd rather stay home with the servants than go with her father to visit relatives, during midsummer! *Sits down at the end of the table, takes off his left boot.*

KRISTIN. She's probably embarrassed after that uproar with her fiancé.

JEAN. Probably. He was a man to stand his ground, though. Do you know how it happened, Kristin? I saw it, you know, though I didn't let on I had.

KRISTIN. You saw it, did you? *Up to the table.*

JEAN. I sure did. – One evening they were down by the stable, and Miss Julie was "training" him, as she called it. *Pointing with his boot.* Do you know what that meant? She made him jump over her riding crop the way you'd teach a dog to jump. He jumped twice, and each time he got a rap. But the third time he grabbed the crop out of her hand, *Makes a sweep with his boot.* hit her with it across the left cheek, *The boot against his cheek.* and off he went.

KRISTIN. Is that how it happened. You don't say!

JEAN. Yes.

KRISTIN. That's why she paints her face white now.

JEAN *bangs his boot against the table, puts it on again.* That's it. – Now, what have you got for me that's tasty, Kristin?

KRISTIN. Oh, just a bit of kidney I cut from the veal roast. *Serves from the frying pan and places the plate before him.*

JEAN. Superb! That's my great *délice! Sniffs the food, feels the plate.* You might have warmed the plate, though.

KRISTIN. You're fussier than the Count himself once you start. *Pulls his hair affectionately.*

JEAN *angrily.* Leave my hair alone! You know how sensitive I am. *Smoothes his hair.*

KRISTIN. Now, now. It's only love. *Fetches a bottle of beer from the ice-box.*

JEAN. Beer – on midsummer eve? No thank you! I can do better than that! *Gets up, opens a drawer in the table and pulls out a bottle of red wine, sealed with yellow wax.* Yellow seal – not bad eh? KRISTIN *puts her beer back in the ice-box. Pointing, as* KRISTIN *hands him a corkscrew.* Bring me a glass! KRISTIN *fetches a beer glass, which she dries on her apron.* A wine glass, of course, when you're drinking *pur!*

KRISTIN *returns to the stove and puts a small saucepan on.* God help whoever gets you for a husband! What a fuss-budget! *Up to* JEAN *with a wine glass, which she dries on her apron and puts down on the table.*

JEAN. Nonsense! You'd be glad enough to get a gentleman like me. And it hasn't done you any harm to have people call me your fiancé. KRISTIN *puts a lump of sugar in her mouth, pours coffee on a saucer and starts to sip it.* JEAN, *standing, puts one hand behind his back, pours wine with the other, tastes it.* Good! Not quite the proper temperature, though. *Warms the glass in his hand.* We bought this in Dijon. Four francs a liter, not counting the bottle, or the customs duty. *Sits down again, puts the serviette around his neck, scrutinizes the knife, clasps his hand for prayer, suddenly turns around.* What are you cooking? The smell's infernal.

Gunilla Palmstierna-Weiss had designed a fairly realistic kitchen, very similar to kitchens in Swedish castles or manor-houses around 1890. And there was a very strong mood of midsummer about it. At the same time it was extremely functional with marked acting areas: the exterior behind the windows, where prying people could be seen off and on; the stove (Kristin's place); the chair in front of it (Jean's place) with the Count's riding-boots in a dominant position downstage, indicative of his presence in the minds of the three characters; the table (for moments of communion), the hierarchical stairs (to indicate social position or for crucial moments in the struggle for power), the empty area between the stove and the table (for Julie's restless moving around – as opposed to Kristin's and Jean's fixed places of work – indicative of her feeling out of place in the kitchen).

There were also naturalistic touches in the opening of the play, such as the smell of kidney from Kristin's frying-pan and Jean's wiping the sweat from his forehead and rushing to the water barrel, thirsty after Julie's wild dancing with him. His glancing at a newspaper was a directorial addition, presumably inspired by Jean's later reference to a story he had read in the paper. The suggestion here seemed to be both that Jean picked up stories from newspapers when they came in handy for him and that his reading was topical and incidental in contrast to Kristin's traditional reliance on one book: the Bible. This contrast was further illustrated by a directorial addition: Jean's prayer at table, a piece of role-playing enacted merely to satisfy Kristin's piety.

Bergman provided Jean with low boots; when compared with the Count's high riding-boots, which figured prominently throughout the production and which were linked especially with Jean, the low boots seemed indicative not only of Jean's modest social station but also of his tendency to identify himself with his master, of his aspirations once to end up as a Count. Significantly, the low boot was figuratively turned into a riding whip, symbol of mastership, as Jean was telling Kristin about how Julie, having forced her fiancé to jump over his riding crop, suddenly saw her engagement broken.

When describing this event, Strindberg had originally written: "But the third time he grabbed the crop out of her hand and hit her with it across the left cheek." He later replaced the last words by: "... and broke it across his knee." Strindberg would have kept the original version, Bergman argued, had he not been afraid that his wife Siri would refuse to do Julie with a scar on her face, since people might think the scar a result of Strindberg's mishandling of her. Bergman therefore restored the original line and even added another, Kristin's "That's why she paints her face white now." This addition relates to Jean's remark about the "powder on the smooth cheek." Bergman here found a way of exteriorizing Julie's schizophrenic state of mind by providing her with a big, ugly scar, which in the beginning was hidden behind a thick layer of make-up. "It becomes completely understandable," he said in an interview, " why she, with a scar on her face, does not go with her father to visit relatives. Instead, she stays in her room until dusk and puts on so much make-up that she looks like a clown: she believes she can hide the scar that way."[6] It may be countered that the broken engagement is enough reason for Julie's not wishing to visit her relatives.

After the intercourse, the make-up came off, and the wounded face became visible. In the Munich production, the scar was very prominent: "... when Jean deflowers her and she is bleeding, the scar on her cheek starts to bleed, too. When Jean gives her this second 'wound' – her second physical humiliation at the hands of a man – it destroys her."[7] However, to see the symbolic connection between the scar and the blood running down Julie's leg, an audience must identify the blood with deflowering rather than menstruation; this is hardly possible in view of Kristin's earlier reference to Julie's imminent "period." In the Stockholm production Bergman significantly abstained from this confusing kind of blood symbolism.

Beer or wine? Strindberg's use of drinking habits to demonstrate a (desired) social status begins already when Kristin intends to serve Jean beer, while *he* finds wine a more appropriate drink on festive occasions. At this early point Jean pretends to be a wine connoisseur with a refined, aristocratic taste. Later we learn that his expertise in this area stems from his time as a wine waiter – a fact which Bergman ironically illustrated by having Jean fill his wineglass waiter fashion; he was here in fact performing a one-man show – being at once master *and* servant – illustrative of his social and psychological middle position. Bergman also enlarged upon the contrast between Jean and Kristin by having her mistakenly bring him a beer glass for his wine; by having her dry it off on her apron; and by having her sip coffee from a saucer – formerly a habit among the rural population in Sweden – while Jean was tasting his wine.

Another marked directorial touch concerned the handling of Julie's and Jean's contrasting, socio-sexual dreams. While telling Jean of her desire to fall, Julie turned away from him in what was obviously a thinking aloud. By contrast, Jean's dream of rising was vividly communicated to Julie. In this way, their very manner of presenting their dreams indicated their contrasting mentalities: her isolation and death urge as opposed to his sociable vitality.

Jean's story of how he, as a boy, once stole into the Count's Turkish pavilion, that is, the privy in his park, has a meaningful relation to the main action. Just as little Jean, when someone enters the privy, is forced to steal out of the pavilion through the latrine hole, so Julie is forced to steal out of the kitchen when the people invade it into the room of her servant Jean.[8] Jean's story thus anticipates Julie's fall, her sexual "beastiality," to use Jean's word. Strindberg has Jean pick one of the lilacs from the vase on the table and hold it under Julie's nose as he tells her of his visit to the Turkish pavilion. The scent of the lilac seemingly serves to soften the unpleasant smell aroused by the story; but in reality it serves, as an aphrodisiac, to stimulate Julie's sexual urge.

Bergman had Jean and Julie handle the lilacs in a way that clearly was a prelude to their sexual intercourse:

> JEAN. ... So gradually I got a longing *Holds the lilac against* JULIE'S *half-open mouth.* to experience the full pleasure of – *Lets the lilac fall, stands up.* – enfin, I stole in, looked and admired. But then somebody came! JULIE *picks up the lilac, smells it.* There was merely one exit for the gentry, but for me there was yet another, and I had no choice but to take it!

A little later the lilac was transformed from male sexual organ into a riding crop, as Jean, pointing with it to the rear door, referred to the broken engagement by the stable. Since the color of Bergman's lilacs matched that of Julie's dress, indicative of her longing for death, the flowers became a pregnant concretization of three fundamental and partly controversial human urges: sexual impulse, will to power, and death instinct.

Strindberg's "Ballet" – the interlude showing how a crowd of "*servants and farm people*" occupy the kitchen – became in Bergman's version almost a play within the play.[9] Rather than a crowd, the audience was confronted with three maids and three farmhands. In the play text we find the following socio-sexual relations:

> Count married to Countess – Brick Manufacturer (her lover)
> Jean 'engaged' to Kristin – Julie (his 'mistress')
> Diana (thoroughbred) – Gatekeeper's mongrel

Julie's social debasement has its antecedent in her mother's unfaithfulness towards her husband with a man of lower social station and in Diana's rutting with the gatekeeper's pug – whereas Jean's unfaithfulness toward Kristin, in a sense mirroring Julie's mother's marriage to the Count, is a step in the opposite social direction. Bergman enlarged upon this socio-sexual scheme by inserting several low-stationed levels between the Cook and the animals:

> Johan, clerk
> Clara, housemaid
> Lars, coachman
> Sofie, scullery-maid
> Nils, cow-boy
> Anna, dairymaid[10]

The relationship Johan-Sofie mirrored, on a lower level, that between Jean and Kristin, while Clara's jealousy of Kristin, similarly, was a low-stationed echo of Kristin's jealousy of Julie. Lars' relationship to Anna signified both a social and a sexual descendance.

Unlike Julie and Kristin, the three female representatives of the people were colorfully, even gaudily dressed, as a testimony to their primitive joy of life; and unlike them, they were not made up, that is, they lacked a social façade. The cut of Clara's blue dress was similar to that of Julie's. Anna's red one, by contrast, was too small for her pregnant body; she clearly typified the village slut. Sofie's dark-green cotton one was a representative folk costume.

The members of Bergman's prying and celebrating 'chorus' not only contrasted with the main figures; in various ways they visualized the actions and feelings of Jean and, notably, of Julie. Thus, the onstage 'coitus' between Lars and Anna was a mockery of what was at that moment taking place on the other side of the wall. Sofie's pregnancy anticipated Jean's and Julie's fear of "the consequences." And Nils' vomiting prepared for Julie's.

With Strindberg, the reason for Jean and Julie escaping into his room is that there is no other exit (except the one to Kristin's room); this idea was in principle retained in the Bergman production. It therefore seemed inconsistent when Nils entered the kitchen from the left – where a pantry was supposed to be located – as though this was another way to enter/leave the kitchen.

The second stanza of the song was cut, and the obscenity of the words, which – as Strindberg points out in the preface – is not very apparent, was indicated by a slow, mocking manner of singing and, in retrospect, by having Julie wipe sperm from her leg, relating to the song's "The one was wet about her foot." The midsummer wreath which Kristin had earlier tried on her head, wishfully thinking of a bridal crown, now figured on the head of the sluttish Anna. Combined with the song's concluding words, it underscored the theme of unfaithfulness.

In Bergman's version, the Ballet served several purposes. It made visible the class hatred of the people; it created a feeling that the "cruel eroticism that runs beneath the surface of the play"[11] can be found at every level; and it integrated this section more firmly in the play.

Unlike Strindberg, Bergman had Kristin enter the kitchen while the people of the estate were still carousing there. The intention of this was apparently to demonstrate Kristin's strength. One by one, the intruders left the kitchen, driven out by her austere apparition; even Clara, her rival, finally succumbed to her. Strindberg's Kristin learns about the intercourse when she enters the kitchen to fetch Jean for church. Bergman's Kristin learned about it the moment it took place – through the prying people. It was a measure of her realistic view of things – and of her strength – that she could keep herself from rushing into Jean's room at this point.

After the intercourse, Jean's sexual urge is again aroused. Strindberg describes this as follows:

> JEAN. ... Miss Julie, you're a splendid woman, much too good for someone like me! You've been the victim of intoxication, and you want to conceal the error by pretending you love me! You don't, unless my looks attract you – then your love isn't any better than mine – but I can never be satisfied by being simply an animal to you, and I can never awaken your love.
> JULIE. Are you sure of that?
> JEAN. You're trying to say it's possible! – I'd be able to love you – without a doubt! You're beautiful, you're refined – *Comes up to her and takes her hand.* – educated, charming when you want to be, and the flame you've aroused in a man will surely never be put out. *Puts his arm about her waist.* You're like hot wine with strong spices, and a kiss from you... *He tries to lead her out, but she slowly tears herself loose.*
> JULIE. Leave me! – You won't win me that way!

There is a correspondence here between Jean's unctuous flattery and his gentlemanly attempt to seduce Julie. Jean is clearly play-acting at this point. As for Julie, her indication that she might, after all, be able to love Jean reveals her need to stick to this illusion to soften her fall and save her honor. When she tears herself loose from him, it is because she senses his hypocrisy.

Compare this to Bergman's version, in which the dialogue was left almost intact but where Jean's behavior differed considerably from that suggested by the playwright:

JEAN. ... *He fondles her breasts.* Miss Julie, you're a splendid woman, much too good for someone like me! *He kisses her neck.* You've been the victim of intoxication, *Kneeling, kisses her breasts.* and you want to conceal the error by pretending you love me! You don't, unless my looks attract you *Puts his hand underneath her dress.* – then your love isn't any better than mine – But I can never be satisfied by being simply an animal to you, and I can never awaken your love.

JULIE. Are you sure of that?

JEAN. You're trying to say it's possible! – I'd be able to love you – without a doubt! You're beautiful, you're refined – *He forces her down backward against the table and straddles her.* – educated, charming when you want to be, and the flame you've aroused in a man will surely never be put out. You're like hot wine with strong spices, and a kiss from you...

JULIE *fights him off and pushes him to the floor.* No, no! You won't win me that way!

In his 1985 *Miss Julie* production, Bergman created an on-stage echo of the off-stage intercourse when Jean, flattering and 'raping' Julie, revealed a marked discrepancy between his words and actions.

As a result of the changed acting directions, there was an almost absurd discrepancy between Jean's romantic flow of words and the raw sexual urge demonstrated in his actions. He said that he could not be content to be but an animal to Julie – and at the same time he behaved like an animal. Similarly, Julie's line about the possibility of love has much less primitive connotations in the text than it had in Bergman's stage version, where it was colored by her sexual excitement. In short, while Strindberg demonstrates the clinging together of a man seeking a sex object (who moreover can satisfy his social careerism) and a woman seeking a love object, Bergman more grotesquely showed how the words of both of them belied the truth that was acted out: the sexual urge. What the audience witnessed was, in fact, a hypocritical version – since man in contrast to animals has the power of speech – of the copulation between the thoroughbred Diana and the gatekeeper's mongrel.

One of the few cuts that were made in the dialogue concerned the hypnosis scene toward the end, which Bergman found "a little bit ridiculous."[12] In the ending, Julie, now married to death, appeared in a white 'bridal' gown, while Jean and Kristin, dressed for church, surrounded her "like two black, deathly ravens" (Palmstierna-Weiss). The ending was done as follows:

In the final mirror scene in the 1985 *Miss Julie* production, Jean showed Julie how to use his razor for her suicide. In the gray kitchen, designed by Gunilla Palmstierna-Weiss, the birch trees on either side of the door and the lilacs on top of the ice-box indicated that it was midsummer. To the right, the door leading to Jean's room.

JEAN. ... I think if the Count came down here now – and ordered me to cut my throat, I'd do it on the spot.

JULIE. Then pretend you're he, and I'm you! You were such a good actor before, when you knelt at my feet – you were the nobleman then – or – haven't you ever been to the theater and watched a hypnotist? JEAN *nods affirmatively.* He says to the subject: "Take the broom!" He takes it. He says: "Sweep!" And it sweeps.

JEAN. But then the other one has to be asleep.

JULIE *whispers.* I'm already asleep. I'm already asleep.

JEAN *up to her, puts the razor to her throat, fetches a mirror, shows her in it how to hold the razor.* Go now – out to the barn – *Whispers in her ear.*

JULIE. Thank you. Now I'm going to rest. But just tell me – that the first can also obtain the gift of grace. Tell me that, even if you don't believe it.

JEAN. The first? No, I can't. *Up to the chair by the stove.* But wait – Miss Julie – now I know! You aren't among the first any longer – since you are among the last!

JULIE. That's true. I am among the very last! – I am the last. JEAN *turns his face away,* JULIE *lowers the mirror, sits down by the table.* But now I can't go. Tell me once more to go!

JEAN. No, now I can't either. I can't.

JULIE. And the first shall be the last.

JEAN. Don't think, don't think! You're taking all my strength from me, too, JULIE'S *head sinks.* making me a coward. Wait! I thought the bell moved. No! Shall we stuff paper into it? – To be so afraid of a bell! But it isn't just a bell – someone is sitting behind it – a hand sets it in motion – and something else sets the hand in motion. JULIE *gradually shrinks.* Just cover your ears, cover your ears! But then he rings even louder! Rings until someone answers – and then it's too late! Then the police will come – and then – *Two loud rings of the bell. Then fiddle music in the distance.* JULIE *straightens herself up, gets up from the table.* JEAN *rushes out left, returns with a lot of banknotes which he nervously lets fall on the floor, gathers them together and stuffs them into* JULIE'S *side pocket.*

JEAN. This is horrible! But there is no other end! *In servile position.* Go!

JULIE *slowly ascends the stairs, turns around, opens the door and backs out. As soon as she has disappeared,* JEAN *starts to cry, then moves to the table. When two loud rings of the bell are heard, he takes up a little pocket mirror and combs his hair. He picks up the bird-cage and hastens out left with it. Returns to take the small copper coffee pot from the stove, pours coffee from it*

into a silver pot. Picks up the riding-boots, puts them under his arm, takes up
the silver tray, clicks his heels together and marches out left. Black-out.

As appears from this transcription, Bergman in addition to Strindberg's acting directions
made an effective and ironical use of mirrors in the ending. The man in black could be
seen closely behind the woman in white, his arms in much the same position as hers, so
that the two seemed to be one flesh. Instead of making Julie imagine that the razor is a
broom, as Strindberg has it, Bergman had Jean hand her the mirror, instructing her in the
art of suicide. To Julie, the mirror signified above all a confrontation with her own self –
a very Bergmanian face-to-face situation – on the threshold of death. When Jean later
took up his pocket mirror to make himself presentable to the Count – compare the Old
Man's adjusting his 'mask' before the mirror in the second act of *The Ghost Sonata* –
Julie's self-confrontation glaringly contrasted with his hiding behind a social persona.
His behavior at this point was completely in line with his attempts to disguise his share in
the theft (the cramming of the bank-notes into Julie's pocket), the planned escape (the
removal of the bird-cage), and the suicide (his ordering Julie to leave the kitchen).

To Bergman, it was of paramount importance that Julie's decision to die
should be seen as a manifestation of strength, not of weakness: "She has the power and
can crush Jean because at this moment she can force him to take part in her death, force
him to give her the order to go out to the barn."[13] To this end her position was substanti-
ated in various ways. Instead of letting Jean hand her the razor, as Strindberg has it,
Bergman's Julie picked it up herself. By replacing part of the hypnosis passage with the
mirror scene, Bergman further strengthened the idea that Julie consciously takes her own
decision. Finally, by increasing Jean's cowardliness and by having him speak the final
line, not as a command but in an appealing, servile manner, he further weakened his
share in her death.

Although Jean has the final line in the play text, the attention at the end is
directed toward Julie and her exit. We know that she is going to end her life with the razor
we see in her hand. Most directors would focus on Julie in the closing moments. She who
is to die is so much more intriguing than he who goes on living.

But a director can also choose to keep the two, and the alternatives they represent, in balance. This is what Bergman did when he added Jean's concluding pantomime
to Strindberg's ending. After Julie had walked out of the kitchen into the morning sunlight, completely absorbed by her decision to die, Jean briefly sobbed; then concealed all
traces of his own part in what had happened; and returned relieved to his everyday domestic duties. In this manner, two contrasting types – the inflexible versus the lenient, the
idealist versus the realist – were pitted against one another. Jean survived by returning to
his subordinate role, while Julie, unable or unwilling to revert, chose death.

O'Neill, *Long Day's Journey into Night* (1988)

O'Neill's most memorable drama, the finest American drama ever written, produced by one of the foremost directors of our time at the theater which has cared more for O'Neill's plays than any other – the success of Ingmar Bergman's production of *Long Day's Journey into Night*, written in 1941 but published, posthumously, not until 1956, opening at the Big Stage of Dramaten on April 16, 1988, seemed guaranteed.

Like O'Neill – another Strindberg devotee – Bergman has always been very concerned, not only with "the relation between man and man" but also with "the relation between man and God."[1] It is therefore surprising that this was the first, and so far the only time that Bergman staged an O'Neill play.

Although O'Neill and Bergman do not belong to the same generation, the gap between the two is not so great that it cannot be bridged. And, of course, Bergman was in 1988 older than O'Neill ever became. This explains perhaps why in his production of *Long Day's Journey* he stressed the "deep pity and understanding and forgiveness for *all* the four haunted Tyrones" that O'Neill speaks of in the dedication that precedes the play. This statement must have meant a great deal to the author of *The Best Intentions*, Bergman's compassionate treatment of his parents' troubled marriage, especially since O'Neill's phrasing seems like an echo of the pity for suffering mankind that forms the central theme of Strindberg's *Dream Play*.

As already indicated, Dramaten has a very special relationship to O'Neill. It was there that many of his plays were performed when his own country seemed to turn its back on him. A few weeks before he died, in 1953, O'Neill told his wife Carlotta that he did not want an American theater to do *Long Day's Journey*, that he wanted it done at the Royal Dramatic "in gratitude for the excellent performances they had given his plays over the years."[2]

The world premiere, directed by the young Bengt Ekerot, took place on February 10, 1956. It was a tremendous success. It is doubtful whether Dramaten has ever launched a more lauded production. The impact was shattering. To an audience familiar with Ibsen's and Strindberg's revelations of complex and painful family relations, Ekerot's *Long Day's Journey* seemed a very familiar variety of the situation in several of their plays.

O'Neill's dialogue was followed to the letter, resulting in a performance lasting 4 hours and 20 minutes. Also, the stage directions were carefully adhered to. The audience was introduced to a very realistic New England living room. The actors, who were the best the country could boast – Lars Hanson as Tyrone, Inga Tidblad as his wife Mary, Ulf Palme as the elder son Jamie, and Jarl Kulle as the younger one Edmund, O'Neill's alter ego – were wonderfully matched, so that the spectator's opportunity to identify with each of them was optimal, a matter of utmost importance in a play where we are asked to share the playwright's willingness to understand *all* four.

The head of Dramaten at the time, Karl Ragnar Gierow, has said that the dialogue of *Long Day's Journey* "is written in such a way that a group of actors who do not stick closely to the text will not manage the task."[3] Florence Eldridge, similarly, who played the part of Mary Tyrone in the first American production, has praised O'Neill's widow Carlotta for rejecting all talk of the play being repetitious and for refusing to have a single word cut. "The more one worked on the play," Eldridge says, "the more one realized that it was a symphony. Each character had a theme and the 'repetitions' were the variations on the themes."[4] Obviously, no one would abbreviate a Bruckner or Mahler symphony. Nonetheless, Bergman shortened the play by about 20 percent or almost an hour. The servant Cathleen's part was reduced considerably. The initial, allegorical pig story was omitted. And the numerous literary quotations and allusions were largely limited to James Tyrone's references to Shakespeare and Edmund's to Nietzsche. Although some of the Irish fragrance and 1912 atmosphere hereby disappeared, few critics felt that these cuts were harmful to this universal version of the play. The omissions seemed wholly in line with Bergman's reductive tendency, his desire to make the truly important aspects stand out by doing away with all paraphernalia.

In contrast to the realistic 1956 production, Bergman presented an existential, stylized version. This appeared not least from the extremely sparse scenery, designed by Gunilla Palmstierna-Weiss, which combined cinematic effects with theatrical ones. It took no fewer than seven models for her to arrive at the final one. Before she discussed the scenery with Bergman, she had the idea that the performance might begin with a realistic environment and end with a vague, hazy one, that is, that the scenery would reflect the change of climate – outer and inner – in the course of the performance.[5]

This idea was not effectuated. Nor was O'Neill's New England living room put on the stage. Instead, the audience was faced with a black 'raft' – a square, raised stage – surrounded by blackness, insisting that although the sun may enter the living room when the play opens, darkness surrounds it. Or as Tyrone's Shakespeare has it, that "our little life is rounded with a sleep." The blackness of O'Neill's back parlor had, as it were, been extended. On the black cyclorama, black-and-white images were projected. Color was added by properties and costumes.

From another, technical point of view, the scenery could be compared to the black interior of an old-fashioned, funnel-shaped grammophone. What the director and the scenographer had in mind was an acoustic box, where every whisper could be heard. Similarly, the practical idea behind the limited, raised stage was to have the actors come closer to the audience, to emphasize the intimacy of the play.

The 'raft' could also be seen as a jetty (we are close to the sea, as the sound of the foghorn keeps reminding us), the two columns at the back of the stage corresponding to piles. Or it could be seen as the dock, from which Mary had once tried to drown herself. The stage in a sense visualized the past which, Mary claims in one of the key speeches of the play, is "the present" and "the future, too."

In the last act, Bergman took the characters to the veranda of the Monte Cristo cottage, the O'Neill summer home in New London, Conn.[6] O'Neill's unity of setting was hereby abolished. The outdoor setting, especially the worn green veranda floor, helped to objectify Edmund's wish that he had been born a fish and his concomitant longing for death by water – as well as the feelings of all the Tyrones that they were lost in the fog. The impression to be communicated was that of a human aquarium.

Bergman's version was a dream-play version, stressing the unreality of life, exceedingly suggestive in its concentration on the four characters, on their gestures, movements and, above all, their faces. And in its use of projections. First, the façade of the house, dreamlike in its low angle perspective, as though floating in the air, dreamlike, too, in its strange combination of exterior and interior in one and the same stage picture.[7] Then a projection of the window in the spare room, where Mary's relapse takes place, a visualization of what is on the mind of all the men. Then a closed double doorway, telling us that no escape, no exit is possible. Subsequently, a grotesquely big greenish wallpaper pattern inviting the audience to enter the fantasy world of the four characters as they succumbed to dreams and drunkenness. Again the exterior of the house, now behind drifting spells of fog. And finally the wallpaper pattern in cold, blue light.

On the black 'raft,' Bergman limited himself to the necessary properties: a worn brown armchair to the left (a quotation from the 1956 production), a round table to the right, surrounded by four chairs. O'Neill singles out the "*varnished oak rocker ... at right front of table*" from the three "*wicker armchairs*" close to it. The oak rocker represents the sturdy nature of the *paterfamilias* – only he sits in it – while the three wicker chairs around the table indicate a certain unity among the other family members: wife and sons. Bergman retained the idea of four chairs. But unlike O'Neill's, Bergman's chairs were all of different shapes: four different human beings, four different fates. And unlike O'Neill's rocker, Bergman's armchair was occupied not only by Tyrone but also by the other family members. While O'Neill by means of the rocker separates the Tyrone from the rest of the family, Bergman emphasized the constant flux between separateness and communion that is applicable to all the Tyrones.

Largely abstaining from atmospheric light, the director throughout the performance had the characters brightly illuminated, as though they were put on a dissecting table or exposed to X-rays. The lighting visualized both their attempts to get at the naked, unashamed truth with regard to the other family members and their feeling of being painfully stripped of their consoling masks with regard to themselves.

In O'Neill's stage directions the mask-face dichotomy of the characters, their façade mentality, is indicated in the contrast between the neat and at times brilliantly lit front parlor and the black back parlor. In Bergman's version, this had its counterpart in the projection in the first act of the exterior – the façade – of the Monte Cristo cottage, as compared with its interior.

There was also an ironical reference to the façade mentality in the Greek imitation column which later was shown to hide a cocktail cabinet.[8] While this piece of property related especially to the men's tendency to embellish their weaknesses, another column, on which a Madonna and a votive candle were placed, visualized both Mary's and the three men's inclination to cling to an empty faith, in her case, a faith in the Holy Virgin, in their case in the holy mother. For both the faith proves illusory. When the stage was revolved in the later part of the performance, the sculpture was shown to be not three-dimensional as we would have expected, but flat and provided with a support at the back. Significantly, the men's discovery of Mary's relapse into morphinism more or less coincided with the audience's discovery that the back of the sculpture was hollow and in need of support. Some spectators may have been reminded of the medieval Madonna sculpture in Bergman's film *The Touch*, where the same dichotomy applies: the interior of the Madonna, whose enigmatic smile recalls the "secret smile" on the face of David's dead mother, proves to be full of beetles.

The Greek column with its Dionysian content (the liquor) seemed an ironic reference to Edmund's – that is, O'Neill's – Nietzschean craving for a rebirth of the Greek spirit, the Greek sense of tragedy. If this symbolized Edmund's, and to some extent Jamie's 'religion,' the Holy Virgin represented their parents' Christian faith. But, as we have seen, both properties were hollow. The four characters were doomed to move restlessly between what used to be the two cornerstones of Western civilization. Toward the end, they were seen – not unlike four Beckett figures – in resigned, frozen positions, waiting for death.

In O'Neill's text there is an interesting contrast between "the four somewhat dissociated lamps in the living room representing the living present" and "the five 'united' front parlor bulbs reminding us of the harmony that might have been,"[9] that is, *all* the Tyrones including the dead Eugene, who is very present in the minds of the four remaining family members.

Bergman opened his performance of *Long Day's Journey into Night* with a *tableau vivant*, in which the communion between the Tyrone family members was stressed. From left to right, James, Mary, Edmund, and Jamie. Behind the stylized Tyrone interior, the projected exterior of their house.

Abstaining from this lamp symbolism, Bergman nevertheless indirectly retained it by opening his performance with a little pantomime. O'Neill has his four characters enter from the same direction, quite logically, since they have just had breakfast together. Bergman had husband and wife enter from one direction, the sons from another. In this way the older generation was immediately separated from the younger one. Yet very soon the four formed a close-knit family group of tenderness and love. In this group, Mary was singled out as the pivotal figure by her central position opposite the three men. While Tyrone and Jamie both took complementary, self-contained positions – the former an authoritarian, the latter a nonchalantly insubordinate one – Mary and Edmund showed gestural compassion. There was no physical contact between Tyrone and Mary on the one hand and Jamie on the other. Edmund bridged the distance between the parents and Jamie. In the rest of the performance, Edmund was embraced by the other three family members, Tyrone and Mary by each other and by Edmund, but Jamie only by Edmund. The opening *tableau vivant* functioned as a proxemic and kinesic image of the fundamental relationships in the family.

In the subsequent action, the four were never seen again in harmonious togetherness. At most there were brief moments of tenderness and love between individual members of the family. Not until the end of the play were all four together on the stage again for any length of time – but then in positions indicating separation, isolation.

The initial pantomime could be interpreted in different ways. It could be seen as a pose, a façade, an expression of how the family was trying to keep up appearances. Or as a sign of how it wished to be seen by others; the momentary immobility was that of a group in front of a photographer. It could be seen as an expression of wish-fulfillment, indicating their common dream of how everything might have been. Or – with an interpretation more in agreement with O'Neill's intentions – as an image of the love that bound the four together in spite of everything. In any case, the menacing sound of the foghorn, heard already at this point, warned the audience that the relative harmony between the four was more apparent than real.

In the end, Mary's moving away from the three men is indicated in the drama text not only in her radically changed outward appearance but also by striking proxemic, kinesic, mimic, and paralinguistic signifiers:

> [MARY] *comes into the room, the wedding gown trailing on the floor. ...* [TYRONE] *gets to his feet and stands directly in her path.... She lets him take [the wedding gown]. ... She moves back from* TYRONE .... *He sinks back on his chair, holding the wedding gown in his arms with an unconscious clumsy, protective gentleness.*

While Jamie recites from Swinburne's "A Leave-taking,"

> *She moves like a sleepwalker, around the back of* JAMIE'S *chair, then forward toward left front, passing behind* EDMUND *. ... She moves left to the front end of the sofa beneath the windows and sits down, facing front, her hands folded in her lap, in a demure schoolgirlish pose.*

Mary's separation could hardly have been suggested more definitely. This is the only time in the drama text that anyone sits down away from the family table. The men immediately recognize her separation and act accordingly:

> JAMIE *pushes the bottle toward* [TYRONE]. *He pours a drink without disarranging the wedding gown he holds carefully over his other arm and on his lap, and shoves the bottle back.* JAMIE *pours his and passes the bottle to* EDMUND, *who, in turn, pours one.* TYRONE *lifts his glass and his sons follow suit mechanically, but before they can drink* MARY *speaks and they slowly lower their drinks to the table, forgetting them.*

After Mary's concluding monologue, the final acting directions confirm that the separation is lethal to all the Tyrones:

> *She stares before her in a sad dream.* TYRONE *stirs in his chair.* EDMUND *and* JAMIE *remain motionless.*

Mary's returning her wedding gown to her husband signifies her separation from him. She has reverted to the time before she met Tyrone, to the time when she dreamed of becoming a nun, of separating herself from the world. In the closing moments the past, Mary says in the play's key line, "is the present."

Bergman's ending was, even more than O'Neill's, choreographed as a contrast to the initial togetherness. The four chairs around the table in the living room had been replaced by three separate chairs – for the men – on the veranda. One chair was missing. Mary's falling flop down became an ironical comment both on her lack of support (cf. the Madonna figure) and on the discrepancy between her aspiring dreams and

Strongly contrasting with the opening scene, the closing scene of *Long Day's Journey* was one of separation. Isolated from each other, the three men listened, immobile, to Mary's drugged dreaming aloud of the time before she met her husband, while he forlornly held her bridal gown, the empty remnant of their marriage, in his hands. Note the Greek column to the left, and the Madonna to the right, turning her back on the disrupted family.

crass reality. Abstaining from the quoting of Swinburne's "A Leave-taking" – this presumably seemed too explicit and pathetic to him – Bergman retained Mary's proxemic leave-taking of each of her men. Cutting out the drinking on their part, he merely retained its essential element, the drunken stupor that turns them into immobile corpses and creates the stillness around Mary's monologue that makes the audience concentrate all the more on it. One after the other, the characters left the lit 'raft' and departed in the same directions from which they had initially entered into the surrounding darkness – as we are all doomed once to leave the raft of life *alone* on our "journey into night."

At the very end, a striking visual note was added. Before Edmund, who was the last to disappear, left the stage, a radiant tree was double-projected on the cyclorama. The tree visualized both the complicated net of nerves within Edmund – the poet figure of the play – and the entangled relations between the family members. At the same time, its radiance seemed to promise that out of these enmeshed relations a soul was being born. When Edmund picked up his black notebook shortly before he disappeared, it was an indication that, like another Trigorin – Bergman staged Chekhov's *The Seagull* in 1961 – he was going to record what he had experienced around him and turn it into dramatic art.[10] The black notebook provided a link between the staged 1912 situation and the play, *Long Day's Journey into Night*, which Edmund's alter ego some thirty years later was to write. Was then the play the audience had just seen enacted but a dream, a fantasy by the burgeoning young playwright? We are not far from the subjective approach in Bergman's 1970 production of *A Dream Play*, where the Poet, Strindberg's alter ego, was turned into the dreamer of the play.

When Edmund, in the last act, tries to tell his father of his pantheistic experiences, he does so in a manner which indicates that, contrary to what he himself claims, he has more than the makings of a poet in him. Edmund's monologue could be recreated as a desperate attempt to establish contact with his father or, on the contrary, as the reverie of someone lost in a dream, forgetful of the fact that he has a listener. In either case his poetical nature would be stressed by the very fact that the speech seems improvised, spontaneous.

Bergman's approach emphasized another aspect. By having Edmund read bits of his monologue aloud from his notebook, the director made the poetical nature of his speech more plausible and indicated furthermore that Edmund was a budding *writer*. Above all, by having him read the key sentence of the speech from his notebook – "It was a great mistake, my being born a man. I would have been much more successful as a seagull or a fish." – Bergman made it clear that this was no sudden emotional outburst but, as we now know with regard to O'Neill, a persistent feeling of alienation. Edmund let, as it were, his father share the secrets of his very private writer's diary.

Edmund's part, in Bergman's production played by Peter Stormare, is perhaps the most difficult one in the play. He has less of a past and less of a profile than the other family members. The least guilt-laden of the four Tyrones, Edmund is the character we can most easily identify with, the character who bridges the distance between stage and auditorium. This was at least the impression brought forth in Bergman's version.

As played by Jarl Kulle, James Tyrone was a big, boisterous child, in need of a mother. He was also a man who was play-acting at home, since he no longer had a stage on which he could perform. Kulle played the part brilliantly, stressing Tyrone's spontaneity and fighting spirit. But, as other Tyrones have demonstrated, it can be done very differently. In the scene where Tyrone tells Edmund about his poor youth, he was costumed, not as O'Neill has it in "*an old brown dressing gown*," indicating his stinginess, but in an elegant dressing-gown which bore witness of his glorious past; his slippers, by contrast, were old-fashioned and ugly – and so his discordant costume testified to his split nature.

In Lars Hanson's 1956 version, James Tyrone's story of his childhood was a very introvert scene, the confession of a broken man. Fredric March, in the first Broadway production, turned it into just one more whiskey-impregnated anecdote. Laurence Olivier, at the New Theatre, made it a forceful apology by a professional actor. Kulle's version was yet another variation, the need of a rather naive man to justify himself to his more mature son.

The most impressive of the four actors, most critics agreed, was Thommy Berggren, who played the part of the elder son Jamie. Jamie is an actor just like his father, but in contrast to him, he is merely a ham-actor. As in several of his films, Bergman here utilized the contrast between stage actors and clowns. Thommy Berggren's Jamie, the least loved of the four family members, was hiding his true self behind the mask of a grinning clown. At the same time, he revealed that behind the clownesque façade, behind his snobbish and vulgar Broadway wise-guy jargon, there was a sensitive human being, more gifted, perhaps, and probing than any of the other Tyrones. Admittedly, in the last act Berggren almost upset the balance of sympathies in his favor.

The focal character in the play is the wife and mother, Mary. Bergman's Mary (Bibi Andersson) was dressed, as were the others, according to the fashion in 1912. Like his Julie, she wore a violet dress throughout most of the play, and here again the color stood for mourning, death. In Mary's case there was, not surprisingly, a gray, foggy tint to it. The color also helped to link her with the whore Fat Violet, a related figure.[11]
At the end, her nightgown suggested the dress of a nun.

When Mary leaves her three men, handing her bridal gown back to her husband, the family loses its center and binding force; this is why her relapse into morphinism is so fatal for all of them. O'Neill has here created one of the most impressive moments in twentieth-century drama, in which past, present, and future for all the four Tyrones converge in a pregnant visual image.

Bibi Andersson is a rather robust, healthy kind of actress, lacking the nervous oversensitiveness of her predecessor Inga Tidblad. Nevertheless she portrayed a very convincing Mary who, like Kulle's James Tyrone, at times seemed to be acting a part. In their play-acting, one sensed both O'Neill's and Bergman's constant concern with the problem of identity.

Jamie's sarcastic comment on Mary's final entrance – "The Mad Scene. Enter Ophelia!" – was cut by Bergman. Presumably, he found it disturbingly explicit – especially since the Dramaten audience might see the connection between the barefoot Ophelia in Bergman's 1986 production of *Hamlet* and his, at this point, barefoot Mary. This kind of auto-intertextuality is not unusual with Bergman.

In his *Hamlet* production Bergman turned the protagonist, played by Peter Stormare, into a transparent counterpart of himself as a young playwright-director. As we have seen, the same actor played O'Neill's – and Bergman's – alter ego in *Long Day's Journey*. Although Bergman cautiously stressed Edmund's quality of being an outsider, not least in his positions and movements, his version was nevertheless an attempt to strike a balance between the four characters, to understand them all. The audience was confronted with an existential, post-Beckettian drama emphasizing – as Strindberg does in his chamber plays – the fundamental representativity of the fateful family interaction.

Play-acting, role-playing is the common denominator of the Tyrones. They all sense the need of putting on a mask which others can accept so that they can feel accepted by others and thus by themselves. We are here very close both to the playwright who wrote *The Great God Brown* and to the filmmaker who wrote and shot *Persona*. Since *The Great God Brown* on a symbolic-existential level dramatizes much the same situation and many of the same conflicts as *Long Day's Journey*, one might even say that Bergman directed the latter play very much in the spirit of the former one, while permeating it with his own vision. In his version, he certainly tried to bring out the classical tragedy that is hidden behind the naturalistic surface layer of *Long Day's Journey*. In a way, it was a reply to O'Neill's worrying question in 1931: "Is it possible to get modern psychological approximation of Greek sense of fate ..., which an intelligent audience of today, possessed of no belief in gods or supernatural retribution, could accept and be moved by?"[12] Bergman's production of *Long Day's Journey into Night* was an impressive attempt to provide a viable answer to O'Neill's fundamental question.

Ibsen, *A Doll's House* (1989)

How do productions of a play presented by the same director in different countries with a time lapse of some eight years compare? Ibsen's *A Doll's House* (1879), staged by Ingmar Bergman first in Germany and then in Sweden, is a case in point.

On April 30, 1981, his *Nora*, as the play is often called in Germany, opened at the Residenztheater in Munich.[1] Virtually the same text formed the basis for his second production of the play, opening on November 17, 1989, at the Big Stage of Dramaten, the Swedish equivalent of the Residenztheater. The play now carried the traditional Swedish title *Ett dockhem*.

A performance intended for a southern German audience in the early 1980s must be different in some respects from one intended for a Swedish public around 1990. Besides the temporal gap, there is the spatial one, the sociopolitical climate in Franz Josef Strauss' Bavaria being rather different from that in Sweden. The theatrical traditions in the two countries are different. And the characteristics of the individual actors necessarily make one Nora differ from the other, one Helmer from the other. There is the linguistic difference, a German translation of Ibsen's play being necessarily more removed from the Dano-Norwegian source text than a Swedish one. Moreover, in Munich Bergman was forced to deal with a language which was not his own. In Stockholm, by contrast, he was in that respect on a par with his actors, who furthermore shared his social and cultural referential system.

In addition to these general distinctions, a more specific one may be added. In Munich, *Nora* was part of a triad, the other plays being Strindberg's *Miss Julie*, there called simply *Julie*, and Bergman's own *Scenes from a Marriage*, a rather radical stage adaptation of the well-known television series[2]. As the titles indicate, the link between the three plays was the focus upon man-woman relations: Helmer-Nora, Jean-Julie, Johan-Marianne. The plays were produced simultaneously, and the triad soon came to be known as "the Bergman project." In Stockholm, by contrast, *A Doll's House* was presented as an independent play.

The focussing upon the Helmer-Nora relationship at the Residenztheater – the characters were played by Robert Atzorn and Rita Russek – meant that the three Helmer children prescribed by Ibsen as well as their Nurse were visibly eliminated in *Nora*. The ruling idea behind the production was Nora's emancipatory conviction that she has a right – nay, an obligation – to leave her husband and the consequences this has for him and him alone.

Ibsen's play was drastically cut; nearly one-third of the text was removed, and both the Nurse and the Maid were omitted.[3] The three acts of the original were replaced by 15 scenes. And Ibsen's unity of setting gave way to the presentation of three different rooms of the Helmer apartment: the living room, the dining room, and the bedroom. Even so, Bergman retained a strong sense of claustrophobia, since both windows and doors were lacking in the tall wainscot surrounding the room; not until the end, when Nora made her exit was a closet door in the background surprisingly revealed. Nora finally found a way out of her somber 'prison.' This device was in a sense a quotation from Strindberg's *The Father*, as performed at the Stockholm City Theater, where Gunilla Palmstierna-Weiss two months earlier had been responsible for another seemingly doorless, imprisoning living room.

A sense of claustrophobia was also ensured by the fact that the whole play was acted out on an inner stage, a quadrilateral platform, surrounded by extremely high walls topped by small barred windows. The intention behind the setting was not so much to suggest that the Helmer marriage was imprisoning, even less to visualize a fear on Nora's part that she might be imprisoned once her forgery was discovered. Since the representative quality of the Helmer-Nora relationship was stressed throughout, and since the high, dark-red velvet walls at the back of the stage were suspiciously theatrical, the audience was invited to mirror itself in what was happening on the stage.

A striking aspect was that during the whole performance the actors never disappeared out of sight. Exits were indicated simply by their leaving the platform stage for the background, where they remained sitting until their next 'entrance.' Disregarding the playwright's realistic motivations for entrances and exits, Bergman had the characters suddenly appear or disappear – as in a dream. With this device, he placed his production in an illusion-breaking Pirandelloan and Brechtian tradition, indicating the constant flux between on-stage and off-stage role-playing, between theater and life. Moreover, by letting the actors, when off-platform, form a stage audience, he provided a link between them and the real audience. Combined with the barred windows of the setting, the impression of the stage audience was one of a jury in a courtroom sitting in judgement on the marital relationship that was acted out before them and in which they themselves, when on-stage, were directly or indirectly involved. The stage audience could in this way mediate between the acting, on-stage characters and the observing real audience, and the idea was conveyed that the spectators in the auditorium, as mentally divided as the characters-cum-actors, were virtually sitting in judgement on themselves.

As in the source text, the action in *Nora* was set around 1880. On the curtain the scene designer had drawn a street in Christiania, showing the exterior of the Helmer apartment house. When the curtain parted, the audience moved, as it were, from the exterior to the interior of the Helmer apartment – a movement reminiscent of that in *The Ghost Sonata*. The characters wore the stiff clothes of the 1880s, high collars and gray or black dresses for the gray-haired men, a corseted wine-red dress for Nora – a vivid spot in a gray world.

The play opened not with Nora's entering the apartment together with the Porter, as Ibsen has it, but with Nora

> already seated, utterly immobile, in the midst of a wilderness of toys, dolls, and other suggestive relics of childhood. Leaning back against the pillows of the [wine-red] plush sofa, she stared out into empty space – virtually the picture of a human doll waiting to be taken up and played with. The very distant and faintly audible sound of an old-fashioned music-box tune [Schumann's "Träumerei" from *Kinderszenen*] added to the strongly oneiric mood of nostalgia and suppressed melancholy that was created by this silent image of her motionless, oddly dejected figure.[4]

With her wine-red dress Nora was at one with the comfortable sofa she was reclining in – a visual metaphor for the confining unity between character and environment. Among the relics of childhood was a doll's bed, ironically foreshadowing the marital double bed shown at the end.[5] Nora's claim that she has been treated as a doll first by her father and then by her husband seemed visually corroborated by this correspondence.

Unlike his *Nora*, Bergman's *Doll's House* was set around the turn of the century. The union flags in the Christmas tree indicated that the action took place not later than 1905, when the union between Sweden and Norway was dissolved. By this change the distance between the original sender (Ibsen) and the receiver (the Stockholm audience) was diminished by some twenty-five years. Moving the play closer to our time not only increased the audience's sense of being in touch with the characters, Nora's emancipatory ideas and her willingness to break out of her marriage also seemed more plausible. The fashion around 1905 also helped to make the bodies, especially Nora's, erotically present. Last but not least, since the opening took place in one of the most beautiful *art nouveau* buildings in Stockholm – Dramaten was completed in 1908 – the period selected was a kind of homage to the theater which Bergman has come to see as his professional home. For once, the blue *Jugendstil* curtain of Dramaten functioned not as a border separating the stage from the auditorium. Rather, it suggested the temporal unity between these two areas.

As in Munich, the play was acted out on a quadrilateral platform, this time surrounded by walls 11 meters high, topped by eight small barred windows. "The little room – the home – is placed inside a larger room which is society," one critic wrote, and this larger room "in the course of the evening is transformed into a universe, a human cosmos, a home on earth."[6] By surrounding the Helmer home with a large dark space, Bergman diminished the characters, turned them into dolls, and set their little world off from the big, threatening one outside. As in Munich, the actors remained visible also when they were off-stage. However, they were this time not seated in the background but on either side, immediately below the raised inner stage.

On this stage, representing the living room, a green *art nouveau* sofa and armchair could be seen, as well as a decorated Christmas tree and a heap of parcels. Behind the platform a green-tinted bourgeois *art nouveau* dining room could be divined: round table, chairs, and above the centrally placed piano a large painting.[7] Reminiscent of a picture out of a photo album, the setting seemed to indicate Nora's dual vacillation between the world of the present and of reality (foreground) and the world of the past and of fantasy (background), the green color bridging the two worlds. The green could be associated both with hope as in Strindberg's *A Dream Play* and with an imprisoning aquarium existence, as in Bergman's production of *Long Day's Journey into Night*.

In the second scene, the foreground shifted from green living room to brown dining room, while the background, still green-tinted, now displayed a sideboard with two candelabras, above it flowery *art nouveau* wallpaper, and as in the former scene, a large painting. The brown color, characteristic of the *Jugendstil* but here associated rather with bourgeois materialism, was now set off against the green of the background. With Krogstad's appearance, the distance between imprisoning, earthy reality and lofty dream – the candelabras turned the background sideboard into a kind of altar – had increased. The round table on the platform was mirrored in an almost identical one in the background 'photo,' creating an eerie, dreamlike effect. The impression that the play was acted out in two different worlds – one three-dimensional and real, the other two-dimensional and imaginary – was hereby strengthened. Since the projected furniture in the background appeared larger than the real pieces in the foreground, the doll's house connotations of the scenery were further underscored.

An aged Rank (Erland Josephson) appeared in an elegant *fin-de-siècle* costume, whereas a young successful Torvald Helmer (Per Mattsson) was fashionably dressed according to the *dernier cri* in *art nouveau*. Krogstad (Björn Granath) could be seen in a mold green coat, while Mrs. Linde (Marie Richardson) was dressed completely in black as though in mourning – although her husband had been dead for 3 years. Her costume was clearly designed to correspond to that of Nora at the end of the play, where it is clear that Nora has taken over the role that Mrs. Linde has outgrown. Nora (Pernilla Östergren) first appeared in a pink dress with a green apron, on which a small N was inscribed inside a big H – one of those meaningful details characteristic of a Bergman stage production. Later, she appeared in her black-and-white Capri costume, underneath which a bright red petticoat could be glimpsed. She also wore a black shawl – as prescribed by Ibsen. When Helmer had read the first, threatening letter from Krogstad, he angrily ordered her to take off her shawl. It was an act of unmasking. When he had read the second, conciliatory letter, he protectively laid the shawl around her shoulders. The mask was put back in place.

Ibsen's Nora leaves not only her husband but also her three small children. Today, when most people would accept that a wife might divorce her husband if she finds their marriage hollow and meaningless, many would still claim that the presence of young children should prevent her from doing so.

The visual absence of the children in *Nora*, Bergman eventually discovered, was a mistake. Yet in a simplified staging, three children plus a nurse is a nuisance. Besides, leaving three – or even two – children 'motherless' is less sad than leaving just one child behind. After all, two or three children have one another. Consequently, in *A Doll's House* Bergman settled for one child, a daughter, Hilde, who looked about 6 years old. Appearing only at the beginning and end of the play, Hilde was nevertheless symbolically present throughout the performance in the form of her doll that was seated on one of the chairs next to the acting area.

When the play opened, Nora was sitting on the sofa reading the end of a fairy tale to her almost identically dressed daughter: "...but a prince and his bride brought with them as much silver as they could carry. And they moved to the castle east of the sun and west of the moon." The reading was accompanied by sweet, romantic piano music, "The Maiden's Prayer," as from a music-box. Having received a goodnight kiss from her mother, Hilde left for bed. Nora lay down on the sofa, whistling the tune that had just been heard, put one arm in the air, then let it fall to the floor as her whistling petered out.

What Bergman presented in this opening was an emblematic situation, a key to Nora's existence: her desire to see life in terms of a fairy tale (with its obligatory happy ending) and her vague awareness that life is anything but that. Very effectively, Bergman demonstrated how Nora who, as a single child, had herself figuratively speaking been brought up on fairy tales by her father now continued this tradition with regard to *her* single daughter. Three generations were implicitly interwoven in this initial *tableau vivant*, suggesting a *perpetuum mobile*.

Sitting on the floor, Nora then began to unwrap the Christmas presents, while calling for her husband: "Come out, Torvald, and see what I've bought." From a realistic point of view, this might seem strange, but what was important here was that the audience should see that Nora had bought her daughter a doll for a Christmas present. The deeper significance of this was not revealed until the end of the performance.

When Helmer joined Nora behind the Christmas parcels, they looked like two little children – in accordance with the Bergmanian idea that grown-ups are merely children masquerading as grown-ups. As we have seen, psychological role-playing was continually stressed in the production.

"As far as I understand," Strindberg writes in his preface to *Getting Married*, "Nora offers herself for sale – to be paid for in cash." Strindberg's idea that Nora 'prostitutes' herself was utilized already in the opening of the performance. After all, Bergman seemed to argue, it is not the Nora-Rank relationship that is corrupt but the Nora-Helmer one. This was demonstrated in the initial monetary scene, which was done as follows:

> HELMER *still sitting on the floor frontstage, takes out his wallet.* Nora, what do you suppose I have here?
> NORA *who has been standing by the Christmas tree in the background, jumps onto the sofa, triumphantly shouting.* Money!
> HELMER. Good heavens, of course I realize it costs a lot to run a house at Christmas time.
> NORA *still on the sofa, picks one banknote after the other out of* HELMER'S *open wallet – after each approving nod by him.* Ten, twenty, thirty. *He closes the wallet but opens it again and lets her have one more.* Forty. Oh thank you, Torvald, thank you. I'll make this go a long way.
> HELMER. And what have you thought of for yourself?
> NORA. What, for me? I don't want anything.
> HELMER. Of course you do. Name something that you'd like to have – within reason, of course.
> NORA. No, I really don't know. As a matter of fact, though, Torvald...
> HELMER. Well?
> NORA *embraces him.* If you really want to give me something, you could of course – you could –
> HELMER *embraces her.* Come on, let's have it!
> NORA *lies back on the floor and drags him with her.* You could give me money, Torvald. *Stretching her legs in the air on either side of* HELMER, *who is lying on top of her.* Only as much as you think you can spare. Then I could buy something for it.

As appears from this transcription, Helmer's and Nora's marriage was emblematically depicted. The coitus position demonstrated how *she* was offering her body in exchange for the money *he* had just been offering her. Representative as it was, their marriage was no more than legalized prostitution. By presenting the Helmer marriage as starkly as this, Bergman provided a logical basis for Nora's decision at the end to free herself from a relationship which was degrading for both of them. The passage seemed choreographically designed to contrast with Nora's attitude at the end, where she refuses to accept anything from her husband.

In his 1989 *Doll's House* production, Bergman suggestively combined the erotic aspect of the stocking scene with Nora's preoccupation with death – Doctor Rank's and her own – as she 'strangled' him with her black stocking in front of the domestic 'altar.'

Strindberg's severe criticism of Nora refers not to the monetary scene but to her exhibiting her silk stockings to Rank. In Bergman's interpretation, this passage suggested anything but 'prostitution' on Nora's part:

> (NORA *is standing behind* RANK, *who is sitting on a chair. Both face the audience.*) *She puts her hands on his shoulders.*
> NORA. Be nice now. *Puts her hands over his eyes.* Tomorrow you'll see how well I'll dance. And that I do it only for you. And for Torvald, of course. *Removes her hands.*
> NORA. I'll show you something. *Takes up one of her black silk stockings, shakes it, has it glide down across his forehead to his eyes.*
> NORA. Silk stockings. *Removes the stocking from his eyes, lifts it up.* Aren't they beautiful? It's very dark in here now, of course, but tomorrow – . But how critical you look! Don't you think they'll fit me? *Puts the stocking around* RANK'S *neck.*
> RANK. I can't really give you a qualified opinion on that.
> NORA *looks at him, smilingly.* Shame on you!

Substituting black stockings for Ibsen's "flesh-colored" ones and omitting Nora's "Oh well, I suppose you can look a bit higher if you want to," Bergman was clearly not interested in emphasizing the erotic relationship between Nora and Rank. Rather, the scene stressed the fact that they have the idea of imminent death in common. When Nora covered Rank's eyes with her black stocking, she visibly turned him into a victim before an executioner. When she put the stocking around his neck, she provided another 'death sentence.' Yet since the stocking belonged to Nora who is herself a victim of circumstances and who may well be contemplating suicide already at this point – a little later this is manifestly so – both gestures applied also to her. The subtext of Bergman's version was not a regret that they could not sleep with one another; it was rather a consoling, and self-consoling, ritual worthy of a Hedda Gabler, suggesting that death can be desirable.

The ending was set in the Helmer bedroom.[8] In the background the living room and the dining room could, again, be seen as huge photographs. As Nora contemplated her past life with Helmer, the three rooms visualized their 8 years together. The photo-album connotation seemed especially relevant when Nora was about to take leave of this existence and transform it into a remembrance of things past. At the end, one critic wrote, Bergman's *Doll's House* "turns into scenes from a marriage, into distant pictures of an old photo album, where soft shades finally change into modern black-and-white."[9]

Nora's leave-taking of Helmer in the 1989 *Doll's House* production. Between them, in the background, their daughter Hilde with her doll, and to the left, ironically, the reunited Mrs. Linde and Krogstad – all three 'off-platform.'

The idea behind the change of setting – in both productions – was that husband and wife have spent a night together. *He* believed that she had reconciled herself with him. *She* was inclined to think that this was their last night together. When the scene opened, revealing a slender white *art nouveau* double bed with a glaring red bedspread, Helmer was seen asleep in it. When Nora entered, dressed in a simple black, timeless coat and carrying a small travelling-bag, he woke up. In the dark part of the stage on the left Nora was now standing, fully dressed in 'mourning.' To the right, bathed in a searing white light, Helmer was sitting in bed, stark naked, defenceless, unmasked. On the bedpost hung the red jester's cap he had worn at the fancy-dress ball the night before. While explaining her new position to him, Nora moved back and forth from the shade on the left to the brightly lit area on the right, from isolation to communion – as though she was struggling with the question: to leave or not to leave. The ending was enacted as follows:

> HELMER *sitting to the right in the double bed, looking down.* Nora, – can I never be anything but a stranger to you?
> NORA *standing on the left, the travelling-bag in her hand.* Oh, Torvald, then the most wonderful thing would have to happen –

HELMER *looks up*. Name it, this most wonderful thing!

NORA *puts the bag down, walks up to the bed.* You and I would both have to change so much that – Oh, Torvald ... I don't believe in wonders any more. *She turns and goes left, half covering her face with one hand. Takes the black shawl in her left hand, the bag in her right one.*

HELMER. But *I*'ll believe in them. Tell me! Change so much that – ?

NORA *turns away from him, wipes her eyes with her handkerchief, picks up her travelling-bag, turns around and looks at him, in a warm but firm voice.* That our marriage could become a life together. *Pause. Turns away.* Goodbye. *Exits left.*

HELMER: Nora. Nora! Nora!! *The front door slams shut. Whispers.* Nora. *Darkness, curtain.*

Bergman's skilful choreography could be sensed in this unconventional way of ending the play. While most directors would have Nora answer Helmer's question concerning "the most wonderful thing" straight away, Bergman inserted a pause at this point to ensure maximum suspense. In this way, the audience was given time to wonder, with Helmer, what the most wonderful thing might be – and so to feel empathy with him. In addition, the pause gave proper weight to Nora's key sentence.

In the source text this line reads: "At samliv mellem os to kunde bli'e et ægteskab." (That our life together could become a marriage.) For Ibsen "marriage" was the viable concept expressed in the line; for Bergman, offering his version to a present-day audience, it was rather "life together." He cleverly updated the play – thereby adjusting it to the changes in man-woman relations during the last hundred years – simply by having the two key words change places: "Att vårt äktenskap blev ett samliv."

Shortly before Nora left, Hilde appeared, silently watching her mother's leave-taking. Woken up by the shouting of the parents, she became a witness to what was nothing like the fairytale ending Nora had provided her with before she went to bed. Hilde now wore a blue dress, similar in style to the one Nora had been wearing in the beginning, and carried the similarly dressed doll she had just received from her mother. The device came close to what the Dutch refer to as Droste effect, named after the chocolate packets showing a nurse carrying a Droste packet on her tray, this packet again showing a nurse carrying a Droste packet on her tray, this packet... – *ad infinitum*. Left alone with her father – just as Nora had once been left alone with *her* father – Hilde seemed doomed to relive Nora's experience. Deprived of her mother and lacking a sister or brother, Hilde would have to console herself by playing the role of mother to her doll. In his ending Bergman clearly outlined the vicious circle in which the child with just one parent finds itself – a central issue in a social environment where divorces tend to be the rule rather than the exception.[10]

When Nora made her final exit from the platform stage, she passed by Mrs. Linde and Krogstad sitting next to it. The happily united couple was proxemically – and ironically – contrasted with the separating marital partners. While the Munich Nora left through a closet door at the back of the stage, the Stockholm Nora left via the auditorium – as if she was a member of the audience, departing from the theater along with them.

Characteristic of both the Munich and the Stockholm production was the reliance on a heavily adapted version, in which much of Ibsen's concern for realistic plausibility – what we now see as surface realism – was done away with. As a result, a stylized psychological drama came to the fore in which the characters via their off-stage counterparts were related to the audience. This attempt to bridge the gulf between stage and auditorium was especially noticeable in the Stockholm version, where the drama was acted out on a timeless, universal platform between the *art nouveau* decor in the background and the *art nouveau* auditorium in front. An earlier plan to have Nora also appear at the end in *art nouveau* clothes was discarded in favor of a more anonymous, less time-specific costume, which could render her more representative and relate her better to the audience.

While Nora's emancipation was the central issue in the version presented to the relatively unemancipated Bavarian audience, it was rather the consequences of her departure for her single daughter – read: the next generation – that formed the final impression in the version offered to the Swedish audience, an audience increasingly aware of the problems pertaining to the children of parents belonging to the divorcing generation. To put it differently: while the Munich production focussed on the marital relationship, the Stockholm one broadened the perspective. At the end, little Hilde vivified not only the present situation. She also represented Nora as a child – Nora, too, having been suddenly bereaved of a parent. By implication – the doll in her arms – she suggested her own future single-parent role. As in the opening of this production, three generations were in this way combined, suggesting a fateful *perpetuum mobile*.[11]

Despite these differences, relating to differences at the producing and receiving ends, both the Munich and the Stockholm versions could be classified as typical Bergman productions in the sense that they signified a skilful orchestration of the many instruments that, properly attuned to one another, result in an outstanding and memorable performance.

An acute sense of rhythm and a careful moment-by-moment distribution of theatrical signifiers are two of the most striking features of Bergman's craftsmanship. As a choreographer of moving stage images – moving in both senses of the word – he holds a unique position in the contemporary directorial landscape. His two productions of *A Doll's House* bore striking witness to this.

Shakespeare, *The Winter's Tale* (1994)

Already in 1932, at the age of 14, Bergman planned "two superproductions for his puppet theatre: on the one hand *The Magic Flute*, on the other *The Winter's Tale*. Both projects collapsed."[1] The former project was realized in 1975, when Bergman's pioneering screen version of Schikaneder's and Mozart's opera was broadcast by Swedish Television; the latter not until 1994, when his equally pioneering version of Shakespeare's play was performed at the Big Stage of Dramaten.

Commenting on the theme of *The Magic Flute*, Bergman writes:

> "Does Pamina still live?" The music translates the little question of the text into a big and eternal question: Does Love live? Is Love real? The answer comes quivering and hopeful: "Pa-mi-na still lives!" Love exists. Love is real in the world of man.[2]

A closely related theme is found in *The Winter's Tale*, where Leontes in the latter part of the play searches for Hermione as Tamino searches for Pamina. Reminiscing about the situation in 1932, Bergman comments: "*The Winter's Tale* is about the death of Love, the survival of Love and the resurrection of Love. It was the resurrection that broke me."[3]

In Bergman's view, not only the theme of *The Magic Flute* but also the handling of it has a close affinity with that of *The Winter's Tale*. In the opera, he says,

> It is the wonderful suddenness of the fairy tale and the dream that we may experience. ... The sweetness of the dream but also the pain and longing of the dream. ... the people in the play ask themselves if they are dreaming or are awake – if this is a dream or reality.... "If it is not fiction, then it is a dream," as Strindberg says in *A Dream Play*.[4]

A major reason behind Bergman's recent production of *The Winter's Tale*, was presumably the feeling that he was now, at the age of 76, ripe both for the autobiographical aspect of the play, the dream aspect, and the ending of it: the resurrection of Love.

Another more obvious reason was that a new Swedish translation of the play by Britt G. Hallqvist and Claes Schaar, commissioned by Bergman, had just appeared. Bergman had earlier asked Hallqvist to make new translations of *King Lear* and *Hamlet* for his productions of these plays. Concerning the former play, he wrote her: "Dear Britt, what we need is an actable, sayable and *above all* understandable version of *King Lear*."[5] His wishes were amply fulfilled. A comparison with the old Swedish renderings of *The Winter's Tale* reveals that the new translation radically differs from them precisely in the ways indicated by Bergman. Naturally, the demand that the text be actable, sayable, and understandable has often resulted in a certain simplification of the meaning and a diminishing of the poetical qualities (the blank verse). But these losses on the verbal side must be measured against the increased accessibility of the text,[6] as well as against the imaginative non-verbal context in which the dialogue is placed.

Shakespeare's text is divided into five acts. We move from King Leontes' Sicilia (Acts I-III.2) to King Polixenes' Bohemia (Acts III.3-IV.4), and from there – with a time lapse of no less than sixteen years – back to Sicilia (Act V). Disregarding the act division, Bergman divided the text into 11 scenes:

Sicilia, winter.

1.   The park of King Leontes' palace.
2.   Queen Hermione's salon.
3.   Outside Hermione's prison.
4.   The park of the palace.
5.   The court room.

Bohemia, spring.

6.   Wild coast.

       Intermission

Bohemia, spring, summer.
7.   Pastoral landscape. Spring.
8.   Pastoral landscape. Midsummer.

Sicilia, summer.

9.   Cloister.
10.   The park of the palace.
11.   Art gallery in Paulina's house.

Actually Scenes 7 and 8 were Bohemian only in a figurative sense; if anything, the pastoral environment of these scenes was Swedish.

Approximately one third of Shakespeare's text was omitted. Leaving out a couple of courtiers, Bergman on the other hand added two women to Shakespeare's cast: Amalia, lady in waiting to Queen Hermione, and the Abbess at the cloister. The latter took over one of Cleomenes' speeches, while he took over some of Camillo's and the third Courtier's speeches.

More than is usually the case, the performance began with the theater program, where Bergman pretends to be the translator of a letter, written in 1925 by a German professor, who was returning a nineteenth-century theater poster to the Royal Library of Stockholm. The poster, reproduced in the program, announces that *The Winter's Tale*, directed by Mr. Richard Furumo, will be performed as part of Miss Ulrika Sofia's birthday celebration, on December 28, in the grand salon of Hugo Löwenstierna's hunting castle.

By this counterfeit on Bergman's part, the audience, many of whom would be familiar with the work of Carl Jonas Love Almqvist (one of the leading Romantic writers in Sweden), was forewarned that the play they were going to witness would be placed within an early nineteenth-century frame. In one of his works, Almqvist has Frans explain to his brother Henrik that their father Hugo has invented "a kind of plays which he wants to call *Songes*," that is, dreams, to be performed "during the informal and modest evenings of autumn and winter."

> The theater – the yellow salon, the length of which is suitable for this purpose – is arranged so that a curtain of white gauze is hung in the middle of the room, dividing it into two parts.... This curtain will never be raised. We spectators are sitting on one side of the gauze. On the other side, furthest back the dream takes place.[7]

Unlike Hugo Löwenstierna, Bergman chose not to separate the audience from the performance but, on the contrary, to integrate them as much as possible. Setting the play in Löwenstierna's salon, the color of which seemed utterly fitting for a play about jealousy, Bergman created a complex Droste effect. The Stockholm audience were introduced to an early nineteenth-century evening of entertainment, the main part of which consisted in the presentation of *The Winter's Tale*, witnessed also by part of the fictive nineteenth-century guests. The actors of Dramaten incarnated nineteenth-century members of the Löwenstierna family, who in turn, as amateur players, incarnated fairy-tale-like, Shakespearean characters living in an unspecified period. (Admittedly, the illusion of amateurism could, for natural reasons, only be kept up in the comical parts of the production, resulting in a mixing of styles similar to that in *A Midsummer Night's Dream*.) At the same time, scenery, properties, and most of the costumes signalled yet another period, early twentieth century, the time when Dramaten was built. Approaching Strindberg's concept in *A Dream Play*, where "time and space do not exist," Bergman in his version of *The Winter's Tale* created a dreamlike "synthetic theater time."[8]

As designed by scenographer Lennart Mörk, Löwenstierna's horseshoe-shaped salon, imitating the form of the auditorium, was a replica of the beautiful *art noveau* foyer of Dramaten. As a result, the audience found itself in a space between two areas mirroring one another, one meant for performances, the other for relaxation between the acts. The scenery in this way contributed to wipe out the borderline between stage and auditorium, while at the same time it created an unreal, dreamlike effect.

To strengthen the feeling of communion between the people on either side of the proscenium, the Löwenstierna family and their guests appeared happily chatting in the staged salon, while the audience were arriving to take their seats. Almqvist himself

The Swedish nineteenth century frame for Bergman's version of *The Winter's Tale*. The guests, all in blue shades, assembled in Hugo Löwenstierna's (in a gray-green blouse to the right) salon, a semicircular version of Dramaten's *art nouveau* foyer. Even the painting on the ceiling was a replica of Carl Larsson's foyer painting. Note the decorated Christmas tree to the left, indicating the time of year.

sat down at one of the two square pianos. A conjurer entertained the double audience with a trick. A female choir sang one of the *Songes*. There was music and dancing. After a while some of the participants, the host being one of them, walked down the steps installed at the front of the stage and sat down in the first row, thereby turning themselves into members of the real audience. After some ten minutes two children – a boy and a girl – with bells in their hands announced that the performance was to begin.

The scenery in the play-within-the-play had an Elizabethan simplicity: a beautiful garden sofa, a big dinner table, a few painted screens, a wind machine visibly cranked, writhing veiled women representing a stormy sea on which a tiny model of a sailing ship was being tossed. It all had the right flavor of amateur theater.

As with Shakespeare, the first part of Bergman's play was set in winter. But while Shakespeare's pastoral scenes play in late summer or even early autumn, Bergman settled for spring and summer. The reason is obvious. Having relocated these scenes from Bohemia to Dalarna, the provincial heart of Sweden, midsummer would have a strong emotional reverberation among the audience, being the most carnivalesque time (in Bakhtin's sense) of the year in Sweden. Consequently, Bergman replaced Shakespeare's sheep-shearing feast with the Swedish midsummer celebration – well-known also in the theater through *Miss Julie*.

Shakespeare's seasonal development reflects the inner change that the protagonist, Leontes, undergoes in the course of the play, which essentially deals with the death, survival and resurrection of *his* love. This connection was strengthened in Bergman's version, where in the final script we move from "*Winter afternoon*" (Scene 2) to "*Sharp winter*" (Scene 3) to "*Cold winter day with snow falling*" (Scene 4).

In the performance, the lighting, similarly, accompanied Leontes' inner development. When his jealousy was kindled, the windows were lit deep-red. Later, when his love for Hermione had died, or rather lay dormant, a cold winter night with a starry sky and a frosty moon above snow-clad trees could be glimpsed outside the windows.[9]

Leontes' sudden and seemingly unjustified jealousy is a classical, and crucial, problem confronting every director of *The Winter's Tale*. Shakespeare has Polixenes visit Leontes for nine months to make it plausible that *he* could be the father of Hermione's child. In performances, her state of pregnancy would usually be indicated from the beginning.

Bergman proceeded differently. He placed Hermione (Pernilla August) on a wooden *art nouveau* sofa between her husband Leontes (Börje Ahlstedt) and their guest Polixenes (Krister Henriksson). She was in red, Leontes in blue, Polixenes in green, the sofa in noncomittal blue-green. Hermione was so intimate with both men that it was difficult to tell whether this was a 'matrimonial' sofa or a sofa meant for a *ménage à trois*.

The troubled quartet in the opening of *The Winter's Tale*: Mamillius was anxiously eavesdropping on his parents Queen Hermione and King Leontes, while King Polixenes jealously looked the other way. Hermione's erotic 'strangling' of her husband was strikingly similar to Nora's 'strangling' of Rank in *A Doll's House*. Both women were played by the same actress.

Confirming his intention to return to his own Bohemia the following day, Polixenes had been provided with a red guest book in which he had just finished writing. The book was handed over to Hermione. After a while Leontes snapped the book from her, looked into it, and abruptly closed it. Hermione, declaring her love for her husband, put her arms around Leontes' neck, while imploring Polixenes to stay with them for some time. Leontes opened the book again and continued to read, then suddenly got up, threw the book on the sofa and left. Here was suggested that Polixenes had praised Hermione in writing to such an extent that Leontes' jealousy, aroused already by her intimacy with his friend, was kindled.

  Leontes returned and hid himself behind the sofa, spying on Hermione and Polixenes. What he heard served to increase his suspicions:

> HERMIONE. ... We freely admit
>   the sins we have seduced you to,
>   if you first sinned with us, and then

remained with us and never slipped.[10]

LEONTES *up behind the sofa with a* "Boo!"

HERMIONE *and* POLIXENES, *who have been sitting close together, surprised fall away from one another.*

Hearing that Polixenes had complied with Hermione's prayer that he remain in Sicilia for a while, Leontes now placed himself on the sofa between Hermione and Polixenes, turning his back on the latter, who looked away to the right. When Hermione put her red shawl around Leontes' neck it was on her part a lovingly playful gesture which, however, was experienced by him as though he was being ensnared. With her shawl around his neck, Leontes, now alone on the front stage, suffocatingly spoke his

> Too hot! Too hot! To go too far in friendship,
> that is the same as mingling blood.

This soliloquy is usually regarded as the first indication in the text of Leontes' jealousy; in Bergman's version, as we have seen, it was preceded by several motivating pointers. Shortly after his jealous outburst Leontes characteristically put the red shawl next to the red book and sat down on both of them.

Highly pregnant with meaning was the situation when Polixenes and Hermione were seen lovingly dancing in the background as Leontes told Camillo (Gösta Prüzelius):

> You think I am so muddy, so unsettled
> that I myself have caused my suffering....

At this moment, it was suggestively unclear, one critic noted, whether the dancing in the background was an objective event or a subjective projection of Leontes' jealousy.[11] When Leontes a little later, another critic observed,

> glimpses Hermione and Polixenes circled in [the] dance ... a rush of stabbing anguish overcomes him; Leontes breaks into the circle, casting Polixenes out and embracing Hermione. He holds her at arm's length while she nestles his hand gently against her cheek. Suddenly, Leontes whispers something obscene to her, and Hermione breaks away. Leontes grabs a nearby female member of the court and begins to rape her.[12]

Beyond the need to revenge himself by humiliating his wife even more than she had – as he believed – humiliated him, this sudden outburst of passion and violence seemed to visualize both "the middle-aged king's unconscious terror of impotence"[13] and, in Bergman's fairy-tale-like terms, "the death of Love."

Much of what took place between the three main contrahents within Bergman's central magic rectangle had its proxemic and kinesic counterpart in the area outside it. Using one of Anna Pavlova's so-called social dances, suited for the balls of the bourgeoisie, as well as various elements from Antony Tudor, choreographer Donya Feuer had the dancers move – and at strategic moments freeze their movements – like blue-gray shadows in patterns hinting at the subtextual drama that was being enacted at center forestage. At the same time, the dancing couples helped to expand, universalize, the man-woman relations demonstrated by the three chief characters – especially when these left their central, well-lit space and joined the dancers in the outer, dimmed area.

Characteristic of his concerns in later years is Bergman's preoccupation with children in his productions. The expansion of Prince Mamillius' part is a case in point. Early in Scene 1, the boy was seen playing with his puppet theater, identical with that of Alexander in *Fanny and Alexander*, that is, modelled on the Royal Theater in Copenhagen with its motto "Not Only for Pleasure" inscribed above the proscenium opening. The scenery in Mamillius' puppet theater was that of the yellow salon surrounding it. Moreover, itself figuring inside a theater, his puppet theater had another puppet theater on its stage, this again a puppet theater on *its* stage.[14] Intervisually connecting the play with the film, Mamillius with Alexander, Bergman by this second Droste effect brought together the boy playing with his theater and the grown-ups – both on the stage and in the auditorium – busying themselves with theirs.

With Shakespeare, Prince Mamillius is sickened to death either because he cannot bear his father's harsh treatment of his mother or, with another interpretation, because, like Hamlet, he cannot bear "the supposed sin of his mother and consequent taint upon himself."[15] Whatever the reason may be, Mamillius' sad fate is included in the play mainly to demonstrate the far-reaching consequences of Leontes' jealousy. With Bergman Mamillius, a boy of 10, played by a girl (Anna Björk), was a representative, because 'androgynous,' *child*. His hair was reddish like that of Leontes' – sufficient proof, it would seem, that the King of Sicilia was indeed his father. Yet Leontes, like Strindberg's Captain in *The Father* – several critics noted the resemblance – had doubts about his own parenthood. Mamillius' loyalty to both parents was indicated both in costume – like Leontes he wore a blue dress in Scene 1; like Hermione he was dressed in red in Scene 2 – and in his attitude to them. Intuitively sensing that something was awry in their marriage, he early in the play was seen moving away from his puppet theater to the sofa where he eavesdropped on their conversation with Polixenes. A little later, he was happily sitting on his father's lap – until Leontes brutally pushed him away. In Scene 2, similarly, he was comfortably 'sleeping with' his mother – until Leontes tore him away from her. Shortly after this, he was again seen eavesdropping as Leontes called his wife a whore. In Scene 3, he was seen outside his mother's prison, suffering with her.

In his description of the dilemma in which a child of disagreeing parents finds itself – a situation vividly experienced by little Ingmar[16] – Bergman gradually added visual information that would motivate what in his version seemed to amount to a suicide on Mamillius' part, the boy who, as one critic put it, was hit by "*too* great a sorrow *too* early."[17]

While Shakespeare's play seems set in a pre- or non-Christian, fairy-tale-like environment, Bergman, in conformance with Almqvist's religious mysticism, made use of a marked Christian frame of reference. It is no coincidence that the performance of the faked program was set on the day that the Catholic church used to celebrate as the Holy Innocents' Day; hereby was suggested that Leontes was another Herod, while Mamillius and Perdita corresponded to the victimized Bethlehem children (Mat. 2.6). The Christmas tree in the wintry part was carried over in the cruciform Maypole in the midsummer part; this again was developed into the cruciform of the Holy Virgin in Scene 9 – transformations in the spirit of *A Dream Play*.

With Shakespeare, Leontes' repentance – after 16 years – is demonstrated in Act V.1, usually set in his palace. Bergman, no doubt recalling the Stranger's penance in the asylum scene of Strindberg's *To Damascus*, staged by him 20 years earlier, instead set the scene in a cloister, showing Leontes, crushed, surrounded by virginal nuns, representatives of that which he had violated. Leontes was seen with his back, streaked with blood, turned to the audience, prostrated in front of a life-like image of the Bleeding Madonna, a sword plunged into her heart – to Leontes clearly an image of the wife he felt he had killed.

When Paulina in the Swedish text reproaches him for what he has done, Leontes submissively answers:

> It is true. Killed! I have killed her,
> yes, but how you hurt me with those words!
> If they are bitter in your mouth, then they are
> much more bitter in my thoughts.
> Please say them seldom!

Showing Leontes as a flagellant, Bergman replaced the escapist "seldom" with the masochist "often."

While the penance scene fittingly was set in a cloister, the resurrection scene was staged in a secular environment: Paulina's art gallery, at night. Hermione was carried in on a catafalque, which was placed in the middle of the room.

> PAULINA. ...   Music, awake her!
> (*Almqvist's Songe No. XV is hummed in the distance.*)
> The time has come. Be stone no more! (HERMIONE *moves.*)
> Look, she moves! (*Silence.* HERMIONE *raises herself to sitting position.*)
> Be not afraid! What she is doing is as holy
> as my conjuring is good.

As in *The Magic Flute*, music worked the magic at the hands of someone steadfast in love.

Providing the scene with a richness of overtones, Bergman was certainly not suggesting that Paulina (Bibi Andersson), although she knew that Hermione had merely been hidden away for 16 years, was performing a trick – as did the conjurer appearing in the pre-play sequence. Rather, he was suggesting that the long survival of love, expressed through wordless art and music, could miraculously lead to its resurrection. The *Songe* that was hummed in the distance was the one that was sung in the beginning, bridging the pre-play and the play proper. This *Songe*, called "The Flower of the Heart," relates a parable in simple words. God has planted a colorless rose in the heart of man. Its thorns wound the heart. When the heart asks God why He has done so, God answers: "The blood from your heart colors your rose for you. / You and the rose of your heart then resemble Me in beauty." Suffering *in imitatio Christi* is the way to salvation. This meaning ties in with Leontes' 16 years of penance, emblematized in his flagellated back, red with blood. Suddenly, the red of Hermione's and Mamillius' costumes in the beginning of the play has gained a deeper meaning.

For the noble Paulina, Shakespeare's play ends happily. Having lost her husband, she remarries; her new husband is Camillo. This solution was not open to Bergman, since he had gradually turned Camillo into a Catholic priest. Instead, he chose an ending where the attention was strongly focussed upon the reunion of Leontes, Hermione, and Perdita (Kristina Törnqvist) – husband, wife and daughter:

> HERMIONE *slowly, gropingly.*
>   Tell me, my child,
> how were you saved, and where have you been?
> How did you find the way to your father's house?

PERDITA *puts her head in* HERMIONE'S *lap.*

PAULINA *up to the trio, puts one hand on* LEONTES' *shoulder, the other on* PERDITA'S.

Tell about that, you may do later.

You fortunate people, go now and share

your triumph with one and all! *Moves to the right.*

I, old turtle, will fly away

to some withered bough, where I will lament

my husband, whom I have lost, until the end of life.

LEONTES *shaking his head.*

No! No! No! Dear Paulina, *Up to her, embraces her, takes her left hand and moves her behind* HERMIONE *and* PERDITA.

accompany us now to some place where we

in peace and quiet, with questions and with answers,

may learn of what has happened to us all

in this long period that we've been separated.

Come, *Reaches his hand out to* HERMIONE *who rises.* PERDITA *takes her right hand.* HERMIONE *lets* LEONTES' *hand loose and takes both* PERDITA'S *hands, then takes* LEONTES' *hand again.* come with us. *They turn away from the audience and are about to leave upstage.*

HOUSEMAID *in from right.* Excuse me, Your Excellency, but the supper is served since quite some time.

LÖWENSTIERNA, *who has been sitting in the middle of the front row, witnessing the performance, enters the stage. Happy mealtime music. Most of the people, who have taken part in the performance whirl around on the stage, now out of their roles. A white-dressed girl jokingly sits down on the catafalque, where* HERMIONE *has just been raised from the dead. Exeunt ALL except the* SINGER. *Starlit night, strong moonlight through the windows.*

SINGER *sitting downstage right, sings a capella Almqvist's Songe No. 1.*

O my Lord, what is it pretty,

to hear music from a holy angel's mouth.

O my Lord, what is it lovely,

to die to music and to song.

Quietly flow, o my soul, in the river,

the dark and heavenly purple river. TIME, *a white-haired lady in a black*

crinoline with a red train enters the stage from the auditorium with a big
alarm clock.

Quietly sink, o my blessed spirit,

in the arms of God, the relieving, good. TIME *puts down the ticking alarm*
clock on the forestage. It shows five to twelve.

O my Lord, what is it pretty,

to hear music from a holy angel's mouth.

O my Lord, what is it lovely,

to die to music and to song.

TIME *leaves upstage. Black-out. The ticking of the clock grows louder.*

By having Time (Kristina Adolphson) – whose only speech (in Act IV.1) is usually given
to a man – reappear at the end of the performance in the form of an elderly woman,
wearing both the color of life and of death, and by providing her with an alarm clock
instead of an hour glass, Bergman could end his *Winter's Tale* with a sound that, like the
allegorical figure herself, bridged stage and auditorium and fused the two areas into a
theatrum mundi, in recognition of the fact that we are all ruled by the Clock of Life and
that the silence of darkness eventually awaits us all.

PART 2

THE SCREEN DIRECTOR

The Seventh Seal (1957)

The theater has long seemed to me, like art in general, a *Biblia pauperum*, a Bible in pictures for those who can't read what is written or printed, and the playwright a lay preacher hawking the ideas of the day in popular form, so popular that the middle classes, the theater's primary audience, can understand the basic questions without too much effort.

Strindberg's condescending view of the theater, in the opening passage of the preface to *Miss Julie*, was more applicable to another art form when Bergman began his career as a director: the film. Here, even more than in the theater, "the ideas of the day" were expressed visually rather than verbally. Moreover, the audience did not have the possibility of reading what was "written or printed," since film scripts were rarely published.

In a more restricted sense, the term *Biblia pauperum* is especially relevant to Bergman's one-act morality *Wood Painting* (1954), which forms the basis for the film *The Seventh Seal*.[1] In *Wood Painting*, which Bergman directed himself, he "moved a medieval church painting to the stage and transformed it into a silhouette-like gothic group in which all the figures ... stiffened into a sculptural pose.... The group was dissolved and the play began."[2] Bergman has himself informed us about his source of inspiration both for the play and the film:

> As a child I was sometimes allowed to accompany my father when he travelled about to preach in the small country churches in the vicinity of Stockholm. ... While Father preached away in the pulpit ..., I devoted my interest to the church's mysterious world of low arches, thick walls, the smell of eternity, the colored sunlight quivering above the strangest vegetation of medieval paintings and carved figures on ceiling and walls. There was everything that one's imagination could desire: angels, saints, dragons, prophets, devils, humans. There were very frightening animals: serpents in paradise, Balaam's ass, Jonah's whale, the eagle of the Revelation. ... In a wood sat Death, playing chess with the Crusader. Clutching the branch of a tree was a naked man with staring eyes, while down below stood Death, sawing away to his heart's content. Across gentle hills Death led the final dance towards the dark lands. But in the other arch the Holy Virgin was walking in a rose-garden, support-

ing the Child's faltering steps, and her hands were those of a peasant woman. Her face was grave and birds' wings fluttered round her head. ...

My intention has been to paint in the same way as the medieval church painter, with the same objective interest, with the same tenderness and joy.[3]

The inclination of the church painters to narrate in series of pictures relates to the epic structure of both the play and the film. And as in the medieval murals, in the film images of the sinful alternate with those of the innocent.

Bergman's choice of historical period, fourteenth century, was determined by the ravages of the plague around this time. Such a fatal epidemic means that the consciousness of death is increased. To him who fears that he is soon to die, the existential questions become burning. Does death mean annihilation or is there a life after this one? If the latter is the case, what is it like? Is there any connection between my life on earth and life hereafter? Will I be punished or rewarded according to how I have lived? Has my life been meaningful? What is the meaning of life?

Being an epidemic, the plague is a threat to everybody, man and woman, young and old, rich and poor, good and evil. The unjust distribution of fortune and misfortune in life is rectified by the democratic death that visits all. Confronted with a collective mortal danger, we strongly experience that we are all subject to the same inevitable fate.

When *The Seventh Seal* was shot, the most serious threat to mankind was the possibility that a nuclear war would annihilate all life on earth. In Sweden, Nobel prize winner Harry Martinson wrote his space epic *Aniara* (1956), which describes various reactions to the catastrophic situation in which mankind suddenly found itself. Ten years earlier, another Swedish Nobel prize winner, Eyvind Johnson, had published his version of *la condition humaine* in the novel *Return to Ithaca*, where the world of *The Odyssey* provides a distancing perspective to what is essentially, to quote the subtitle, "a novel about the present," dealing with, to quote another Johnson title, "the return of the soldier." In *Barabbas* (1950), a third Swedish Nobel prize winner, Pär Lagerkvist, depicts the title figure, representing man as imprisoned in himself, as a person who longs for a faith but who has no god to believe in. Below its historical surface layer, Lagerkvist's novel, too, focusses on a dilemma characteristic of modern man.

It is in this tradition we must place *The Seventh Seal*. In the words of Bergman himself: "It is a modern poem, presented with medieval material that has been very freely handled. The Knight of the film returns from a crusade as a soldier in our times returns from a war."[4] At home, his faithful wife is waiting for him, a medieval Penelope or a timeless Solveig.[5]

The film describes what is happening to the Knight (Max von Sydow) from his first to his last meeting with Death (Bengt Ekerot), who is here as in *Everyman* depicted as a concrete figure approaching man to end his life. When the death of the Knight is postponed, it is not, as in *Peer Gynt*, because someone in love with him has interceded. It is rather because Death enjoys playing chess with man – as the cat enjoys playing with the mouse before killing it. Ironically, the presumptuous Knight imagines that he can beat Death: "If I win, you will release me." His hubris – the sin of the tragic protagonist – is an expression of man's dream for the impossible: the abolition of death. His desire to go on living is representatively selfish.

After the meeting with Jof (Joseph), Mia (Maria), and Mikael (child Jesus) and their attitude to life, the situation changes. The Knight realizes that a postponement of his death would give him time to perform a truly good deed, so that he can die with the consoling thought that his life has not been meaningless. The good act consists in saving Jof (Nils Poppe), Mia (Bibi Andersson), and Mikael from Death.

If the Knight's metaphysical search is one pervading theme, the inevitability of death is another. In accordance with this, there is a 'Shakespearean' alternation in the film between stylized scenes, focussing on the protagonist, and realistic collective scenes; between tragedy and comedy, between 'verse' and 'prose.'

The modern equivalent of the medieval plague, Bergman has himself pointed out, is the nuclear war which in a few minutes may extinguish all of humanity.[6] This threat remains and will remain. There is, alas, no risk that the film in this respect will become dated.

In recent years, the fear of a nuclear war has been overshadowed by two other dangers threatening mankind: the destruction of natural resources and AIDS. These two dangers, especially AIDS, which threatens to kill millions of people within the next few years, may be seen as a modern equivalent of the medieval plague. Like the victims of the plague, AIDS victims tend to be shunned by their fellows. Moreover, like the plague, AIDS is regarded by many as a punishment for a sinful life. As a result of this development, *The Seventh Seal*, far from being dated, has remained relevant over the years.

Behind the film title, which is a quotation from Revelation (8.1),

one must imagine the prophet's idea of God's reply to humanity's questions about the ultimate things as a secret message written on the parchment scroll of ancient times and sealed with seven seals. Even if six of these seals are broken, the scroll remains sealed and God's secret preserved. Not until the seventh seal is broken may we learn about the secret of existence.[7]

What is said here refers to the situation of *mankind* at the Last Judgement. But the concept 'the Last Judgment' may also be related to *the individual human being* and be understood as his or her last moment in life. Viewed in this way, the breaking of the seal happens at the moment we die.

In the film we follow Antonius Block and his squire Jöns (Gunnar Björnstrand) on their way home from the Holy Land. As they journey forth, they are confronted with various situations and people. Bergman here relates both to the medieval station drama and to its modern equivalents: *Peer Gynt* and *To Damascus*.[8] Characteristic of these plays is that the looseness of structure – there is unity of neither time nor place – is counteracted partly by a thematic density, partly by an almost ever-present protagonist, necessarily someone who is on the move, a traveller.

In *The Seventh Seal*, we deal with a double protagonist, a concretization of Faust's declaration that "zwei Seelen wohnen, ach! in meiner Brust," a split within the self, indicated by the master-slave relation and by the fact that Jöns lacks a surname. In Bergman's words:

> To the fanatical believer [Antonius Block] physical and spiritual suffering is beside the point, compared with salvation. That is why, to him, everything happening around him is irrelevant, a mirror-image, a mere will-o'-the-wisp. But Jöns, he's a man of the here-and-now. He feels sympathy, hatred, and scorn;[9]

The thinker is pitted against the man of feeling, he who is concerned with a transcendent reality against him who lives in the visible present, the fanatic against the realist. The classical paradigm of this antithesis is, of course, Don Quixote and Sancho Panza.

Although Jöns is the more active of the two, the Knight is not completely passive. In the scene where the witch, Tyan (Maud Hansson), is being burnt, it is (in the script) the Knight who is acting out of compassion. Neglecting the Soldier's warning not to come too close to the witch, he

> *cups his hand, fills it with water from the skin and gives it to* TYAN. *Then he gives her a potion.*
> KNIGHT. Take this, and it will stop the pain.

In the film, it is Jöns who hands Tyan the water, but it is still the Knight who gives her the sedative potion. Here the two cooperate in their assistance of the 'crucified' witch. In a striking two-shot, where the faces of Jöns and the Knight are seen side by side gazing up at the dying Tyan, Jöns points out the connection between the two: "we see what she sees, and our terror and hers are the same." Similarly, Jöns' saving of Jof's life in the inn compares with the Knight's saving of 'the holy family' from Death.

Around the Knight and Jöns, the other characters are grouped. On the side of the Knight we find Tyan, the Girl (Gunnel Lindblom) and Karin (Inga Landgré); on Jöns' side, the rest. Jof takes a middle position. As an artist, he can enjoy this life and yet be in touch with another reality. Jof is the visionary of the film either because he is clairvoyant or else because he has a very lively imagination. In accordance with this typology, the film alternates between realistic close-to-life scenes and stylized metaphysical scenes – everything within the framework of the Revelation.

The Seventh Seal is a black-and-white film. Rarely have these colors been more adequate. It opens with a title frame – white text on a black screen – accompanied by a somber, reverberating sound, followed by deathly silence. A black frame, representing Black Death, is accompanied by ominous instrumental music. The music swells and turns into the singing of *Dies irae* as the director cuts to a low angle shot of restless, towering clouds, sunlit to the left, threateningly dark to the right – a weather contrast anticipating that of the final dance of death. When the words "*dies illa*" are heard, Bergman cuts to a low-angle shot of a sea eagle, dark against the light-and-dark sky. Then abrupt silence. After this, a cut to an extreme long shot of a mountainous coastline, black against the light sea and sky. An off-screen voice, soon to be identified as the voice of Death, reads from Revelation 8.1,[10] "And when he [the Lamb] had opened the seventh seal, there was silence in heaven about the space of half an hour." There is a cut to a high-angle extreme long shot of waves breaking on a beach, where the black silhouettes of two horses are seen. As the voice continues – "And the seven angels which had the seven trumpets prepared themselves to sound." (Rev. 1.6) – the surge of the waves is heard faintly.

The film, it will be seen, opens with a sequence which seems to fuse the Day of Creation with the Day of Judgement. We recall the words of Genesis 1.1-2: "In the beginning God created the heaven and the earth. And the earth was without form, and void; and darkness was upon the face of the deep. And the spirit of God moved upon the face of the waters." Earth, heaven, sea are what we see in the opening shots. The soaring eagle is reminiscent of "the spirit of God," especially since the optical point of view in these powerful pictures of nature seems to be that of the eagle. But the bird also relates to the Last Day. In Revelation 8.13, it says: "And I beheld, and heard an angel flying through the midst of heaven, saying with a loud voice, Woe, woe, woe, to the inhabiters of the earth by reason of the other voices of the trumpet of the three angels, which are yet to sound!" The silhouetted horses, finally, are reminiscent of the ghostly horses of the Apocalypse.

Alternating with the divine bird's-eye view, there is the low human perspective: shots of clouds and of the soaring eagle from beneath, providing visual backing for "the Knight's hopeless search for God, who remains distant and silent"[11] – an interpretation supported by his position: lying on the beach, his glance is directed upwards. Apart from its cosmogonic function, the landscape by this arrangement illustrates the Knight's – modern man's – existential sense of desolation. This is scenery mirroring a state of mind – in imitation not only of a playwright like Strindberg but also of a film director like Victor Sjöström. When the camera descends, it takes in two human wrecks on the beach.

The introductory biblical text indicates that while the film's 'human' playing time seems to be a few days – from sunrise to sunrise – its 'divine' playing time is merely half an hour, that is, the time from the breaking of the seal to the sounding of the trumpets of Judgement.

When Bergman has Death read the text of the Revelation, he relates his film to the Prologue of medieval morality plays such as *Everyman*, a drama which also in other respects has much in common with *The Seventh Seal*. Moreover, Death is here given divine status; compare Genesis: "And God said," etc. Jöns is, significantly, asleep when Death speaks His prophetic words.

Like the Death figure in the medieval moralities and murals, Bergman's Death is a metaphysical power, visibly incarnating the condition of being dead. But unlike them, He is an enigmatic, contradictory figure. We do not even know if He is omnipotent or merely the tool of a higher power. The only time He speaks of God, He questions – dressed as a monk! – God's existence. Does this imply that existence is ruled by an evil power, the Devil, or by blind Fate? The Death figure in *The Seventh Seal* can be identified with both. He has diabolic traits; and he claims to be "ignorant." Bergman's Death is at once all-seeing – "Nothing escapes me" – and blind.

Ordinary people cannot see Death until they are face to face with Him, that is, at the moment of death. This is true also of the Knight. When he first meets Death on the beach, it is because Death has come to fetch him. When Jof, who on two occasions sees Death although he is not personally confronted with Him, it is because, being clairvoyant, Jof senses that Death is hunting him. The first appearance of Death has been called "one of the most dramatic 'entrances' in all cinema."[12] In the script this is described as follows:

> A cloud hangs mute and dark over the western horizon. High up, barely visible, a sea bird floats on motionless wings. Its cry is weird and restless. The KNIGHT'S large gray horse lifts its head and whinnies. ANTONIUS BLOCK turns around.

Behind him stands a MAN *in black. His face is very pale and he keeps his hands hidden in the wide folds of his cloak.*

KNIGHT. Who are you?
DEATH. I am Death.
KNIGHT. Have you come for me?
DEATH. I have been walking by your side for a long time.
KNIGHT. That I know.
DEATH. Are you prepared?
KNIGHT. My body is frightened, but I am not.
DEATH. Well, there is no shame in that.

The mute and dark cloud here anticipates the appearance of Death. The restless crying of the sea bird and the neighing of the horse reveal that the animals have already felt Death approaching. The neighing makes the Knight turn around. What does he see? His surprise is shared by the spectator. Death appears simultaneously to him and to us – an effective way of turning the Knight into Everyman. Significantly, Death approaches from behind, like a traitor.

The Knight makes a distinction between the body's fear of death and the soul's longing for it, and in the Swedish original there is an untranslatable pun on the words 'beredd' (prepared) and 'rädd' (afraid), indicating that the Knight, consciously or unconsciously, does not answer Death's question but answers a question never posed by Him. The presence of Death makes the Knight feel cold. When Death opens his cloak to put it around him, it is both a possessive and a warming gesture.

Let us now see how this sequence is recreated in the film. Here the chessboard, which we have already linked with the Knight, appears in close-up. With its black and white chessmen, it signifies the struggle for survival that the Knight is soon to fight with Death. The metaphysical function of the game is clarified when Bergman has the chessboard dissolve into an extreme long shot of the roaring sea. In the distance the sun rises out of the sea. When the image of waves breaking against black rocks dissolves into the black shape of Death, the roar of the surf is replaced by complete silence. Where the sun was seen, we now see the white face of Death. There He suddenly stands, in long shot, in a black, long, hooded cloak – a gigantic hangman with the face of a corpse, in the boundary between the dark earth and the light heaven. There is a cut to a long shot of the Knight, in profile, squatting on the beach. He is looking for something in his "*big bag.*" Suddenly he looks into the camera, as though he sensed the presence of Death. Then follows the dialogue between the two, ending with the Knight's assurance that he is himself not afraid of Death. As he gets up to approach Death, dull, ominous music is intoned. Death raises his right arm to a horizontal position, so that his wide cloak falls out like a black wall. There is a quick zoom-in on the pale, clownesque face of Death, surrounded by the black hood.[13] He looks cruel. After this shot, which makes us share the Knight's fear, Bergman cuts to an even more radical point-of-view shot: a completely black frame. Along with the Knight, we are enclosed in Death's black cloak. In the next shot the blackness, the cloaked arm of Death, is lowered – the camera is now behind Him – and the Knight's face appears in the upper part of the frame as he says: "Wait a moment." Then the pact with Death is concluded that provides the Knight with a respite covering the playing time of the film.

The difference in this sequence between the script and the film is considerable. Both in the script and in the film, the arrival of Death is presaged through realistic, contextually determined, diegetic on-screen sounds (the crying of the sea eagle, the neighing of the horse). But in the film the roar of the sea ceases as soon as Death appears. The switch from an outer, recognizable reality to an inner, metaphysical one becomes in this way more strongly emphasized in the film. The discrepancy between script and film concerns also the relation between the sun and the figure of Death. In the script, the different positions of the sun are carefully noted. It is here not only a question of indicating the progression of time. In the metaphysically waste landscape, the sun receives apocalyptic dignity. This can easily be made clear verbally. But how does one visually depict a sun "which wallows up from the misty sea like some bloated, dying fish" or, in a black-and-white film, a sun which has "lost its red light"? The earlier noted dissolve from the sun to the face of Death at least indicates the transcendental nature of this celestial body.

Once the Knight and Death have sat down by the chessboard – "a striking quasi-surrealist image, the transitory and fragile game of life played out against eternity"[14] – there is a slow dissolve into a long shot of sea and sky, emphasizing the metaphysical significance of the chess-playing.

There follow a series of shots in which the Knight and his Squire are seen journeying forth on horseback; the conventional dissolves here indicate the discrepancy between implicit and visualized time. Although the difference in status is indicated by the Knight riding ahead and Jöns behind, what is striking, through the choice of extreme long shots, is rather their minute equality in a 'divine' perspective. They are seen at first from a bird's-eye view as tiny creatures moving forward along the beach; then in another extreme long shot as they keep riding between and behind high black rocks, reminiscent of a medieval hell mouth; finally in a low angle extreme long shot as they proceed across a heath, silhouetted against the sky, a shot anticipating the dance of death at the end.

Suddenly we see the back of a man sitting by the road, with a dog nearby. Jöns dismounts his horse to ask him about the way. When the man does not react to Jöns' tap on his shoulder, Jöns jokingly grasps his hood and turns his head. In a shocking point-of-view close-up, reminiscent of the one we have just seen of Death, a face "*with empty eye sockets and white teeth*" suddenly stares simultaneously at us and at Jöns. This is the first testimony in the film to the ravages of the plague. But why the dog? The contrast dead human being/living animal returns later in connection with Skat's death, but then with a different meaning. The significance of the dog is clearer in the script, where it says: "*Close by a scrawny dog is whining, crawling toward its master....*" The symbolism is here the same as in Hjalmar Söderberg's short story "A Dog without Master" (1891), where the death of the dog's master corresponds to man's existential desolation following upon the death of God. After the confrontation with the dead man, Jöns no longer rides behind but side by side with the Knight. Death extinguishes all class differences.

Masked as a monk receiving confession, Death makes the Knight reveal his strategy at the chessboard. "Why should Death cheat on certainties?" a critic asks.[15] Do we deal with the hangman's cruel game with his victim? Does the confession scene serve to illustrate the Knight's hubris, his vain belief that he can outwit Death? Or is Death's behavior in this scene merely an expression of the Knight's *feeling* that he is being cheated?

The confession scene is interesting in several respects. Its inclusion is in the first place motivated by the Knight's need to confess his sins now that he knows that he is soon to die. In that sense, it is highly archetypal. The sin that burdens him is selfishness, indifference to his fellow men. But this is also the 'sin' that God, according to the Knight, is guilty of vis-à-vis mankind. The question is then: Is man's selfishness the cause or the result of God's selfishness?

A confession is a speech between monologue and dialogue. The confessing person has a speaking partner, but this partner, the confessor, functions primarily as a listener. Moreover, it is his duty not to reveal the content of the confession to others. In these respects, a confession comes close to a monologue. Bergman visually supports the idea of someone primarily speaking to himself by having the Knight's face surrounded by bars. By means of a strong side light, the bars separating the Knight from his confessor (Death) are reflected on the opposite wall. The chapel is turned into a prison cell, in accordance with the Knight's feeling that he lives "in a world of phantoms. I am imprisoned in my dreams and fantasies."[16] The room, in other words, recreates a mental condition.

It is, of course, ironical that the confessor is identical with Death. Instead of providing consolation, He extracts the chess secret from the Knight. Again, he appears as the Knight's opposing player, as well as a cheater. There is also an irony in the Knight's longing that God "uncover his face" – at the moment when we see Death hiding His face from him.

The stylized description of Skat's (Erik Strandmark), the jester's, death is like a church mural in black-and-white. While Skat is planning for the next day, we who have seen Death approaching him from behind, know that there will be no next day for him. When Skat discovers that Death is sawing away at his tree, he tries to negotiate with Him. Bergman here intercuts between Skat's optical point of view from above and Death's from below. One would expect the same distance between the two point-of-view shots. Instead Bergman alternates between medium shots of Death and close-ups of Skat. The difference in distance illustrates how Skat psychologically is much closer to Death than he wants to admit. The end of this scene reads as follows in the script:

> DEATH *begins to saw again. The tree creaks.*
> SKAT. Isn't there any way to get off? Aren't there any special rules for actors?
> DEATH. No, not in this case.
> SKAT. No loopholes, no exceptions.
>   DEATH *saws.*
> SKAT. Perhaps you'll take a bribe.
>   DEATH *saws.*
> SKAT. Help! Help!
>   *The tree falls. The forest becomes silent again.*

We notice how Death, who has earlier answered Skat's questions, toward the end ceases to do so and exclusively pursues his work.

In the film, this passage is recreated in a different way. Instead of audible cries for help, we here merely see Skat screaming. The effect, not unlike that of Edvard Munch's famous *Scream*, is more terrifying when we have to fill in the sound ourselves. In Bergman's case, the muteness of Skat's scream is motivated also by the fact that it is the scream of someone dying, a unique situation. It is as though Skat has already taken a first step into the mute realm of the dead.

We then witness how the tree falls. The crash is followed by three light, clock-like strokes – an inversion of Death's three dull knocks on the gate at the end of the film – and immediately a squirrel jumps onto the stump and begins to nibble it. Life goes on as if nothing has happened. Or is it a playful reminder of the possibility of transmigration? The conventional sequence of the script – scream (life) followed by silence (death)

– is expressively inverted by the addition in the film of the squirrel. We have silence where we expect a scream and a non-diegetic sound (the hopeful clock-like strokes) where we expect silence.

The Church Painter's (Gunnar Olsson) remark that people are more interested in "a skull" than in "a naked woman" sums up the thematic poles of the film: Thanatos and Eros. His remark is verified when the jesters' erotic stage performance is suddenly interrupted by the flagellant procession which attracts the attention of everyone. Here art is confronted with reality, the hedonism of the theater with the asceticism of the church. But the two events may also be seen as two different types of performances. The jesters perform their pantomimic farce on a stage, separated from the audience which keeps mocking them.[17] By contrast, the flagellant procession passes through the crowd of villagers, who mutely kneel to the Crucified, clasp their hands and make the sign of the cross in the hope that the self-mutilation of the flagellants will turn away God's wrath and spare them also from the plague.[18] The awkward song that the jesters have just been singing and in which joy of life is contrasted with awareness of death is now replaced by the monks' somber *Dies iræ*.

The black Dominican monks, with their hoods pulled down and carrying swaying censers, are first seen at a distance. As they approach the low camera and grow in size, the rows separate, so that the spectator feels squeezed between them. "*After the line of monks*," it says in the script, "*comes another procession. It is a column of men, boys, old men, women, girls, children. All of them have steel-edged scourges in their hands with which they whip themselves and each other, howling ecstatically.*" The procession stops at the open space of the village. A raised skull to the left and a crucifix to the right are the focal points in a carefully composed *tableau vivant*.

Then follows the Monk's (Anders Ek) fire-and-brimstone sermon on the theme today red, tomorrow dead, yelled out next to the face of the Crucified, a visual *memento mori*. Just as Death, disguised as a monk, in the confession and witch-burning scenes, appears close to the cross, so the inexorable Monk close to the crucifix bears a striking similarity to Death.[19]

When the flagellants proceed, singing and screaming, they are seen from a bird's-eye point of view. In a slow dissolve, they disappear into the ground. There is a moment of absolute silence. It is the film's most radical expression of the idea that we are all doomed to end underground. The drastic compression of time combined with the bird's-eye view gives the impression that the transformation from life to death is seen from the perspective of a Higher Power. To God, a human life lasts but the fraction of a second.

As often with Bergman, life and theater, reality and fiction ironically mingle in *The Seventh Seal*. For example, Jof's, Mia's, and Skat's pantomime on the theme of the deceived husband, his wife, and her lover is repeated in reality when Skat – while Jof and Mia continue their performance with blacksmith Plog (Åke Fridell) among the audience – behind the stage seduces, or is seduced by, Plog's wife Lisa (Inga Gill). When he learns about this, Plog challenges Skat in the nearby forest. Each of them tries to surpass the other in abuses. Skat seeks moral support from Lisa, Plog from Jöns. But very soon Lisa changes side and is reunited with her husband. The whole scene is a piece of stylized theater – with Jöns as a willing prompter and predicter of the outcome. Reality here appears to be just as crude and human relations just as simple as in the pantomime we have just witnessed. When Skat finally fakes a suicide, Lisa and Plog characteristically mistake play-acting for reality.

The same reversal is seen a little later; just as Skat's sham death appears very real, his real death is a piece of stylized theater. Jof's enforced bear dance on the table in the inn – a torture scene linking it with Tyan's martyrdom – is a spectacle to the customers more relished than the one he has just performed on the stage. Why? Because Jof's suffering this time is genuine. Like the child Tyan, the innocent Jof functions as a scapegoat on whom the audience can project their fear.

The paradisaic wild strawberry scene in *The Seventh Seal*, a secular communion. From left to right Jöns, the Girl, Jof, Mia, and the Knight.

In the famous wild strawberry scene, the five characters are symmetrically grouped in a half-circle: Jöns and the Girl to the left, the Knight and Mia to the right, Jof with his lyre in the middle and a little behind the others. On the wagon in the background Skat's mask of death is a reminder of the presence of death even in the happy moments of life. Or is it there to exorcise death? The evening sun sheds its soft light on the five. Jof plucks his lyre and hums the romantic ballad he has been singing before, "On a lily branch a dove is perched." The central part of the scene, as it is recreated in the film, is as follows:

> *Long shot of* MIA *and the* KNIGHT. JOF *in the background.* MIA, *the bowl of wild strawberries in her hands, picks a few berries from the bowl and hands them to the* KNIGHT.
> MIA. Do you want some wild strawberries?
> *The* KNIGHT *shakes his head, raises his clasped hands, looks at them.* Faith is a torment, did you know that? It is like loving someone who is out there in the darkness but never appears, no matter how loudly you call. *Takes a berry from* MIA'S *hand.* How meaningless and unreal all that seems to me when I sit here with you and your husband. How unimportant it suddenly becomes.
> MIA *smiling.* Now you don't look so solemn.
> *Medium shot of* JOF *with his lyre; the skull of death and the wagon are in the background.*
> *High angle long shot of* MIA *and the* KNIGHT, JOF *figuring in the background.*
> *The* KNIGHT *with the bowl of wild strawberries in his hands.* I shall remember this moment. The silence, the twilight, the bowl of wild strawberries, *Hands the bowl to* JÖNS. the bowl of milk, *Track-out of the group.* JÖNS *hands the bowl to* MIA, *who in turn hands it to the* GIRL. your faces in the evening light. Mikael sleeping, Jof with his lyre. MIA *picks up the bowl of milk.* I'll try to remember what we have talked about MIA *hands the bowl of milk to the* KNIGHT. *Frontal medium close-up of the* KNIGHT, *holding the bowl of milk in front of him.* And I shall carry this memory between my hands as carefully as if it were a bowl filled to the brim with fresh milk. *Drinks from the bowl.* And this will be a sign to me *Hands the bowl back to* MIA, *cut to the group.* and a great sufficiency.

This is a democratic meal, in which the participants address each other informally and eat and drink out of the same bowls. It is also a secular counterpart of the Holy Communion. This is indicated by the semicircular grouping, which resembles the grouping round the altar rails; by the presence of death in the form of the mask; and by Jof's humming and plucking of the lyre, which correspond to the subdued singing and organ playing accompanying the Communion.[20] In this secular communion out in the open, the wild strawberries and the milk – equivalent of the bread and the wine – work a transubstantiation on the part of the Knight. He discovers the meaning of life.

Significantly, it is Mia – a young, warm woman, pure of heart – who officiates. Wild strawberries are sometimes in Christian iconography linked with the Virgin Mary. The milk connotes woman as a nourishing mother. When the bowl of milk is raised and held between the hands, like a Communion cup, it relates both to Jof's early vision, where he saw the Virgin Mary holding "the Child between her hands," and to the ending, where Jof and Mia, in a similar light and environment, one after the other lovingly hold Mikael between their hands.

These allusions and correspondences give emphasis to the Knight's newly gained conviction that his metaphysical search has been "meaningless" and that the love radiating from Mia and Jof will be "a great sufficiency" to him.

The meal of love out in the open contrasts with the gluttonous eating and drinking in the dark inn. Here a living pig is running around, while a dead one is turned on a spit, a drastic variation on the theme "Today red...." The morning meal at the end of the film is a third variety, an ascetic last meal – and in this sense another Communion – while waiting for Death.

The text of the Revelation returns at the end of the film. However, it is now read, not by a metaphysical off-screen figure but by a human on-screen one: the Knight's wife Karin. The Knight has just arrived together with his four travelling companions: Jöns and the Girl, Plog and Lisa. Now they are all waiting that the prophecy of the Revelation about the Last Day will come true. *"Three mighty knocks"* on the door of the gate announce the arrival of Death. Jöns gets up to open the door. When he returns, the Knight asks: "Was someone there?" Jöns answers: "No, my lord. I saw no one." This is said with a facial expression that makes one doubt Jöns' sincerity. Psychologically, it is a white lie. Jöns wants to spare the others. Metaphysically, it is a truth. Jöns, the atheist, claims that death, rather than being "someone," is "no one," definable only as a negation, as the absence of life.

When Death finally appears – this time only as a vague, dark shape at the other end of the room – the six get up from the table and "stand close together," face to face with Him – and us. The grouping, suggesting how the six "form a single body" – to quote from a similar situation in *Cries and Whispers* – to protect themselves against "the ultimate loneliness," illustrates both the equality and the communion before death. The

The six characters facing Death at the end of *The Seventh Seal*. From left to right: Lisa, Plog, Karin, the Knight, the Girl, Jöns. The six are actually never seen exactly like this in the film, where Bergman has the camera pan across them.

grouping is highly symmetrical: three men and three women, metonymically representing humanity. But there are also individual differences. While five of them retain the frontal position, the Knight kneels down in the background; in semi-profile he holds his hands pressed together as if in prayer, his gaze turned to the bit of sky that can be seen through the small window. While the light from the window falls on his face, the others remain more or less in the darkness. In accordance with this visual contrast, the dialogue turns into a 'quarrel' – to use a term common in medieval *conflictus* literature – between the two halves of the double protagonist:

> KNIGHT. From our darkness, we call out to Thee, Lord. Have mercy on us because we are small and frightened and ignorant.
> JÖNS *bitterly*. In the darkness where you claim to be, where all of us probably are... In that darkness you will find no one to listen to your cries or be touched by your sufferings. Wash your tears and mirror yourself in your indifference.

Contrasting with the Knight's *de profundis* appeals for mercy is Jöns' stoic attitude. Facing the inevitability of death squarely, his protest does not concern Death or God, as the American translation misleadingly suggests, but the Knight's attitude to death. The Knight's indifference to his fellow men – this is what Jöns implies – has its counterpart in God's indifference to man. While the three men in the background vary in their attitude to Death – Plog is apologetic, the Knight appealing, Jöns protesting – the three women in the foreground take a joint attitude. Karin bids Death informally but "courteously" welcome; Lisa curtsies speechless to "the great lord"; and the Girl falls on her knees and says: "It is finished." This is her first and only speech in the film.[21] The three words, being the last words of Christ (John 19.30), give a special dignity to her utterance.

The Girl is an early exponent of a type of woman appearing in several Bergman films: she who does not express herself through words but through loving action, the paragon being the mute Milkmaid in *The Ghost Sonata*. The Girl, who has so far had a rather subordinate role in the film, is the central figure in the final confrontation with Death. It is she who first turns her glance to the door through which Death is to enter. It is she who first gets up from the table to kneel to Death. It is across her face, in close-up, that the shade of Death is spreading. It is she who with her animated, radiating face expresses a transformation from anguish to affirmation. When her face is dissolved into that of Mia, it is as though longing for death was fused with life affirmation – a subdued counterpart of the polarity between the Knight and Jöns.

The last we see of the six characters, in search of an 'Author,' is a low angle extreme long shot showing how they, guided by Death, "tread the dance in a long row ... toward the dark lands." In this famous shot,[22] anticipated by the church painter's dance of death mural, the human figures move like silhouetted tiny creatures in the metaphysical borderland between heaven and earth, in a dance from dawn to darkness – a pregnant image of the life-long movement towards death. As silhouettes, the six have been deprived of their individuality[23] and transformed into representatives of humanity. Jof speaks, with a variation of the words from Revelation, of how "the rain washes their faces and cleans the salt of tears from their cheeks." This is how it appears in Jof's subjective vision, but since we participate in his vision, it is objectified into a 'truth.'

What we logically expect is that the six dancers are identical with the six who have just been facing Death. Their silhouetted clothes should reveal that we deal with three men and three women. But what we see are four men and two women. To complicate the matter further, we have Jof's statement that the dancers following Death are "the smith and Lisa and the Knight and Raval and Jöns and Skat," that is, five men and one woman. It has been said that the reason why Jof does not mention Karin is that he hardly knows of her existence. One critic believes that the reason why the Girl is left out is that, like 'the holy family,' she may have been saved from Death.[24] Another critic imagines that Jof has developed "a mental block in imagining death for someone resembling Mia."[25]

A more likely reason why Bergman presents no less than three different versions of the six dancers is that in this way the spectator becomes at once mystified and actively involved. Our logical expectations are contradicted by what we see. And what we see agrees neither with Mia's view – she does not see anything – nor with Jof's vision. This leads to the conclusion that there is no objective knowledge, merely subjective 'visions.'

As for the visual correspondences between the Girl and Mia and, we may add, Karin, whose dress is remarkably like Mia's, the simplest explanation is that all three represent an archetypal feminine affirmative attitude to life and death, contrasting with the archetypal male attitude of questioning (the Knight) or protesting (Jöns) – similar to the male-female grouping in *A Dream Play*.

However, *The Seventh Seal* does not end on a note of death. In Revelation we are told that Archangel Michael conquers the dragon (the Devil) and that God after the Day of Judgement shall dwell among humanity and "shall wipe away all tears from their eyes; and there shall be no more death, neither sorrow, nor crying, neither shall there be any more pain: for the former things are passed away." (Rev. 21.4) Bergman shows how 'the holy family' – Jof, Mia, and their son Mikael (!) – are saved from Death as Joseph, Maria, and child Jesus were saved from Herod when they fled to Egypt. The final shot of the film shows how the three move away from the dark realm of Death. The contrast with the opening of the film is striking. There we saw the Knight and Jöns in a low position, surrounded by a sterile landscape, a gray light of dawn and a sea in turmoil. Now we see Jof, Mia and Mikael and their horse and wagon high up on a plain overlooking a quiet sea, bathed in soft sunlight; and we hear the warbling of birds, the notes of harps, and the singing of angels. Do these celestial sounds refer only to the blessed trinity? Or do they indicate that also the six will eventually be saved? The ending is, no doubt deliberately, unclear on this point. But it may be noted that even after the light frame of 'the holy family' has been replaced by a final black frame, corresponding to the one opening the film, the hopeful singing of the angels can be heard: *Soli Gloria Deo.*

Wild Strawberries (1957)

Many film directors have stressed the connection between the film medium and the nocturnal dream. No one has done it as frequently and as emphatically as Ingmar Bergman.[1] One of his most explicit statements on this matter reads:

> No other art-medium ... can communicate the specific quality of the dream as well as film can. When the lights go down in the cinema and this white shining point opens up for us, our gaze stops flitting hither and thither, settles and becomes quite steady. We just sit there, letting the images flow out over us. Our will ceases to function. We lose our ability to sort things out and fix them in their proper places. We're drawn into a course of events – we're participants in a dream.[2]

To Bergman, literary reception is primarily intellectual, while filmic reception, like the reception of music, is mainly an emotional experience: "The sequence of pictures plays directly on our feelings."[3] In film, we deal with "a language that literally is spoken from soul to soul in expressions that, almost sensuously, escape the restrictive control of the intellect."[4] Since Bergman feels attracted to the film medium because of its ability to create a dreamlike mood – direct contact with hidden psychic levels – it is logical that he makes maximum use of this possibility. Strindberg's importance for him is here evident. Not least in *Wild Strawberries*, Bergman resorts to dreamlike changes of time and space, recalling the technique of *A Dream Play*. As in Strindberg's case, these changes serve to evoke the feeling that life itself is dreamlike. As Eva in *Shame* puts it, echoing the Poet in *A Dream Play*:

> Sometimes everything seems like a long strange dream. It's not my dream, it's someone else's, that I'm forced to take part in. Nothing is properly real. It's all made up. What do you think will happen when the person who has dreamed us wakes up and is ashamed of his dream?

The idea is here that life is a nightmare dreamed by God. And that mankind is forced to exist in this nightmare. We do not usually call a person to task for what (s)he is dreaming. But that is precisely what Eva is doing here with God.

Similar though they may seem, there is a marked difference between an ordinary dream and a film dream. We can never directly experience each other's dreams. Only indirectly, by telling each other about them, can we 'experience' them.

One of Jung's best known, and most controversial, ideas concerns the hypothesis of the collective unconscious, the idea that we all, irrespective of time and place, have certain unconscious drives in common. It is interesting in this context to note that a film performance is perceived collectively. When a dream is made visible in the cinema, deep levels of our psyche, levels that we share with our fellow-men, are activated. The collective unconscious becomes almost perceptible.

Both the verbal dream report of everyday life and the audiovisual dream creation of film are, in different ways, imitations, incomplete reconstructions of the authentic dream. Moreover, unlike its prototype, the nocturnal dream, the film dream is to a great extent an aesthetic phenomenon, thematically and structurally related to other parts of the film to which it belongs. It is true that the purely verbal dream report can also be an aesthetic phenomenon when it is part of a novel or a play. But often, for example in a therapeutic situation, it has quite another function.

Wild Strawberries deals with a professor emeritus in bacteriology, Eberhard Isak Borg (Victor Sjöström),[5] who undertakes a journey from Stockholm to Lund, where he is going to be promoted to jubilee doctor at the solemn degree ceremony in the cathedral.[6] Like Saul's journey to Damascus, paraphrased by Strindberg in his trilogy, Isak's trip turns into a penitential journey, working a conversion. Isak Borg's career has been based on a reckless attitude to his fellow-men. Now, on the threshold of death, he begins to suffer from pangs of guilt. The trip to the south is interrupted by a dream or daydream as Isak revisits the summer house of his childhood. Discovering the old wild strawberry patch, he nostalgically returns to the innocent period of his life. A little later he has another nightmare in which he is confronted with his own egoism. While the former dream deals with a lost, innocent paradise, the latter deals with the circumstances leading to the loss of this paradise. The cause is simply growing up, that is, growing sinful and guilt-laden. Just before Isak undertakes his journey, he has a nightmare. When the journey is over he again revisits, in a dream, the summer paradise of his childhood. And there the film ends.

The pattern is: nightmare, nostalgic dream, nightmare, nostalgic dream. Isak is alternately haunted by erinnyes and eumenides. Altogether, the dream sequences take up about one-third of the film. The balance between dreams and reality results in a meaningful floating between these two areas of experience. After Strindberg, Freud, Proust, and Joyce, we are inclined to see this floating as realistic. A great part of our life is spent on dreams and fantasies – especially when we grow old and the past has more to offer than the present.[7] Nostalgically we turn back to the light memories, often connected with childhood. Frightened we await the approaching darkness. With his 78 years – in the script he is two years younger – Isak Borg has reached this marked point in life.

Bergman's handling of the continual alternation between, and merging of, dream and reality calls for a complex narrative structure. Apart from the author, Bergman, who is telling the story about Isak Borg, there is the narrator, Isak, recounting in voice-over his diary notes about himself; there is further the Isak of the present, meeting various people during his automobile trip; and there is the dreaming Isak, who as an old man meets various people looking just the way they did when he was young.[8]

The first dream follows immediately after Isak's introductory presentation of himself. In the script, this prologue is actually an epilogue, for the introductory diary notes have obviously been written down *after* the journey from Stockholm to Lund, as appears at the end of the notes when it is stated that the rest of the story is "a true account of the events, dreams and thoughts which befell me on a certain day." This can only refer to the journey to Lund.

It is not unimportant that the prologue here in fact turns out to be an epilogue. For if the journey means that Isak gains new insight and matures, we expect this to be reflected in his initial characterization of himself. But this is not the case:

> Nevertheless, if for some reason I would have to evaluate myself, I am sure that I would do so without shame or concern for my reputation.

> All I ask of life is to be left alone and to have the opportunity to devote myself to the few things which continue to interest me, however superficial they may be.

> ... I detest emotional outbursts, women's tears and the crying of children.

The first quotation indicates self-satisfaction rather than self-knowledge, the other two suggest passive egocentricity. In short, these descriptions reveal that Isak has not changed. What seemed like a conversion proves to be no more than a temporary change of mood. The script shows an Isak who is back in his old egocentric role.

In the film the introductory autobiographical sketch is offered the day *before* the journey to Lund. In the expository pre-credit text it here says: "Tomorrow I shall be promoted to jubilee doctor in the cathedral of Lund." Subsequently, the film demonstrates that Isak undergoes an inner change during his journey south. Where the script reveals man's inability to change in any profound way, the film indicates that this is indeed possible.

After the credits, the film proper begins with the nightmare Isak had "in the early morning of Saturday, the first of June." Then follows the journey and the degree ceremony in Lund. And the film ends with Isak's paradisaic vision in the night after the degree ceremony. That the introductory nightmare in the film precedes the journey is confirmed by Isak's statement during the trip: "I suddenly remembered my early-morning dream: the blank clock face and my own watch which lacked hands, the hearse and my dead self." The journey begins on Saturday, June 1, around 3 a.m. and ends the same day around 5 p.m., when the ceremony in Lund takes place. That the trip is undertaken by car instead of airplane, as Isak had originally planned, is motivated by the fear of death that the nightmare has given rise to. Although he is a scientist, Isak is obviously superstitious.

Had Bergman chosen to let the nightmare follow after the journey, some of the events during the journey might have been explained as reminiscences of the experiences of the day before. This has obviously not interested him. By turning his nightmare into a traditional, anticipating type of dream, he gives it a metaphysical rather than a psychological status. Also, it adds an aura of mystique to the events during the journey. Thus, the ringing of church bells in the nightmare sequence anticipates both the bells at the degree ceremony in the cathedral and, hypothetically, the funeral bells which are soon to ring for Isak. The latter is particularly emphasized, since the ringing in the nightmare is combined with a shot of the man who drops dead immediately before the arrival of the black hearse,[9] which corresponds to Isak's old black car.[10] The accident of the hearse anticipates Alman's (Gunnar Sjöberg) driving his car into the ditch; when one of the wheels of the hearse in a low-angle shot rolls towards Isak, so that he "had to throw [himself] to one side to avoid being hit," the situation corresponds to the crash with Alman's car which Isak barely manages to avoid.[11]

That the nightmare precedes rather than follows the journey also means that this dream together with the journey and the concluding paradisaic vision becomes an inner journey à la *Divina Commedia*. Borg is first punished with a vision of hell (Inferno), is purged during the journey with its different 'stations,' among which there is one gas station (Purgatorio), and is finally rewarded with heavenly grace (Paradiso).

The calm pre-credit sequence, which recreates a completely realistic environment (Isak's study), is followed by the strongly contrasting nightmare. In this manner, Bergman already at the outset of the film demonstrates the division between Isak's seemingly harmonious, conscious ego and his repressed, guilt-ridden anguish.

The initial nightmare could, in principle, be recreated in three different ways. Bergman could let Isak, in close-up, relate his dream. He could visualize the dream, with or without sound effects. Or he could combine these two approaches, that is, provide the visualized dream with a narrative commentary. Not surprisingly, Bergman on the whole settles for the most dreamlike alternative: direct visualization – with sound effects.

Nowhere is the distance between script and film as striking as in the initial nightmare sequence. While in the script the dream is narrated by Isak, in the film it is shown. The transient passage is:

> In the early morning of Saturday, the first of June, I had a strange and very unpleasant dream. I dreamed that during my morning stroll I had gone astray and arrived in a district, unknown to me, with deserted streets and dilapidated houses.

Via a close-up of the dreamer's, Isak's, face combined with his retrospective commentary just quoted, we move into his dream.

After Freud's *Traumdeutung*, we know that dreams are often initiated by outer stimuli. We remember the little boy whose urge to pee results in a dream beginning with a small stream of water and ending with an ocean. Similarly, in the script, Isak's dream is determined by the rising sun. "It was three in the morning and the sun was already reflecting from the rooftops opposite my window," it says as soon as Isak has woken up. Shortly before this he dreams that

> High above me the sun shone completely white, and light forced its way down between the houses as if it were the blade of a razor-sharp knife.

Here is implied that the sunlight, suddenly streaming in through Isak's window, functions both as a dream stimulus and as an alarm clock. In the film, where Isak sleeps with drawn curtains, this indication of a visual dream source has disappeared, while an acoustic stimulus has been preserved. The ticking of the alarm clock, which is heard when Isak wakes up, has visually initiated both the clock outside the optician's shop and Isak's own pocket watch, while acoustically it makes him hear his own heartbeat.

All these ingredients are highly symbolic. In most cases, we deal with death symbols – whether we think of Isak's approaching physical death or his present state of being a spiritually dead or dying man. Each symbol in the nightmare sequence must be seen from this both/and perspective. Whether Isak looks forward or backward, he is confronted with death in one form or another. Take, for example, the description in the script of the optician's sign: "The dial was blank, and below it someone had smashed both of the eyes so that they looked like watery, infected sores." The absence of the hands indicates that time has ceased to exist for Isak, that life has been replaced by death. When we die, the eyes burst. But the blank dial and the wounded eyes staring at Isak also mirror his frigid egoism. The connection is even more obvious in the film, where only one of the eyes is wounded – to indicate Isak's mental one-eyedness. The symbolism here corresponds to the one in the film's second nightmare sequence, where Isak in a microscope only manages to see his own eye. The big optician's spectacles may be seen as a visualization both of Isak's social persona and of his spiritual nearsightedness, of his egoism. Similarly, the man without a face, whom Isak takes to be alive but who appears to be dead, is obviously his double. They are significantly dressed in much the same way. The empty face of the man with its desperately closed mouth and eyes resembles the face of a fetus. A grown-up man and yet a fetus is a rather adequate description of Isak who emotionally has remained at a rudimentary stage. Alternatively, the face can be seen as Isak's true, grim appearance beneath the mild persona he shows to the world. When the man without a face turns his back to Isak, his attitude reflects both Isak's experience of his father as being constantly absent and his own attitude to his son Evald (Gunnar Björnstrand).[12] The man without a face may even be seen as a metaphor of *deus absconditus*, the god who collapses – 'dies' – when you regard him,[13] a reversal of the biblical idea that he who has seen God must die.

If the man without a face is a living dead, then the corpse in the coffin is a person refusing to die. By having the same actor play both Isak and the corpse, Bergman indicates the connection between the two.[14] This is further strengthened by the series of shots/reverse shots, in which we see the corpse with Isak's eyes, and Isak with the eyes of the corpse. At gradually shorter intervals, the camera approaches the two faces, until they nearly blend. Via a zoom-in, we are returned to Isak's sleeping face. The strength of this sequence depends upon its ambiguity: we cannot say for certain whether it is Isak who tries to pull the corpse out of the coffin or the corpse that tries to pull him into it. Fear of death and longing for death intermingle.

Very striking are the contrasts between the initial nightmare and the paradisaic vision with which the film concludes. Here a sterile urban environment is pitted against open, smiling nature; an Isak surrounded by tall buildings closing him in and making him small – indicative of an imprisoning existence – against an Isak up on a hillock in a high and free position; sharp sunlight and black shadows against shadeless mild sunlight; and loneliness against communion: in the paradisaic vision of the end we see, for the first time, in a point-of-view shot, Isak's parents, be it at a distance.

When Isak is left alone by the wild strawberry patch of his childhood in front of the house, where he spent the first twenty summers of his life, the memories crowd in on him. The transition from reality to dream is again mediated by the retrospective narrator; in the version of the film:

I don't know how it happened, but the day's clear reality flowed into the even clearer images of memory, which arose with the force of real events.

When we first saw the summer house, with Isak's and Marianne's eyes, it "slept behind closed doors and drawn blinds," as it says in the script, as desolate and silent as the houses in Isak's initial nightmare with their boarded windows. The realistic motivation is that the house is empty this summer. The underlying reason is that in this way an effective contrast could be established between the silent house of the present (reality) and the living house of the past (remembrance). Via Isak's nostalgic reliving of the past, we experience how the house suddenly seems "bursting with life" and sound: piano music, happy voices, laughter, footsteps, children's cries, singing.

Why then a wild strawberry patch? In Sweden, wild strawberries are associated with summer, childhood, and happiness. What Proust's madeleine cake is to the first-person narrator of *A la recherche du temps perdu*, the wild strawberry patch is to Isak Borg. The sight, smell, and taste of wild strawberries arouse the memory of the wild strawberry patch of childhood, similar to the one Isak now has before him and yet, in the light of memory, quite different. In the film, the transition from the wild strawberry patch of the present to that of the past is marked by a couple of dissolves showing trees in the wind and moving white summer clouds.

The fact that in Christian iconography wild strawberries signify good deeds and righteousness further supports the idea that these berries symbolize the innocence of childhood. In the last instance, we deal with Isak's – an ageing man's – nostalgic attraction to childhood because it represents innocence, purity. But this longing for a return to a paradisaic state of innocence is also mankind's. We have all, like Adam and Eve, dwelt in an innocent, happy Eden. We have all, by growing up, eaten from the tree of knowledge of good and evil. We have all been driven out of Paradise. That Bergman had the biblical situation in mind appears from the script, where it says: "I sat down next to an old apple tree that stood alone and ate the berries, one by one." But how are we to interpret the Bergmanian variant? Do the wild strawberries correspond to the biblical apple? Hardly. Rather, they symbolize a purity contrasting with the knowledge of good and evil represented by the apple. As a scientist, Isak has devoted himself to the fruits of knowledge. At this late stage of his life, he returns to the pure wild strawberries of childhood.

It is characteristic that the beloved woman of his youth, Sara (Bibi Andersson),[15] who soon appears in his remembrance, devotes herself to the picking of wild strawberries. Everything indicates that Sara is still a virgin. She is secretly engaged to Isak, he too erotically inexperienced – rather than innocent. The wild strawberry patch is theirs. When Isak's elder brother Sigfrid (Per Sjöstrand) appears and kisses Sara, the Fall is a fact. This is how Isak, in the words of the script, remembers it:

> She was carried away by this game and returned his kiss with a certain fierceness. But then she was conscience-stricken and threw herself down on the ground, knocking over the basket of strawberries. She was very angry and began crying with excitement. ...
>
> SARA. You've turned me into a bad woman, at least *nearly*.

Confronted with Sigfrid, the seductive 'serpent,' Sara cannot resist the erotic temptation. Partly responding to his seduction, she reveals herself as unfaithful towards her 'fiancé' Isak. Herein consists her true Fall, made visible when the wild strawberries are spilt on the ground. That Sara is a sinning Eve appears from her reaction: "And look, I have a spot on my gown." This is the wording of the script; in the film, the "gown" has significantly been replaced by an "apron."

In Bergman's version, the Fall is connected not with erotic extravagance but with the guilt feelings resulting from it. Retrospectively, we realize that it has less to do with Sigfrid's way of acting than with Isak's way of thinking, Isak who "likes to kiss only in the dark" and who frequently speaks "about sinfulness." Sara finds herself torn between Sigfrid's active hedonism and Isak's passive moralism.

When Isak, in the foreground, is a passive observer of Sigfrid's seduction of Sara in the background, the reason is of course that he, belonging to the present, cannot intervene in a situation of the past. What is more, Isak never witnessed the seduction; at most, he heard it described by the gossiping twins. What takes place between Sara and Sigfrid at this point therefore essentially takes place in Isak's imagination. The arrangement is akin to that in Edvard Munch's *Jealousy*, where in the foreground we see the face of the jealous husband and in the background the love-making between his wife and her lover the way he imagines it, here, too, with the universalizing biblical reference: the lover stands close to a half-nude Eve who picks an apple from a tree.

When the gong sounds, everybody runs indoors for the family breakfast. For a moment Isak is left alone with Sigbritt's little child. A connection between the old man and the little child is indicated. As Sara is soon to state, Isak is "a child," a circumstance implied also by their names: the biblical Sara was Isaac's mother.

Soon Isak finds himself alone in the dark hall, looking into the light dining room, where his nameless aunt and uncle Aron, his cousin Sara, and his many brothers and sisters are seated. The present is spatially contrasted with the past. Remarkably, neither Isak nor his parents are present at the breakfast. The authoritarian aunt, who

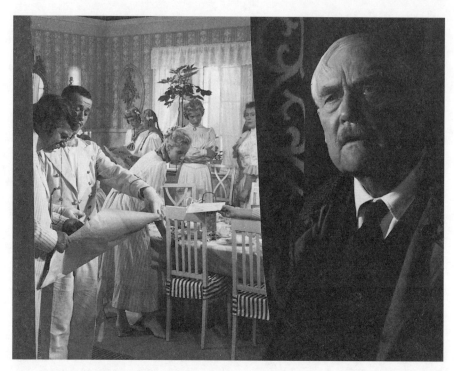

Wild Strawberries: Isak Borg as a lonely outsider in the dark hall representing the present, reminiscing the idyllic togetherness of his childhood.

continually keeps exhorting the young members of the family, communicates as badly with them as the "stone deaf" uncle. The division mother's sister/father's brother is significant. Isak's mother is later revealed as a cold woman, disliked by the children, while his father, on the contrary, is liked by everyone. The aunt and the uncle are apparently parental substitutes.

Why, then, do we not see the young Isak at the breakfast table? Just as in the case of the seduction at the strawberry patch, Isak was not present at this particular breakfast. But since he has experienced many similar ones, the breakfast may be seen as a synthesis of all the breakfasts in the summer house. What we witness is a representative, Oscarian, upper class breakfast.

However different the parents may be, they have one thing in common: their absence. While the mother's absence is not regretted, "daddy" is eagerly searched for. Even to the old Isak the message that his young counterpart is "out fishing with Father" gives rise to "a secret and completely inexplicable happiness." Being alone with father must have been something exceptional in a family with ten children. The lack of contact between parents and children seems to be at the root of Isak's problem.

After the painful confrontation with the Alman couple which also means a confrontation both with the past (Isak's bad marriage with Karin) and with the present (Marianne's problematic marriage with Evald), Isak falls asleep. In his dream, he is back by the wild strawberry patch he has just visited in his imagination. This time he can communicate with Sara. The wild strawberries appear again, now no longer in their natural surroundings but picked and put into a basket. Next we see the basket turned over and the wild strawberries – innocence – spilt. In the mirror that Sara holds up to Isak, he can see his own guilt-ridden face.

The mirror sequence is seemingly constructed as a continuous dialogue between Isak and Sara. On closer inspection, four stages can be discerned, marked by Sara's alternate turning to the young and the old Isak – while for the spectator he remains visibly the old Isak of the present. Through this technique of condensation, it is indicated that Isak is a man who has stagnated in his growth.

When Sara hears the crying of Sigbritt's little boy, she hurries to the child. In the script, it says:

> She lifted the crying child and cradled it in her arms. The sky turned black above the sea and large birds circled overhead, screeching toward the house, which suddenly seemed ugly and poor. There was something fateful and threatening in this twilight, in the crying of the child, in the shrieking of the black birds. Sara cradled the baby and her voice, half singing, was very distant and sorrowful.
>
> SARA. My poor little one, you shall sleep quietly now. Don't be afraid of the wind. Don't be afraid of the birds, the jackdaws and the sea gulls. Don't be afraid of the waves from the sea. I'm with you. I'm holding you tight. Don't be afraid, little one. Soon it will be another day. No one can hurt you; I am with you; I'm holding you.
>
> But her voice was sorrowful and tears ran down her cheeks without end. The child became silent, as if it were listening, and I wanted to scream until my lungs were bloody.

The child is rocked to sleep. But the old man, who is also a 'child,' is left alone with his anguish. Isak's scream is not heard. Unlike Peer Gynt, he has not yet deserved a Solveig's maternal care.[16]

When Sara a little later is called to the house by Sigfrid, she runs to him and hands him the child. Together, they disappear in the house. We here seem confronted with a dreamlike reduction of time. Before our eyes Sigbritt's little boy is turned into Sara's and Sigfrid's newly born baby.

In the film, this passage is done as follows. While the camera is panning with Sara as she is running towards the cradle, we hear agitated music, soon mixed with the cries of birds. Not until she arrives at the cradle do we hear the crying of the child – mixed with that of the birds. Sara has, in other words, heard the crying of the child before we do – an indication of her maternal instinct. Sara bends over the cradle, picks up the child, and speaks calmly to it. We see her in a medium shot; behind her face there are two dead branches resembling a pair of claws. The child and the birds have ceased crying, but the agitated music remains below her consoling words.

After Sara has disappeared into the house, there is a low-angle shot of swarming, crying jackdaws against the dark sky. The cradle is seen again, now in silhouette under huge branches, black against the light evening sky. Isak approaches it as a black silhouette. The crying of birds continues, now amplified by regular 'heartbeats,' reminiscent of those in the initial nightmare. Isak's anguish has become audiovisualized. He looks into the empty cradle, then turns his glance toward the house. The camera tilts upwards to the claws of the dead tree, black against the light sky. Slow dissolve to Isak's 'wandering' face, which now seems caught by the claws.

The newborn child and the old man under the dead tree become an image of life from birth to death. In the approaching darkness and the restless circling of the black birds, we divine the proximity of death. Sara 'saves' the little child from the claws of death, but old Isak is caught by them. The dead tree returns later in the confrontation between Evald and Marianne (Ingrid Thulin) by the sea. As in the earlier sequence, Marianne's affirmation of life, concretized in her pregnancy, is contrasted with Evald's longing for death, significantly voiced by a dead tree. In this way, Bergman weaves a complicated pattern of fertility versus sterility symbols.[17] The living trees are pitted against the dead as the living human beings are pitted against the living dead.

When Isak approaches the illuminated house in the twilight, we first see him standing outside a window with a drawn, illuminated blind – an image of the outsider. From inside, piano music can be heard. Isak moves to another window. And here we see, with him, Sara sitting by the piano and, behind her, Sigfrid. Sigfrid walks up to Sara, kisses her neck, then her mouth. She responds to his kisses. The situation is a repetition of the earlier seduction scene. While this happens, the diegetic piano music is replaced by the non-diegetic playing of a violin. The camera pans with them as they walk to an elegant dinner table further inside, a spatial change that may suggest a temporal one. Sigfrid in tails and Sara in a white, low-necked, silk dress are costumed like Marianne and Evald later, when they are leaving for the solemn degree dinner, an indication that Sara in Isak's dream mingles with Marianne, Sigfrid with Evald, the past with the present. Significantly, Isak is not present at the dinner following the degree ceremony, although it is partly given in his honor. Feeling now that he is not worthy of what is bestowed on him, he remains an outsider even at the end.

We see Sigfrid and Sara with Isak's eyes, as he stands outside the window. His face is illuminated partly by the warm light from inside, partly by the cold moonlight outside. The divided light emphasizes how Isak is left alone with the man in the moon, once more separated from the communion of the young couple.

The image of the two at the dinner table slowly dissolves into one of dark clouds and moonlight, reflected on the window pane. There is a shot of the moon gliding behind dark branches and a close-up of Isak's anguished face, his glance turned upwards towards the moon. Silence. The camera pans with Isak as he moves, past a protruding nail, to another, completely black window. He knocks loudly on the window pane, touches the nail with his palm (in the script it is glass splinters), looks at his wounded palm, behind which his dark face, as reflected in the pane, can be divined. Again, we hear the regular, somber 'heartbeats.' Then Alman's face appears behind the window pane where we just saw Isak's. Alman invites him to enter through what now appears to be a door with a window up above. The moonlight through the door-window forms a cross on the floor of the hall next to Isak's dark silhouette.

The window sequence is metaphorically very pregnant. Here is demonstrated how the 'imprisoned' Isak experiences himself as excluded, how his egocentricity leads to self-pity. The Narcissus motif is combined with the motif of stigmatization. Again we hear the anguished beating of his heart. And we see how his face is mirrored in that of his alter ego: Alman.

Then follows a new dream transformation. The corridor which in the former dream led to the light dining room now leads to "a large, bare windowless room," resembling an anatomy theater. In this closed, windowless room, corresponding to the lecture room where Isak used to examine his students, he is now himself to be examined – in the presence of ten young students, among them the three he has taken into his car, the hitchhikers Sara, Anders (Folke Sundquist) and Viktor (Björn Bjelvenstam). The situation corresponds to the one in the asylum scene of *To Damascus I*, where the Unknown is held responsible before those against whom he has sinned in the past, the difference being that there the victims appear in ghost-like dresses, while in *Wild Strawberries* they are dressed normally, realistically. The sequence also corresponds to the school scene in *A Dream Play*, where the Officer who has just received an honorary degree finds himself returned to the primary school. Here, surrounded by school children, he must "ripen."

Isak's examiner appears to be the cynical engineer Alman, his alter ego. The questioning seemingly concerns Isak's professional knowledge, but in reality it concerns his attitude to his fellow men. When in the microscope he sees only his own eye "in an absurd enlargement," it is an expression of his own one-eyedness, his egoism. And when he proves unable to read the text on the blackboard, saying that "a doctor's first duty *is to ask forgiveness*," it symbolizes his unwillingness to admit his own guilt. By letting us see what Isak sees – the eye in extreme close-up; the text on the blackboard that is unintelligible also for us[18] – Bergman makes us identify with him. We, too, are selfish. We, too, find it hard to admit our guilt. Isak's role of Everyman is marked also by the accusation that he is "guilty of guilt," meaning that he shares the guilt tainting all mankind: Original Sin.

When Isak is asked to diagnose a patient, he declares that the patient is dead. At the same moment, the woman, who turns out to be Berit Alman (Gunnel Broström), opens her eyes and laughs loudly. Since she was earlier linked with Isak's dead wife Karin (Gertrud Fridh), the diagnosis sequence indicates that Isak's wife, although she has been dead for thirty years, continues to haunt Isak in the form of guilt feelings he tries to repress. The connection is clarified when Alman orders Isak to revisit a traumatic memory of his wife. In the erotic sequence that now follows, Karin's laughter is an echo of Berit's. Alman takes Isak to a glade, where once more he is forced to witness how his wife gives herself to another man.

The sequence is a development of the earlier Sara-Sigfrid seduction. Sara responds to Sigfrid's kiss. Karin receives a bestial lover "between her open knees" (this according to the script; in the film the coitus is toned down). While Isak has *not* witnessed his fiancée's unfaithfulness, he *has* witnessed his wife's copulation with the lover – without intervening.[19] This second seduction is therefore much more aggravating for Isak than the first one – and consequently more traumatic, more repressed. The two sequences are visually linked through the ladder, set up against the apple tree, figuring in both, and behind which Isak takes protection in the latter case. But the ladder has changed; it is now burnt – again a transformation of a prop in the spirit of *A Dream Play*.

The universal-biblical aspect is carried through in the script, in which the coitus between the wife and the lover takes place in cold moonlight in a glade surrounded by "fallen down dead trees" (omitted in the American translation) and marshy ground with lots of snakes. Afterwards Karin complains that she "is bitten by a snake" (omitted in the American translation). Whether we associate this with the biblical or the phallic serpent, the symbolism is so explicit that Bergman has abstained from it in the film. As a result, the connection between the two seductions is to some extent obscured.

The second nightmare ends with Alman's conclusion that Isak has "removed" his own guilt, that he is punished with loneliness, and that it is uncertain if there is any grace to be found for him.

The question of grace comes to the fore in the film's last dream sequence, which coincides with Isak's falling asleep the night after the degree ceremony. The following motivation is given by the retrospective narrator:

> Whenever I am restless or sad, I usually try to recall memories from my childhood, to calm down. This is the way it was this night too...

We notice the iterative formulation. Like his creator, Isak lives very much in his childhood.

There is a dissolve to the summer house. Children pour out of it. They are on their way down to the landing-stage. Sara, in white summer dress, leaves the others and approaches Isak, in black suit and dark overcoat, with the message that there are no wild strawberries left and that he should go looking for his father. Isak answers that he *has* been looking for him but that he can find neither him nor his mother. Sara says that she will help him. Down by the landing-stage, a boy has been pushed into the water. A life-saver is thrown out. Sara and Isak regard the intermezzo. Isak's face lights up. Perhaps there is a life-saver also for him.

Isak's nostalgic, soft-focus vision of an idyllic vacation existence at the end of *Wild Strawberries*, a vision which, relating both to the past and to the future, stresses his desire to establish contact with his parents.

Sara takes Isak by the hand and leads him through the forest up to a hillock from where there is a wide view over the bay. We hear the joyful singing of birds – contrasting with the shrill crying of jackdaws earlier – and a harmonious harp chord. When they arrive at the hillock, Sara points to the bay. A new harp chord forms a transience to an extreme long shot of the bay, in dreamy soft focus. Far away, a man (Isak's father) is sitting by the shore with a long, bent fishing-rod. His reflection is seen in the still water. Further up sits a woman (the mother), knitting. Both wear white summer clothes. Both look in Isak's direction and wave to him. Sara leaves Isak. Again, we see the bay and the parents. The singing of the birds, mingled with harp chords, is now very loud. Track-in on Isak's transfigured face in an extreme close-up, singing of birds, harp chords. Slow dissolve to Isak's 'real face' on the pillow, still in a transfigured light. He opens his eyes. Harp chord. Fade-out of Isak's face.

In the final images, it will be evident, we are brought back to reality, but to a reality marked by the vision we have just shared with Isak. Even if the film's pre-credit sequence clarifies that Isak does not die at the end, the final images suggest that this is precisely what happens. In the image of the parents, the past (the childhood memories) and the future (the hope for a happy reunion with them after death) mingle.[20] The image of them surrounded by a lovely summer archipelago is an image of paradise pointing in two directions. The spatial distance between Isak and the parents corresponds to the temporal distance, backwards towards childhood, forwards towards life hereafter. The distance is further emphasized in the script, where the outsider theme is stressed even at the end: "I dreamed that I stood by the water and shouted toward the bay, but the warm summer breeze carried away my cries, and they did not reach their destination."

Wild Strawberries is usually described as a film in which the search for God and for a meaning in life are replaced by more immanent questions. This is not altogether true. The metaphysical questions appear also in this film. Isak Borg's behavior during a long life cannot be separated from his existential situation in the shadow of death. Like *The Seventh Seal*, *Wild Strawberries* is in its essence a filmic counterpart of *Everyman*, the medieval morality play about Man who in the face of Death is confronted with his deeds in life, a theme that is penetratingly dealt with in Ibsen's *Peer Gynt*, the play that was on Bergman's mind when he wrote the script for *Wild Strawberries*. The final images of Isak's transfigured face are both thematically and emotionally close to Solveig's concluding song in Ibsen's drama: "I shall rock you, I shall watch you; – / sleep and dream, my dearest boy!" As for the paradisaic final vision, it relates very closely to the Student's vision of a paradisaic Isle of the Dead at the end of *The Ghost Sonata*. In his third staging of this play Bergman rearranged, as we have seen, the ending and had, to the accompaniment of harmonious harp chords, a celestial light of grace shine on a reunited family – an ending very similar to that of *Wild Strawberries*.

Earlier in the film, we witnessed another paradise: the beautiful view of a huge sunlit lake seen from a terrace high up. At this occasion, a hymn by Johan Olof Wallin, beginning "Where is the Friend for whom I'm ever yearning?," is quoted by Isak, Marianne and the young theology student Anders.

The friend for whom Isak is yearning is the constantly absent father. When Isak on one occasion is out with the father fishing, he experiences a brief moment of reunion with this friend. The episode points forward to the end's relished fishing together with the father, who even has a catch: the fishing-rod is bent.

The hymn speaks of a "Friend": God; and the script of a "friend": the father. When the word is uttered in the film, we cannot tell if it is capitalized or not. This is meaningful, for in *Wild Strawberries* the father is in fact – just as in *Through a Glass Darkly* – at least in part the equivalent of the heavenly Father. This explains why everybody is so concerned with the father rather than the mother and why it is always him they are looking for. Little Isak's search for an earthly father, who for the child has divine status, blends with old Isak's search for a heavenly Father, a forgiving God. When the sun of grace in the final frames illuminates Isak's face, it is a confirmation that he has finally found – or believed he has found – the Friend he has been seeking all his life. One can hardly imagine a more pregnant expression of the Freudian idea of the dream as wish-fulfilment.

We can now see the connection between the wild strawberries and the father which earlier seemed somewhat cryptic. Both are gone. It is not just the happy safety of childhood that Isak has lost when growing up. The wild strawberries also connote purity, the purity which Isak has gradually lost – as we all do when we grow old. It is this imagery which is suggested in the gradual change of the wild strawberries from naturally growing berries to picked, spilt, and absent ones. When the wild strawberries are gone, dark clouds gather in the sky. It is then high time to seek a forgiving, loving Father.

Although the final images of Isak's face bring us back to reality, on another level they connote death and reawakening to life hereafter. Only in this way can one satisfactorily explain why Bergman in the final frames does not have Isak fall asleep with a transfigured face but wake up with such a face. The wish-fulfilling dream has, objectified, been transmitted from Isak to the spectator.

Strindberg, *Storm* (1960)

In the spring of 1955, Victor Sjöström, the grand old man of Swedish silent cinema, performed one of his last stage roles, that of the Gentleman in Strindberg's *Storm* (1907).[1] Two and a half years later, *Wild Strawberries* had its world premiere. The lead was played by Victor Sjöström, his very last role.

About two years after this, Ingmar Bergman launched his TV production of *Storm*.[2] The performance met with great enthusiasm among the critics. A Danish critic called it a milestone in the history of the teleplay and even went so far as to claim that not until now, when shown on the small screen, had Strindberg's chamber play fully come into its own.[3]

It is well-known that Bergman's chamber films in the 1960s have an affinity with Strindberg's chamber plays. It is less well-known that *Wild Strawberries* in many ways resembles the first of the chamber plays.[4] In the following, Bergman's production of Strindberg's *Storm* will be examined with special attention to its relationship to *Wild Strawberries*.

Both the Gentleman in *Storm* and Isak Borg are old men with unhappy marriages behind them. Preparing themselves for the final rest, they long for "the peace of old age," to quote the Gentleman's reiterated phrase. Both imagine that they have reached a stage in life where loneliness, as a preparation for the ultimate loneliness, can be calmly accepted. Both live in apartment houses, surrounded by other people. And both have a housekeeper, who obviously functions as a substitute wife. In short, both men lead an existence bordering on that of a hermit, a choice indicative of their vacillating attitude to loneliness and togetherness, respectively. Like the Gentleman, Isak has the habit of strolling "along a broad, tree-lined boulevard," another indication that both of them cherish a *flaneur* existence of observation, of noninvolvement.

Both men are self-centred and highly subjective. Yet both Strindberg and Bergman disguise this initially by having us share the protagonist's point of view. For a long time we tend to side with the Gentleman against his wife Gerda – until we discover in the course of the play that he gives different reasons for his divorce from her. It is only after we have come to doubt his judgement that Strindberg has the Brother, his closest friend, reveal that neither Gerda nor her new husband are as wretched as the Gentleman would have us, or rather himself, believe. Then comes the Brother's weighty remark: "You only see things from your viewpoint." Suddenly we realize that the Gentleman has been an unreliable, highly subjective narrator of his own life story.

The Brother's key line is echoed, sharpened, and expanded by Marianne in *Wild Strawberries*, when she tells Isak, her father-in-law:

> You are completely inconsiderate and you have never listened to anyone but yourself. All this is well hidden behind your mask of old-fashioned charm and your friendliness. ... We who have seen you at close range, we know what you really are. You can't fool us.

The question may be posed: Has the Gentleman in *Storm* ever listened to anyone but himself? Strindberg has structured his play in such a way that he is not seen "at close range" by the audience until fairly late, at which time his mask of friendliness is dropped, and he reveals his bottled-up aggression toward his fellow men. Marianne's portrait of Isak *could* be read as Bergman's interpretation of the Gentleman. But whereas Isak in the course of the film grows – or is revealed as – more human than we had expected, the Gentleman grows – or is revealed as – less so.

In both play and film, the aged protagonists live more in the past than in the present. Says Isak:

> I have found that during the last few years I glide rather easily into a twilight world of memories and dreams which are highly personal. I've often wondered if this is a sign of increasing senility. Sometimes I've also asked myself if it is a harbinger of approaching death.

A twilight world is precisely what we have in *Storm*, set on an August evening shortly before the gaslamps are lit. As a result, the expression fits the Gentleman even better than it does Isak, whether we think of old age as the twilight of life or of memories as belonging naturally to the crepuscular light.

Since *Storm* is a text intended for the stage, the memories of the protagonist could not be made visible in the form of flashbacks – as is done in *Wild Strawberries*. In a screen version, this is theoretically possible, but Bergman – unlike Alf Sjöberg, for example, in his well-known film adaptation of *Miss Julie* – has abstained from such excursions into the past.

Strindberg's play opens with an empty stage:

> *The façade of a modern house. The subsection, below ground level, is of granite; the upper part of brick, covered with yellow stucco. The surrounds of*

the windows, and other ornamentations, are in sandstone. In the middle of the granite subsection is a low porch leading to the inner courtyard; it also contains the entrance to the café. On the right of the house is a garden plot, with roses and other flowers. In the corner a letterbox. Above the subsection is the ground floor, with big windows standing open; four of these belong to a dining room, elegantly furnished. Above the ground floor can be seen the first floor, the four central windows of which are covered by red blinds, illuminated from within. In front of the house is a pavement lined with trees. In the foreground, a green bench and a gas lamp.[5]

Bergman's performance opens with a series of stills. Accompanied by the somber tolling of church bells, there is the the iconic photo of a thundercloud with the title of the play, the genre (chamber play), and the name of the author in his own handwriting written into it. The somber cloud dissolves into a low-angle still of a church tower (Hedvig Eleonora in the opulent Östermalm part of Stockholm) with a prominent old-fashioned lamppost in front of it. There is a dissolve to a high-angle photo of a marketplace (Östermalmstorg) taken from the church tower. Then another dissolve to a picture of an avenue with apartment houses and a row of high lampposts in the middle of the avenue. Finally, a dissolve to a row of stately apartment houses behind a line of trees.

Via this authentic material, the play is firmly located in the Stockholm of the turn of the century. In biographical Molander fashion, we are introduced to Strindberg's 1907 environment. To those who are familiar with the author's life at that time, Bergman strongly suggests that the Gentleman is Strindberg's alter ego.

As the last still dissolves to a high-angle close-up of a gas lamp, the somber tolling of the church bells is replaced by a cheerful waltz played on a piano, Waldteufel's *Plui d'Or*, prescribed by Strindberg later in the play. The high camera tracks in on the ground floor of an apartment house and pans right. Through the open window, the Gentleman (Uno Henning) is seen reading a paper. Another pan right reveals him through another window, now with the young Louise (Mona Malm) next to him serving him after-dinner coffee.

The transference from the initial authentic stills to a studio-built apartment house immediately creates the impression that the building before us, in which the Gentleman lives, is not a real house but an illusory one. In this way, Strindberg's idea of life's unreality is retained. But unlike Strindberg's house, which faces a street, Bergman's seems to face a narrow courtyard, that is, a claustrophobic environment.[6] In the play text, Gerda at one point refers to her marriage, and by implication also to her life, as an imprisonment. Similarly, when the Confectioner (John Elfström) comes out of his dwelling below ground level, sighing and wiping his neck, the claustrophobic scenery helps to suggest that he is not so much suffering from the heat as from infernal life.

Unlike the stage, the small screen allows Bergman to focus immediately on one of the central symbols of the play: the gas street lamp. This lamp clearly relates to the street lamps we have seen in the stills. All the street lamps are found in an intermediate area between heaven and earth. But unlike the lamps in the stills which were seen from below, from a human perspective, this one is seen from above, from a celestial one. The still of the church and the tolling of the bells have already provided a religious atmosphere. This is retained when Bergman has the camera lower itself and track in on the house behind the uppermost part of the street lamp, the lantern. Like another Indra's Daughter, the camera here descends to Earth to visit the House of Life. This is synchronized with the sound effects indicating a similar dichotomy between death and postexistence on the one hand – since the sound of the church bells suggests a funeral – and life (the dance music) on the other.

It is in view of this emphasis on metaphysical aspects surprising that Bergman has not retained the Gentleman's initial stage business as indicated by Strindberg. In the text it says:

> The GENTLEMAN is seen at the table in the dining room. ... A YOUNG GIRL, dressed in light colors, is serving him the final course. The BROTHER (outside the house) enters left, and knocks with his stick on the window-pane.
> BROTHER. Have you nearly finished?

Not only is the Gentleman being served his *last* course by an angelic figure; he is also being asked if he will not be *finished* soon. From the very beginning Strindberg implies that the Gentleman's life is coming to an end. Bergman's Gentleman, by contrast, is simply reading a paper by his after-dinner coffee. Realistic or practical concerns here seem to have prevailed over metaphoric ones, hardly transferable to the spectator.

The somber tolling of church bells heard in the opening of Bergman's *Storm* is heard also in the nightmare sequence opening *Wild Strawberries*. Here, too, we see curtained – even boarded – windows which, combined with the intense silence, inform us that we are in the realm of the dead. The prominent street lamp is found here, too, now seen in a more dramatic situation than in the play. With the symbolic significance of the street lamp in *Storm* at the back of our minds, we realize that when the horse-drawn hearse crashes into the lamppost, it is metonymically and by way of contiguity suggested that death overtakes life. When one of the carriage wheels, that has come loose, in threatening low-angle perspective rolls straight towards Isak, we realize that the collision represents his moment of death.

In the nightmare sequence, we recall, Isak Borg is confronted twice with his double, first in the form of an almost identically dressed dummy, then in the form of a corpse looking exactly like himself. Similarly, in the *Storm* production, the Gentleman and his Brother (Ingvar Kjellson) are dressed almost identically as though they were twins. The sameness is further emphasized by their identical way of walking, as we see them side by side leaving for their evening stroll, one hand carrying a cane, the other a pair of gloves behind the back – a slightly comical touch. While Louise in the play text says that the brothers *may* be twins, Bergman strongly suggests that they *are*. The visible identity of the two brothers indicates that they incarnate two attitudes of the same ego, of Man on the threshold of death, one calm (the Brother), the other worried (the Gentleman). One is reminded of the double protagonist in *The Seventh Seal*.

Bergman rehearsing Act II of *Storm*. From left to right: the Brother, the Gentleman, Bergman, the Confectioner, and Louise.

In the second act of *Storm*, the Gentleman at one point finds himself alone in his apartment. The act opens with Louise's playing chess with the Gentleman. When she has to leave, the Gentleman asks the Confectioner to play a game with him, but the Confectioner cannot leave his "saucepans." The Gentleman is left alone for a few moments. Strindberg's text reads:

> GENTLEMAN *alone, moves the chessmen for a few seconds, then gets up and paces across the room.* The peace of old age! Yes! *Sits at the piano and strikes a few chords. Gets up and starts to pace again.* Louise! Can't you leave that laundry?
> LOUISE *in the doorway.* I mustn't do that. The woman's in a hurry. She has a husband and child waiting for her....
> GENTLEMAN. I see. *Sits at the table and drums on it with his fingers. Tries to read the newspaper, but tires of it. Strikes matches and blows them out. Looks at the clock. There is a noise in the hall.* Is that you Karl Fredrik?

In Bergman's production the pantomime sequence is done as follows. The Gentleman sits down again at the chess set, his sherry glass next to it. Deep sigh. He moves the chessmen to an opening position. Loud ticking of the grandfather clock. He impatiently drums his fingers against the table, gets up, walks over to the piano, strikes a few keys. The clock is heard loudly. As Louise 'dismisses' him, he walks into his study, which is considerably darker than the dining room, sits down at his desk, puts on his glasses, picks up the evening paper but almost immediately puts it back on the desk. Another clock, ticking faster than the one in the dining room can be heard. The Gentleman, now in close-up, lights a match, blows it out, lights another match, blows it out. Takes out his pocket watch. Gets up as he hears a noise from the front door and leaves the room.

The position in front of the chess set, indicating the lack of a partner, the listless striking of the piano keys, the interrupted newspaper reading – all these signs in the text of an old man who is bored with his lonely existence are found in Bergman's version, too. But in addition we are here confronted with a picture of Man sensing how his life is passing away, minute by minute, and how death is approaching. By having the Gentleman move from one room to another, from one clock to another, Bergman can quite naturally change both the lighting and the sound. It is by such realistically moti-vated audiovisual changes that the Gentleman's increasing anguish is expressed. While in the nightmare sequence of *Wild Strawberries* a visual link is provided between the optician's clock and Isak's pocket watch, in the pantomime sequence of *Storm* an aural link is provided between the two clocks and the Gentleman's pocket watch.

The climactic moment of the pantomime sequence, indicated by showing it in close-ups, is the lighting and blowing out of the matches. The matches are here comparable to the street lamps which, as we know, are lit and extinguished daily. Clearly, both the matches and the lamps stand for the flame of life.[7]

The pantomime sequence may also be compared to the pre-credit sequence of *Wild Strawberries*. Here again, we have a lonely man sitting at the desk in his study, his sherry glass next to him, listening to the ticking of a grandfather clock. Just as the Gentleman has photos of his ex-wife and daughter like treasured memories "on the stove, between the candelabra," so Isak has his family members surrounding him in the form of photos. And just as the thermometer in *Storm* measures the unstable relations between husband and wife, so in *Wild Strawberries* the aneroid barometer close to the globe measures the unstable relations between Isak and the rest of the world.

As we have seen, Bergman's *Storm* opens with Louise treating the Gentleman to his after-dinner coffee. *Wild Strawberries*, similarly, opens with Agda's calling Isak to the dinner table. On his way to the dining room he stops in front of the stove and his chess set – properties which we recognize from *Storm* – indicating with his fingers that he wants to move one of the chessmen. But instead of doing so, he signals to his dog – another female servant – to come with him. The sequence ends with a long shot of the desk and Isak's chair, now empty. The low-angle perspective suggests that the dog has lost her master. It is a shot anticipating Isak's death.

The reversal in *Storm* comes close to the end when Louise tells the Gentleman: "Madam has gone to her mother in Dalarna to settle there with the child." Strindberg's Gentleman receives this message standing by the window outside the house. Bergman's receives it in the dining room. As soon as the Gentleman has told Louise to switch out the lights in the apartment above and lower the curtains, we see how he himself switches out the lights in the dining room, so that, in a close-up, the portrait of Gerda is blotted out. He then switches out the lights in the hall. Through the darkened hall, the two brothers leave the house to the celestial adagio (muted strings and harpsichord) of Vivaldi's "Autumn," the third movement of his *Quattro Stagioni*. The non-diegetic music emphasizes the peace that has come over the Gentleman now when he knows that his child is "in a good home." What we witness in Bergman's performance, more extensively than in Strindberg's text, is a symbolic leave-taking from the house, from life. The Gentleman's last weighty line – "And this autumn I'll move out of the silent house." – has been ritually dramatized.

Once outside the house, the brothers sit down next to each other on the bench to the left, while the Confectioner remains on his chair to the right. Three old men who have experienced the storms of life are waiting for the Lamplighter – and for the full moon. This is Strindberg's way of dramatizing – between Maeterlinck's *Intérieur* and Beckett's *Waiting for Godot* – Man's inevitable waiting for death. The Gentleman's phrasing – "Look! Here comes the Lamplighter. At last!" – indicates his longing for death. Bergman stresses this longing by having the Gentleman stretch out his arms as though he wanted to embrace the Lamplighter. The Gentleman's desire is fulfilled. Bergman's Lamplighter, though dressed in black – as Death should be – is by no means the frightening figure we remember from *The Seventh Seal*. On the contrary, his shining Father Christmas face looking upwards to the lantern – and, like Isak, to the moon – seems to incarnate the wisdom of old age that the Gentleman identifies with the blind lantern, whose light can be shaded so that it does not shine on the carrier. This is a suggestive metaphor for the idea that the flame of life is hidden – this is the Gentleman's hope – rather than extinguished when we die.

The Gentleman's mentioning of the blind lantern coincides with the lighting of "the first lantern,"[8] as he calls the street lantern. As a result, the street lantern becomes – in our imagination – a blind lantern, a source of hidden light, of life transcending death.

The Lamplighter's arrival implies that "det börjar skymma," as the Gentleman puts it, indicating not only that "it is beginning to grow dark" but also that he is getting dim-sighted. The moment of death is near at hand. Bergman's choice of turning out *all* the lights in the apartment house points in the same direction. His version ends as it began with a high angle shot of the lantern in close-up. The lantern, which we saw unlit in the beginning and which has remained so throughout the performance, is now being lit. If we agree that the lighting of the gas lantern at the end of *Storm* symbolizes the moment of death, then the position of the lantern between earth and heaven is certainly meaningful. Behind the initially unlit lantern, we discerned two people inside the house. Now, behind the lit one we discern two people walking away from the house, visibly moving off-screen – a visual pun, it seems, on the euphemistic Swedish expression for dying: "gå bort" (lit. go away). The last we see of the two is their backs, out-of-focus, shadowy.

The Gentleman in *Storm* does not visibly die at the end of the play. Similarly, Isak does not visibly die at the end of *Wild Strawberries*. Nevertheless, here as there, the ending carries strong overtones of death. What is more, both men reveal an intense longing for it.

Nineteen days before *Storm* was transmitted, Victor Sjöström died. Some six weeks after his death, Bergman delivered an address at the Swedish Film Academy commemorating him. It consisted mostly of passages from the diary Bergman had kept during the shooting of *Wild Strawberries*. The speech ended:

We have shot our final supplementary scenes of *Wild Strawberries* – the final close-ups of Isak Borg as he is brought to clarity and reconciliation. His face shone with secretive light, as if reflected from another reality. ... It was like a miracle. ... Never before or since have I experienced a face so noble and liberated. ... In the presence of this face I recalled the final words of Strindberg's last drama *The Great Highway*, the prayer to a god somewhere in the darkness.

"Bless me, Thy humanity,
That suffers, suffers from Thy gift of life!
Me first, who most have suffered –
Suffered most the pain of not being what I most would be."[9]

A face shining "with secretive light, as if reflected from another reality" – the lantern seen in close-up at the end of Bergman's *Storm* has found a human equivalent in the close-up of Isak's face at the end of *Wild Strawberries*. In addition to this 'dissolve,' there is the one between Isak Borg, initially called Isak Berg, and the Hunter in *The Great Highway*, who, like the Gentleman in *Storm*, is very much Strindberg's alter ego. Dissolves, confluences everywhere. In more senses than one, the film *Wild Strawberries* and the teleplay *Storm* are twin creations.

Persona (1966)

Persona, which shares its central interaction between one speaking and one silent character with Strindberg's monodrama *The Stronger*,[1] is arguably Bergman's most daring and most enigmatic film. This is especially true of the cryptic introductory sequence, the suite of images preceding and intertwining the credits.[2] In the following, I shall focus on this sequence and its relationship to the film proper.

Although the sequence contains disparate images and abrupt transitions, it is not lacking in structure. The various images tend to form image clusters. There are images of film equipment, of people, of nature, or, more specifically, images of faces, of hands. Some images are recurrent. In some places, we may speak of audiovisual intensification. There are subliminal correspondences, for example, between the anguished white-clad man in the film farce who pulls the spread over his head to hide himself from Death and the boy who pulls the white sheet over his head in order not to hear the telephone and who then adopts a fetal position. Here is a parallel-by-contrast between the man who does not want to die and the boy who does not want to live. Sound and image may also, in combination, evoke a certain impression. For example, when we see the high, gray tree trunks, the chiming makes us associate them with the columns in a church. The living columns in the temple of nature, to paraphrase Baudelaire, by implication form a contrast to the 'dead' stone columns of a church. More obvious is the connection between the slaughtering of the sacrificial lamb, the pierced hand, recalling the crucifixion and the awakening of the boy in the morgue (the resurrection). Add to this the title of the book the boy is reading, *The Hero of Our Time*, and it seems evident that Bergman in this sequence of images has depicted a piece of religious development away from Christianity[3] – on the part of the boy, who here seems to function not only as his alter ego but also as a representative of mankind.

In its interaction between heterogeneity and homogeneity, the pre-credit sequence anticipates the fundamental theme of the film: the problem of identity. The questions provocatively posed in the introductory sequence – What is the connection between the images? What separates them? – are posed again in the film proper with regard to the two women.

The introductory sequence already reveals that *Persona* is a metafilm, a film dealing with itself, its origin, its relationship to other Bergman films, its media conditions, its characteristics as an artistic product. Significantly, the original title of the film was *Cinematography*; the title *Persona* was chosen as a concession to the producer.[4] However, the meta ingredients are not included to indicate in any narrow sense what film is. Rather, they function as alienation effects, as reminders that what we are witnessing is not life but art. By elucidating, and complicating, the relationship between life and art, reality and the artistic adaptation of reality, they concretize a theme that has constantly preoccupied Bergman.

One of the meta ingredients is the image of the animated woman, whose inversion is an indication that the frame of her has not yet passed the projector lens; when this happens she will be turned the right way around.[5] Is this Bergman's version of Indra's Daughter's Platonic view, in *A Dream Play*, of the world as turned around the wrong way, a "wrong copy" of the original world?

Another meta aspect concerns the many white frames in the introductory sequence and the fact that some of the pictures do not fill the whole frame but are "written into the whiteness."[6] The whiteness can be interpreted in several ways. It may be seen as the pure, transparent film strip on which the director inscribes his images or the white cinema screen, the white 'paper,' on which his inscribed images are projected. By intermingling the film images with white frames, Bergman is again reminding us that we are watching a film, an artifact, something constructed, composed. Moreover, he is suggesting a correspondence between the cinematic contrast of image-filled frames and imageless (i.e., white) frames in the pre-credit sequence and the psychological dichotomy mask-face in the film proper.

Towards the end of the sequence the white frames grow into a gigantic 'white frame.' This happens when the boy (Jörgen Lindström) stretches out his hand towards us. Although Bergman was forced to make this frame transparent to enable us to see the boy, it is evident that especially this frame represents the cinema screen. This is evident not least from the fact that the size of the frame as compared with the boy, when the 'screen' in the next shot is again found behind the boy, approaches the proportions between cinema screen and spectator. The gigantic face watched by the boy now corresponds to what we, as spectators, experience as a close-up on the screen.[7] However, the boy's groping makes it clear that the fluctuating female face is not touched by his hand. It is apparently to be found behind the transparent 'screen.' Yet that is where we found ourselves a second ago. By turning the image, Bergman has suddenly placed the projected woman in the auditorium.

Contrary to what one might expect, the boy is no internal narrator. In the main part of the film, he is totally absent. Who then is the boy, and whose are the faces of the diffuse women? What does he seek? Clearly, he is identical with Elisabet's (Liv Ullmann) son,[8] who has been rejected by his mother and who therefore, we may assume,

The nameless boy in the pre-credit sequence of *Persona* reaches out to or wards off the huge female face which alternately carries the traits of Elisabet and Alma.

either hates her, takes an ambivalent attitude to her, or tries to re-establish contact with her – in her imagination.[9] Figuratively, he also represents Alma's (Bibi Andersson) aborted child. (The female face he keeps watching alternately carries the traits of Elisabet and Alma.) The boy incarnates guilt feelings on the part of the two mothers. This explains why he appears so frequently in the introductory sequence, usually frontally and looking straight into our eyes. It is as though the identical images of the boy in this sequence coalesce into one image, as though we are watching a photo that has traumatically settled in the memory of a guilt-laden mother. There is an inner correspondence between the boy in the prologue and the rejected and doomed Jewish boy in Albert Cusian's photo,[10] a photo that Elisabet constantly carries with her and that she contemplates in the film proper. Significantly, Bergman in an extreme close-up isolates one of the Jewish boy's raised arms to provide a link with the boy's raised arm searching for or warding off his mother in the pre-credit sequence.

We can now see that the purpose of the double placement of the female face is to draw the audience into the action, to make it identify with the two guilt-laden women, to make it co-responsible. Human evil that is so obvious in the authentic pictures from

Vietnam and Warsaw (reality) is via the fictive figures (the two women and the boy) transmitted to reality (the cinema audience).

From a meta-filmic point of view, the boy is identical with the director, the narrator of the film. In the "reflection" preceding the script, Bergman describes himself as a child. He was, he says, "a contact-seeking child, beset by fantasies" – an adequate characterization of the boy in the introductory sequence. Being the narrator of the film, the boy is frequently seen, once, as we have noted, in a key position between the spectator and the 'screen.' It is as though Bergman wants to remind us that what we see is reality filtered not only through a cinematic but also through a human medium: the director's mind and feelings.

The boy who gropingly strokes the gigantic female face could also, psychoanalytically, be seen as an image of man's regressive longing for the maternal womb or, religiously, as his longing for a mild, cosmic mother. But the mother or maternal god remains unattainable. Momentarily, the female face may seem to come closer, but it remains diffuse, enigmatic and alienated, and at last it closes its eyes, stops seeing – an image of how Elisabet (I quote a description of her) "withdraws from the world into disengaged observation and silence in order not to compromise herself, make herself part of the violence surrounding her in the world."[11] Or is it an image of blind Fate?

The introductory sequence anticipates the film proper in various ways. In that sense, it demonstrates "the film's impatience to get started" and "how, from scattered images, a film is born."[12] Thus, the pierced palm anticipates Alma's turning of her hands which, in turn, suggests that the back and the flat of the hand have their counterparts in the left and right half of the human face, so spectacularly contrasted in the film. The dripping sound in the morgue sequence can be compared to the script's reference to words "*dropping with empty intervals.*" Suddenly, we realize that the relation word/silence in the film proper is equivalent to the relation image/nonimage – the latter appearing as either a white or a black frame – in the wordless introductory sequence. It is significant that the mute Elisabet in her letter to the doctor describes herself as "blank," a *tabula rasa*. The alternation between images and non-images in the introductory sequence thus in a way corresponds to the two women of the main film, one speaking, the other silent. There are also more incidental correspondences. Alma, who is linked both with sensuality and cleanliness (bathing, washing), is anticipated by the very earthy woman washing herself in the animated film fragment. But when the image of this woman is suddenly frozen and then again begins to move, it foreshadows Elisabet's sudden silence when she is acting in *Electra*. "She ... was silent," it says in the script, "for more than a minute. Then she went on playing, as if nothing had happened." The animated woman is, in other words, an amalgamation of Alma and Elisabet, anticipating their symbiotic relationship.

Elisabet in *Persona* falling silent and turning away from the audience when acting in *Electra*.

At one point in the film proper, we see Alma in bed, her face frontally turned toward us but upside down. This frame points back both to the animated woman, also shown upside down, and more obviously to the inverted face of the woman in the morgue. As a result, two contrasting impressions are conveyed. Is Alma comically inverted like the buxom animated woman or tragically like the dead woman? Alienation or intensification – that is the question. The situation may be compared to Elisabet's inclination, in the script, to laugh in the middle of the tragedy *Electra*. Whether you laugh or weep at life is a question of your point of view. This is what Bergman seems to imply when he inverts both Alma's and our way of looking at the world. However, in the film there is no sign of laughter in Elisabet's face at this point. What strikes the spectator here instead is that as she turns silent, she turns away from the theater audience to face us – the film audience.[13] In a single shot, Bergman suggests not only her position between stage and screen but also her rejection, by means of the silence, of both of them and, by implication, of art in general.

When Elisabet, because of Alma, is wounded in her foot by a glass splinter, which in the script is described as "*a protruding spearhead*," it is a combination of the pierced hand, the spearhead railing, and the bare feet in the introductory sequence.

A more cryptic prolepsis is the spider, which anticipates Elisabet's remark in her letter to the doctor that she feels "curiosity in a fat spider" – a remark omitted in the film. The verbal spider in the script has turned into a visual one in the film. Both spiders point to the relationship between Elisabet and Alma. Elisabet is curious about the spider – as she is about Alma. But she is herself, like the spider, a (Strindbergian) vampire when she sucks Alma's blood and when she wraps her hair, her 'net,' around Alma. (Significantly, both women are busy taking up fishing-nets in the script.) It is also important that the spider is seen through a microscope. The spider, which is viewed behind glass from below, it has been said, is "ready for scientific examination, a detail which ironically foreshadows the cold, clinical, and calculating ways in which Elisabet will study Alma and Bergman his characters."[14]

Even the opening frames – the explosive contact between the carbon rods of the projector – are meaningfully connected with the violent confrontation, in intense sunlight, between Elisabet and Alma at the end of the film. And just as the two women 'separate' in the end, we witness how the two carbon rods recede from one another.

This is also saying that *Persona* has a striking circular composition, in several respects. In the concluding frames, we see how the fictive characters, Elisabet and Alma, return to their former occupations: those of the actress and nurse, respectively. We see how the actresses creating these roles finish the shooting of the film we have just been viewing. Liv Ullmann's inverted face in the film camera now corresponds to the three inverted faces we have seen earlier. We see how the film strip that curled into the projector in the beginning now curls out of it. And we see once more the boy groping with his hand towards the gigantic female face. Illusion, reality, and medium are intertwined in a manner reminiscent both of Strindberg's *Dream Play* and Pirandello's *Six Characters in Search of an Author*.[15]

The oscillation between illusion and reality, authentic 'truth' and fictive 'lie,' is a fundamental theme in *Persona*. In the film proper, the authentic, meaningful suicide of the Vietnamese monk is contrasted with the planned, meaningless one of role-playing, inauthentic Elisabet. The implication is that Elisabet only commits fictive suicides – on the stage. On the television screen, she is confronted with a piece of authentic reality so frightening that one is inclined to regard it as fictitious. Similarly, we cannot immediately decide whether the dead people in the morgue are authentically or fictively dead, whether we are witnessing a documentary fragment or a piece of feature film. In the same way, it is not always possible to decide whether we are watching Elisabet Vogler's or Liv Ullmann's face, Alma's or Bibi Andersson's. The boundary between what is authentic and what is fictitious is eliminated.

By its position, the introductory sequence points with its Janus face in two directions: backward to Bergman's earlier films and forward to the film that is to emerge. The sequence is found in a border area, and Bergman has indicated this by turning what

is a prologue also into a kind of epilogue. As has often been pointed out, several ingredients in the sequence may be seen as quotations from earlier Bergman films. Thus, the
silent film farce derives from *Prison*. Its protagonist, the man in a nightshirt and night-
cap, appears in *Smiles of a Summer Night*. The spider is reminiscent of the spider god in
Through a Glass Darkly, while the slaughtering of the lamb reminds one of Märta in
Winter Light, the Christ figure who is 'sacrificed' by Tomas and who appears in a furcoat
made of sheep skin when the Eucharist hymn "God's pure, innocent lamb" is sung in the
opening of the film. The piercing of the hand – reminiscent of the Crucifixion – turns up
in *The Seventh Seal*, *Wild Strawberries* and *Winter Light*. The young boy is not only
played by the same actor doing the boy in *The Silence*; he is also reading the same book
as him, Lermontov's *The Hero of Our Time*.

What then does Bergman wish to communicate through this kind of auto-
intertextuality? His intention with the introductory sequence, he says, was

> to make a poem, not in words but in images, about the situation in which
> *Persona* had originated. I reflected on what was important, and began with
> the projector and my desire to set it in motion. But when the projector was
> running, nothing came out of it but old ideas, the spider, God's lamb, all that
> dull old stuff.[16]

This statement indicates that the purpose of the auto-quotations, at least partially, was to
take an ironical attitude to earlier all-too-explicit symbols, symbols that are totally lacking in *Persona*. In line with this, the sequence may be seen as a thematic demarcation, an
indication of how the new film differs from the earlier ones.

The introductory sequence has also been regarded as a summary of
Bergman's involvement with film, from the animated films and silent film farces of his
childhood to his own serious sound films. Or even as an indication of the birth and development of film generally.

Bergman wrote the script of *Persona* in the Sophia Hospital in Stockholm:
"My life just then consisted of dead people, brick walls, and a few dismal trees out in the
park. ... Besides which I had a view of the morgue...."[17] This must have given him certain
déjà-vu feelings. In his autobiography, it says: "When I was ten, I was shut inside the
morgue at the Sophia Hospital. ... I was alone with the dead or the apparently dead. At
any moment one of them might rise up and grab hold of me."[18] The brick wall, the trees,
and the dead or seemingly dead people all appear in the pre-credit sequence. Although
the hospital has thus been a source of inspiration, it does not explain how the ingredients
just mentioned fit into Bergman's film. It is not the morgue Bergman could see from his

window but "this morgue of a world," to quote the Student in *The Ghost Sonata*, that is here of significance. Indeed, Bergman's morgue is not an ordinary one. Containing sleeping rather than dead people – compare Elisabet's remark that Alma "lives like a sleep-walker" – it is a metaphor for life, its inhabitants for the living dead. The cinematic and the religious spheres can also be combined. The creative human being – the artist, in this case the film *auteur* – has creativity in common with the Creator:

> In the beginning God created the heaven and the earth. And the earth was without form, and void; and darkness was upon the face of the deep. And the Spirit of God moved upon the face of the waters. And God said, Let there be light: and there was light. (Gen. 1-3)

The cosmic contrast between light and darkness which is here described verbally is produced audiovisually in the explosive opening frames of *Persona*. Here we find Bergman's – the film creator's – "Let there be light." Here, in this variety of the Creation, the 'dead' filmstrip of *Persona* comes alive in the light of the arc-lamp. The cosmic antitheses heaven-earth, light-darkness soon appear to have their counterparts on the inter- and intrahuman level. Already in the introductory sequence we see Elisabet/Liv with a light-and-dark face.

But there is also a sexual component in the opening images. Film arises when two carbon rods come together, in a moment of 'fertilization.' It is no coincidence that the pillar of light in one of the early frames is strikingly similar to the erect penis shown a little later. Similarly, the rounded quadrangle towards which the pillar is directed can be combined with the image of the vertical lips, representing the vagina. Does Bergman wish to indicate that artistic creativity is related to divine creativity? That just as the world has come into being through "contact between divine and earthly substances," as it says in *A Dream Play*, so the birth of a piece of art is determined by a 'sexual' union? Or does he merely wish to indicate that artistic activity is a sublimation of sexual activity? Here, as elsewhere in this enigmatic film, Bergman invites, as he says in the note preceding the script, "the imagination of the ... spectator to dispose freely of the material [he has] made available."

But why is the male organ shown directly, the female only indirectly? In the latter case, we touch on a pregnant visual metaphor related to the fundamental theme of the film, a theme developed as Alma tells Elisabet of her beach orgy. Once when sunbathing, she met Katarina. Shortly afterwards two young boys, unknown to both of them, showed up. Katarina was soon "helping" the older one to put his penis into her vagina. She then took the semen of the younger boy "in her mouth," that is, her mouth functioned as a vagina. The vertical lips in the introductory sequence anticipate this situation. What is then the significance of the combination lips-pudenda? In a film dealing with the relationship between speech and silence, the human speech organ, the mouth, gains a special significance. A closed mouth connotes silence, an open mouth speech. However, Katarina's mouth was open not to produce words but to receive semen. Katarina here showed the same "ravenous hunger" (script) as Elisabet.[19] The mouth is reduced to a consumptive, vampiric organ. (Later, Elisabet, as we have noted, literally sucks blood from Alma's arm.) This is figuratively true also of Alma's and Elisabet's wombs. The former has had an abortion, the latter has given birth to an unloved son. Their vaginas have played the same consumptive role as Katarina's mouth. The mouth imagery, we can now see, deals in the last instance with the relationship between giving and taking, love and lovelessness.

It is possible that the sexual ingredients in *Persona*, just like the sadistic ones, aim to activate the spectator. This is completely in line with the contemporary *nouveau roman* doctrine about the recipient as co-creator of the artistic work. Bergman has also declared that he is in favor of Buñuel's method of shocking the spectator with brutal images.[20] However, in a film dealing with identity problems, the sexual and sadistic elements function above all as emotive expressions of mental conditions. The painful nail-through-hand sequence, for example, is a brutal expression of the sadomasochistic relationship between Alma and Elisabet. As we have seen, the sexual elements have a similar metaphoric function.

Through its seemingly capricious, associative, wordless stream of images, the introductory sequence may seem like an attempt by Bergman to create a cinematic counterpart of Joyce's stream of consciousness in *Ulysses*. But the sequence is rather a pictorial poem, an audiovisual alternative to the verbal poems of the modernists. "I wanted to make a poem," Bergman said himself about the sequence, "not in words but in images, about the situation in which *Persona* originated."

Poetry, dream, reality – the sequence contains all these elements. For as the author of *A Dream Play* demonstrates, it is difficult to keep the three concepts apart. Strindberg's drama is certainly closer to Bergman's film than Joyce's novel. What *A Dream Play* has meant for the development of drama, *Persona* has – possibly – meant for that of film.

Cries and Whispers (1973)

Cries and Whispers begins and ends in the park of a stately mansion. Between these two exterior sequences the action, except for one brief flashback, takes place inside the mansion, primarily in one room. The space is, in other words, exceedingly restricted.

Four women form the nucleus of the action: Agnes (Harriet Andersson), who is dying; her sisters Karin (Ingrid Thulin) and Maria (Liv Ullmann); and the maid Anna (Kari Sylwan). The cries and the whispers belong to them. As in a string quartet, we listen to four different 'instruments' somehow attuned to one another in this 'chamber film.'[1]

Karin and Maria have come to the mansion, the home of their childhood, to keep watch at Agnes' bedside.[2] The film describes the last two days of Agnes' life, her death, funeral, and 'resurrection.' These events are intermingled with flashbacks of situations or events in the past, showing Agnes' relationship to her mother, Anna's to her child, Karin's and Maria's to their husbands.

The script begins with a declaration by the director which provides a key to the film:

> *As I turn this project over in my mind it never stands out as a completed whole. What it most resembles is a dark flowing stream: faces, movements, voices, gestures, exclamations, light and shade, moods, dreams. Nothing fixed, nothing really tangible other than for the moment, and then only an illusory moment. A dream, a longing, or perhaps an expectation, a fear, in which that to be feared is never put into words.*

Like the author of *A Dream Play*, Bergman in *Cries and Whispers* strives to "*imitate the disconnected ... form of the dream.*" The most spectacular dream element in the film is Agnes' continued life after death. But there are several other sequences which are almost as dreamlike: Karin's mutilation of herself, Joakim's suicide attempt, the Chaplain's self-reproaches. We must constantly ask ourselves whether the situations and events describe an objective reality or whether they express the characters' subjective versions of reality. Rarely does Bergman indicate that we are dealing with dreams, fantasies. Yet the descriptions are such that we find it difficult to accept them at face value. The borderline between dream and reality is blotted out.

In the centre of the film, we find Agnes, "*the intended owner of the estate.*" In the script, it says:

She has vague artistic ambitions – dabbling in painting, playing the piano a little; it is all rather touching. No man has turned up in her life. ... At the age of thirty-seven she has cancer of the womb and is preparing to make her exit from the world as quietly and submissively as she has lived in it. ... She is very emaciated, but her belly has swollen up as though she were in an advanced stage of pregnancy. ...

AGNES' *painting is generously colorful and somewhat romantic. Her main subject is flowers.*

Agnes strikingly resembles the Young Lady, Adèle, in *The Ghost Sonata*, the intended owner of the beautiful *art nouveau* building on the stage. Neither the Young Lady's nor Agnes' illness – cancer of the uterus – should be taken literally. Just as the Young Lady is "withering away in [an] atmosphere of crime, deceit and falseness of every kind," so Agnes is surrounded by faithlessness and emotional chill. Neither her mother, now dead, nor her sisters have given her the warmth she longs for. Both Karin and Maria are unhappily married, both have been unfaithful to their husbands, both are anxious – as are their husbands – to show an immaculate social persona. Agnes cannot thrive in such surroundings.

However, she has one friend who is pure of heart and able to feel love. Anna, it says in the script,

> *is very taciturn, very shy, unapproachable. But she is ever-present – watching, prying, listening. Everything about* ANNA *is weight. Her body, her face, her mouth, the expression of her eyes. But she does not speak; perhaps she does not think either.*

Like the Milkmaid in *The Ghost Sonata*, Anna incarnates altruistic love. And just as the Milkmaid's profession indicates her nurturing function, so Anna's role of maid is a sign of her willingness to serve – feel compassion for – her fellows. In both the play and the film, the person who is socially the most unassuming is ethically the most high-minded. Characteristically, Bergman cast the same actress in both parts and provided her with virtually the same costume and hair (pigtail) in both.

Anna is the only one who hears Agnes' crying; who consoles her with the warmth of her maternal bosom; and who is willing to stay with her when she is dead. But Anna is herself in need of human warmth. Functioning as a mother substitute to Agnes, she has herself found a substitute in Agnes for the little daughter she has lost.

Early in the film we see Anna in her simple room praying for her dead daughter. Next to her, there is a lit candle, flowers in a vase, and apples in a bowl. A close-up of Anna is followed by one of a photo of her and her daughter, this again by a close-up of

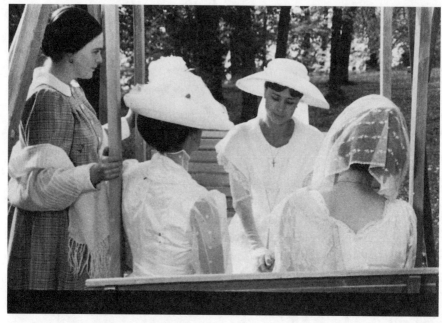

At the end of *Cries and Whispers* Agnes' diary, recording a blissful moment, comes alive in Anna's memory. The three sisters – Karin, Agnes, and Maria – seated in the old swing, are rocked by Anna.

the daughter on the photo. When the praying Anna returns in view, the frame is supplemented by nondiegetic piano music, a melancholy Chopin mazurka. Anna blows out the candle and begins to eat an apple while she regards the photo of herself and her daughter. She then gets up and leaves the room past an empty child's bed.

The sequence is carefully composed. The flowers, the apple, the candle, the photo, the bed – nothing is there by coincidence. The eating of the apple links Anna, whose dead daughter was undoubtedly an illegitimate child, with the Eve of the Fall, with Original Sin. The photo, which is framed by flowers on one side and by a card showing a butterfly, symbol of the resurrection, on the other, bears witness of her longing for the dead daughter – as do the prayer and the empty bed. The lit candle represents her hope that her little girl has risen from the dead and that God's angels are now protecting her in heaven.

The melancholy Chopin mazurka continues as Agnes, dressed in white, is framed next to a bowl with big, white, cultivated roses (contrasting with Anna's more modest wild flowers). Agnes takes one of them, smells it, looks thoughtful, then very sad. The fragrance of the rose evokes the image of her beloved dead mother. There is a slow dissolve from the white rose to the mother's white dress, as she is walking, alone, in the park of the mansion, surrounded by shadows as though she were a prisoner of the park.

While Agnes and Anna relate to *The Ghost Sonata*, Maria is linked with *A Doll's House* and *Miss Julie*. This is especially obvious in the sequence showing Maria lying in the bed of her old room. With a thumb in her mouth and a doll next to her, regarding her old doll's house, she is still a doll's wife, a child. The camera follows her glance from the elegant upper floor of the doll's house to the kitchen in the basement – the class society in one tilt. The close-up of a cook by the stove, a servant in livery, and a bird's cage clearly refers to *Miss Julie*, while the mother looking down on her daughter from the painting on the wall resembles the final shot in Alf Sjöberg's film version of Strindberg's play, where Julie's portrayed dead mother looks down on her daughter. Bergman frequently makes use of this kind of allusions. Apart from amusing the initiated, they economically enrich the action.

The environment in *Cries and Whispers* may in the first place be associated with decadent aristocratic life around the turn of the century, as described in Chekhov's *Three Sisters* – an adequate title also for Bergman's film – or in *Miss Julie*. But very soon we notice that the social aspect is not central to the film, which deals more with the shortcomings of humanity than with those of the bourgeoisie.

The most striking aspect of the scenery is that the interior is constantly kept in various shades of red. Moreover, the different parts of the film are separated by slow dissolves containing intermediate red frames. Red is the color of blood, of life but also of sacrifice, of death. It is the color of erotic love, passion. In addition to these conventional meanings, there is a more esoteric significance, indicated by Bergman himself. In the script, he informs us that "*ever since [his] childhood [he has] pictured the inside of the soul as a moist membrane in shades of red.*" It is obvious that Bergman's "*soul*" is very similar to the uterus.[3] In *Cries and Whispers*, we not only find ourselves in the sisters' home of childhood, this alone a sign of their inability to escape the early phase of their life; we find ourselves in the original 'home' of us all, the maternal womb, the only place where two human beings are in true communion with one another. As David tells Karin in *The Touch*: "You can never live inside me. It's only for short, hopelessly short moments that we imagine the prison has been opened. ... I think it's some dim memory from the womb. That's the only fellowship there is...." Both in the red interior and in the reddish dissolves, we should sense the blood pulsating in each of the four women, driven by the beating of the heart, just as the many clocks of the mansion are driven by their clockworks. At the same time, the redness makes visible the psychoanalytic idea that our lives are determined by what we have experienced in the maternal womb. The dissolves combined with whispering voices – equivalent of fetal membranes and fetal sounds and/or sounds heard by a fetus – suggest both a prenatal existence and, in the context of the film, the alienation from life felt by someone dying.[4]

Of the many clocks in the mansion, *"the mantelpiece clock, with a flute-playing shepherd,"* associated with Agnes, *"is the only one not going."* The symbolism is obvious. As in *Wild Strawberries*, the ticking and striking clocks represent the living, while the silent clock indicates that Agnes' time on earth is up.[5] When she sets it moving again, her action, comparable to Peer Gynt's appeals to the Buttonmolder or Antonius Block's chess-playing, is a prayer for respite.

The four women, who receive about equal attention, represent four different types, outlooks, temperaments. Agnes is mild, Karin cold, Maria superficial, Anna warm. They appear in costumes suiting their mentality: white for the virginal Agnes, black for the life-denying Karin, red for the erotic Maria, gray for the serving Anna. Turning to their wombs, we may speak of a virginal but sick (Agnes), a frigid (Karin), a sensual (Maria) and a maternal (Anna) one.

What then does Agnes' sick womb represent? It has been suggested that the disease relates to that "of being a woman and of not fulfilling a woman's function by bearing a real child."[6] However, the reason why Bergman has selected cancer of the uterus is not that it is an illness restricted to women but that it is an illness located in the original home of all of us – both in the biblical and in the psychoanalytical sense.

Through her cancer, Agnes, like the Young Lady, reveals that she is subject to Original Sin. Anna's eating of an apple and Karin's and Maria's 'sickly' wombs amount to the same. Yet, like Eve they have all begun life as innocent creatures – as their names indicate: 'Agnes' and 'Karin' both mean 'chaste'; 'Maria' carries, through the Holy Virgin, the same meaning; and 'Anna,' being the name of the Virgin Mary's mother, points in the same direction. Rather than being subject to *Original* Sin, Bergman's women seem to be victims simply of life; growing up means growing sinful. Life has turned the firm Karin into a hard and bitter person, who declares herself "rotten to the core." Similarly, the chameleonic Maria has become a cynic below her smiling persona. In contrast, Agnes and Anna have retained more of their original identity, each in their own way accepting life on its own terms.

Faced with Agnes' illness, science (the Doctor, Erland Josephson) is powerless. Once she has died, faith (the Chaplain, Anders Ek) proves as powerless when it comes to offering hopes for a blessed after-life. The representative fellow-creatures (Maria and Karin) distance themselves from the dead Agnes even though they are blood relations, thereby demonstrating the shortcomings of human love. Only Anna has the strength to console Agnes. In her alone does love prove triumphant.

The theme of isolation-versus-communion pervades the film. Both the dinner between Fredrik (Georg Årlin) and Karin, husband and wife, and the family gathering after the funeral signal the frozen relations that are typical of humanity. After Agnes' death, the weather has, significantly, suddenly turned colder and it has begun to snow. The funeral guests, unable to warm one another, *"are warming themselves with a cup of tea and a glass of sherry."*

Physical proximity is the symbol of communion. One of Anna's good memories, omitted in the film, is that of how she, her little daughter, and Agnes once built a house under the dinner table. *"There they are as close as a single body.... In this way, they forget their fear."* The situation anticipates the pietà scene between Anna and Agnes. Similarly, Maria reminds Agnes: "Do you remember when we were little and played together in the twilight? Suddenly, and at the same moment, we felt afraid and cuddled together and held each other tight."

One of Agnes' good memories is the one of how she once was allowed to stroke her mother's cheek: "We were very close to each other that time." Its counterpart is the scene in which Maria is allowed to touch Karin who never wants to be touched and who nevertheless nourishes "a longing for nearness." In the script, this sequence is accompanied by tender words between the sisters. In the film, the words are reduced to inaudible whispers which, along with their caresses, express the tenderness between them. In addition, there is music: a fragment of the sarabande from Bach's suite for cello in C minor – dark, warm, lofty music for *one* instrument, close to the human voice, an adequate expression of spiritual communion between people. (The sarabande returns later in the film, this time to illustrate the communion between Anna and Agnes.) However, this moment of tenderness between the sisters proves to mean much more to Karin than to Maria, who later denies its significance.

The theme of communion culminates in the final sequence. For the first and only time, we see the four women *"as close as a single body."* The sequence clarifies a passage from Agnes' diary:

A summer's day. ... My sisters, Karin and Maria, have come to see me. It's wonderful to be together again – as in childhood. ... We slowly strolled down to the old swinging seat in the oak tree. Then the four of us (Anna was there too) sat in the swing and let it rock to and fro, slowly and gently.

I closed my eyes and felt the breeze and the sun on my face. All my pain was gone. The people I am most fond of in the world were with me. ... I felt the presence of their bodies, the warmth of their hands. I closed my eyes tightly, trying to cling to the moment, and thought: This is, indeed, happiness.

This ending is quite similar to that of the final vision in *The Ghost Sonata*, the way Strindberg originally imagined it. But what with Strindberg is a journey into life hereafter, or rather the hope for such a journey, with Bergman it is at most an indication in that direction. Like the paradisaic final vision of *Wild Strawberries*, the ending of *Cries and Whispers* points to the past, to a paradisaic existence in *this* life, to the communion inherent in childhood that has later been lost. Nevertheless, the final visions of both films – since both Isak and Agnes are tormented by *"the ultimate loneliness"*: death – connote a hope that the communion of childhood will return in a coming life. It is precisely this ambivalence that makes the final visions in these films so meaningful.

What is the significance of the film title? We learn that Maria and her mother, who were very close to each other, *"kept whispering"* to one another. Anna *"whispers inaudible, consoling words"* to Agnes. When Karin and Maria after Agnes' death for a moment are close to one another, they keep whispering. The whispers which, as we have noted, also accompany most of the reddish dissolves, function as caresses. They express tenderness, love, communion.

The cries relate to the opposite emotions: anguish, impotence, loneliness. Maria's attempt to establish contact with her sister suddenly fails:

> "I can't," KARIN *cries.* "I can't. All that which can't be altered. All the guilt. It's constant anguish. It's like in hell. I can't breathe any more because of all the guilt.

The crying and the feelings of suffocation indicate that Karin's inability to respond to Maria's attempt at contact is based on guilt feelings at least partly connected with the recently dead sister. For this is how Agnes' moment of death is described:

> *Suddenly she cries*: "Can't you help me? Help me, I don't want to. I don't want to." *She utters a piercing scream and beats about her with her arms until a new attack of choking cuts off her shrieks and she bends backward, mouth agape.*

The closest formal connection with the title we find in the following passage, testifying both to Agnes' anguish and her longing for communion as well as to the sisters' lacking sense of her needs: "AGNES *calls to her sisters faintly, her lips move and she calls in a whisper, but they don't hear her."*

Already in *Through a Glass Darkly*, Bergman touched on this theme. After incest with his sister Karin, Minus falls to his knees, clasps his hands, and prays *"whispering. God ... God ... help us! Like a cry and a whisper."* Naturally, these *de profundis* situations are designed with regard to the biblical archetype, Christ's sense of desolation at the moment of death:

And about the ninth hour Jesus *cried* with a loud voice, saying, Eli, Eli, lama sabachtani? that is to say, My God, my God, why hast thou forsaken me? ... Jesus, when he had *cried* again with a loud voice, yielded up the ghost. (Mat. 27.46, 50; italics added)

That Agnes' suffering and death are modelled on the Passion appears from a number of circumstances. Sharing her name with that of Indra's Daughter in *A Dream Play*, Agnes functions as an *agnus dei*, a sacrificial lamb, the symbol of Christ's *satisfactio vicaria*.[7] Like Jesus, Agnes is pure, chaste. Her suffering at an age comparable to that of Jesus seems altogether unjust and can therefore be seen as vicarious. When the Chaplain states that Agnes' faith is stronger than his own and that God has found her "worthy to bear a heavy and prolonged suffering," he has the parallel to Christ in mind.

Already in the beginning of the film, we see how Maria, who is to keep watch over her sister, has fallen asleep in a chair. It is instead Agnes, who has just stood up, who keeps watch over *her* – with a smile expressing both disappointment and forgiveness. This is Bergman's variant of Jesus' disappointment at the disciples, when they had fallen asleep in the garden of Gethsemane: "What, could ye not watch with me one hour?" (Mat. 26.40) Before this happens, we see Maria's face in close-up, overcome by pain as she is drinking a glass of water – Bergman's allusion to the bitter chalice. When Agnes later "*has bent her head against her chest*," her position resembles that of the Crucified. The same is true of the following description: "*Her eyes are closed and her forehead has beads of sweat on it. Her mouth is bitten and covered with sores. Now and then her body shudders with the constant pain.*" When "*she asks for something to drink*," it corresponds to Jesus' "I thirst" (John 19.28). Quite grotesque is the contrast between her quietly suffering Christ-like face, in close-up, and Maria's off-screen reading aloud from *The Pickwick Papers*.[8] The washing and shrouding of Agnes' emaciated body has a sacred character. Just before she dies, the fingers of one of her hands are twisted like those of the Crucified. When she is laid out, there is a high-angle shot of her emphasizing the cruciform of her body.[9] The most obvious parallel is, of course, the famous pietà scene with its complex fusion of death and birth.[10]

What is the purpose of all these allusions to the Passion? Is Agnes a Christ figure? Does Bergman wish to indicate that there are people – Agnes has a kinsman in Algot Frövik in *Winter Light* – who, like Christ, have a scapegoat mission? Do the allusions serve to give fundamental human feelings – pain, fear of death, sense of abandonment – a higher dignity? Or do they merely serve to create an archetypal object of identification, an emotional correlate? Perhaps something of all of this.

The contrast between mask and face forms a pervading theme in *Cries and*

In the pietà scene of *Cries and Whispers* Anna warms the dead Agnes, in fetal position, with her maternal body.

Whispers. The bedroom of the parents, it says in the script, is beautiful but overloaded. The dining room has "*heavy furniture and dark-red, gilt-leather wallpaper*," "*thick window curtains*," and "*solid silver*" on the dinner table. Karin, loaded with jewels – gifts from her husband while he still loved her or, more likely, gifts to disguise his withering love for her – fits into this environment.

"*The women's clothes*," Bergman points out, "*are lavish, expensive, concealing and revealing*." By appearing in a social persona demanding respect, people try to keep up their self-respect. But the self-respect is undermined by their awareness that they are not what they pretend to be.

Sitting before the mirror, Karin is ironically watching her own "*irreproachable façade*" in no fewer than three mirrors. Similarly, Maria early in the film

> *walks over to a large mirror which is tilting out from the wall; it has panels of blurred glass, a marble ledge, and an ornamental gold frame. She stands before the mirror for a moment, turns her face toward her image and smiles quickly...*

Being "*blurred*," the pretentious mirror in which she sees herself provides poor possibilities for self-knowledge. This applies not only to Maria as an individual; it applies also to her as a representative of humanity; in the words of St. Paul: "For now we see through a glass darkly; but then face to face" (1 Cor. 13.12). True self-knowledge is not possible in this life.

The alternation mask-face is found also in some of the monologues. After Agnes' death, Karin tells Maria:

> We were so fond of her. *Suddenly in a different voice.* Nothing, no one can help me. *Again in her usual voice.* When the funeral is over, I'll ask our solicitor to arrange all the legal formalities. ... I think that *With a change of voice.* yes, it's true, I've thought of suicide many times. ... It's everlastingly the same, it's *In her normal voice.* nothing. I mean it's not a serious problem.

Similarly, the Chaplain, "*enclosed in the black uniform of office*," in the beginning of his speech sticks to the traditional funereal ritual:

> May your Father in Heaven have mercy on your soul when you step into His presence. May He let His angels disrobe you of the memory of your earthly pain.

But he soon drops the ritual, and despite its rhetorical anaphorae, the rest of his speech carries the note of sincere despair at the conditions of mankind:

> *The* CHAPLAIN *falls silent, as though overcome. He stands perplexed with his eyes shut. Then he kneels down stiffly; ... He passes a hand across his eyes and supports himself against a chair with the other.*
> If it is so that you have gathered our suffering in your poor body, if it is so that you have borne it with you through death, if it is so that you meet God over there in the other land, if it is so that He turns His face toward you, if it is so that you can then speak the language that this God understands, if it is so that you can then speak to this God. If it is so, pray for us. Agnes, my dear little child, listen to what I am now telling you. Pray for us who are left here on the dark, dirty earth under an empty and cruel Heaven. Lay your burden of suffering at God's feet and ask Him to pardon us. Ask Him to free us at last from our anxiety, our weariness, and our deep doubt. Ask Him for a meaning to our lives. Agnes, you who have suffered so unimaginably and so long, *you must be worthy to plead our cause.*

The Chaplain's split prayer may be compared both to the contradictory speeches of the split protagonist at the end of *The Seventh Seal* and to Tomas', the vicar's, opening and closing prayers in *Winter Light*, the first showing how he clings to the traditional formula, the second how he gropes for a faith.

The end of the first part, quoted here, sounds like the Student's intercession for the recently dead Young Lady at the end of *The Ghost Sonata*: "may you be greeted by a sun that does not burn, in a home without dust...." The next part resembles the Poet's appeal to Indra's Daughter in *A Dream Play*: "Child of the gods, will you translate / our lament into language / the Immortal One understands." The Chaplain's prayer is crammed with "ifs" – as though he doubted the existence of a benevolent god. In line with this, the perspective of the introductory ritual part is reversed. No longer praying that God take mercy on the dead woman, the Chaplain asks her to intercede by Him for the living. To speak with the author of *A Dream Play*: It is not the dead but the living who are pitiable.

When the sisters after the funeral talk to one another, their veils function as masks. The black-toned sequence, alternately showing their faces, contrasts with the earlier red-toned communion sequence, in constant two-shot.

A striking characteristic with Bergman is his predilection for mystifying doublings. In *Cries and Whispers*, one actress (Liv Ullmann) incarnates both Maria and her mother. The outward resemblance serves to point to an inner one, which in turn explains their closeness to one another. In addition, the film contains another, less obvious doubling: the parts of Anna's and Maria's daughter are played by the same actress, Bergman's own daughter Linn. In this case, the reason for the doubling seems to be that it enhances the contrast between the two mothers. To Maria, the living daughter is merely a doll; in the scene where they appear together, the daughter significantly carries a doll, indicating that it is to her what she is to her mother. To Anna, by contrast, the dead daughter is fully alive.

One of the most enigmatic elements of the film is Karin's self-mutilation. Karin's and Fredrik's dinner – dressed in black, they eat fish and drink red (!) wine, for *"perhaps it is Good Friday"* – is marked by cold phrases between moments of icy silence. A meal of hatred rather than love, their dinner is an anti-Communion, revealing their complete lack of contact. Suddenly, Karin fumbles with her glass. It shatters and the red wine is spilt on the white table-cloth, an ironic visual comment on the formula of the Communion: "The blood of Jesus, shed for you." Here, it is instead purity that is stained, perhaps at the moment when Karin is thinking of her secret lover. Alternatively, the spilt glass and the shed wine (the blood) could be seen as expressions of her longing for death. Her spilling of the wine is visibly linked with Joakim's (Henning Moritzen) suicide attempt: when he has driven the knife into his breast, the blood spreads across his clean, white shirt.

Karin takes a splinter from the broken glass and says, obviously with reference to life: "It's nothing but a tissue of lies." Once inside her boudoir, she *"inserts the splinter in her vagina."* When Fredrik appears, she shows him her bleeding womb, then smears the blood from it around her mouth, declaring again: "It's nothing but a tissue of lies."

Karin clearly wants to make herself sexually inaccessible to her husband. But the sequence means more than that. Having brought the glass in touch with her mouth (the organ of verbal contact), Karin brings it in touch with her womb (the organ of sexual contact). The red wine is figuratively identified with the blood that is moved from womb to mouth. The repeated expression "a tissue of lies" is put in a visual context which makes it pregnant, indicative both of verbal (spiritual) and sexual (sensuous) contact. To Karin there is no true communication. Man is hopelessly lonely in life.

When Agnes dies, it is Anna who closes her eyes. We hear someone weeping, and since Anna, turned away from the camera, is in frame, we believe that it is she. We soon discover that it is Maria, at the other end of the room, who is weeping. The arrangement of sound and image emphasizes how Anna's unsentimental closeness to Agnes contrasts with Maria's sentimental distance.

When Agnes is dead, Anna hears *"a peculiar sound – very faint, very remote,"* soon identified as the desperate crying of a child. Hurrying to Agnes' bed, she discovers *"that the dead woman has been crying; the tears have run down her cheeks."* In the film, Anna's emotional experience of the dead woman is expressed through a subjective camera movement, a swift zoom-in on Agnes' face. Agnes wears a baby's hood on her head, indicating that Anna now merges her with her own dead daughter. It is one of the most dreamlike passages in the film.

For Agnes' miraculous 'resurrection' Bergman gives the following explanation:

> Death is the ultimate loneliness; that is what is so important. Agnes's death has been caught up halfway out into the void. I can't see that there's anything odd about that. Yes, by Christ there is! This situation has never been known, either in reality or at the movies.

But it has been known on the stage! In *The Ghost Sonata*, the ghosts (the Milkmaid, the Consul) are nothing but people whose death has been *"caught up."* However, just as these characters are no real ghosts but incarnations of the Old Man's guilt feelings, so we should not take Agnes' resurrection literally. Rather, we may imagine that whatever Agnes is doing after she has died is communicated solely through internal narrators. Anna's compassion for Agnes here converges with the guilt feelings of the sisters. In different ways, their thoughts revolve around the recently dead woman. Significantly, Agnes in the Swedish original uses the plural form of the pronoun when she tells Anna: "For you [Sw. 'er'] perhaps it is a dream."[11]

Actually, Agnes' 'resurrection' serves primarily to express, in a pregnant way, the three women's attitude not to an abstract character called Death, as in *The Seventh Seal*, but to a dying and dead person. The purpose, however, is the same. In either case, it concerns man's confrontation with "*the ultimate loneliness.*" Like most of the characters in *The Seventh Seal*, Karin and Maria try to escape a confrontation with what eventually will become their own fate. One is reminded of the medieval idea of the dead as a *speculum*, a mirror, of the living: "What you are, I have been. What I am, you will be."

Like the nameless, mute Girl in *The Seventh Seal*, Anna accepts death. It is she who hears Agnes' crying. It is she who remains with the dead woman, both literally by keeping watch over her, and figuratively by keeping the memory of her alive. When the sisters and their husbands depart, in a very Chekhovian scene, Anna is left alone with the memory of Agnes merging with that of her daughter: "*Faintly, very far away and scarcely discernible, she hears the* CHILD'S *crying.*"

The contrast between life and death is expressed also spatially. While Agnes is still alive, her black sick-bed with its blood-red spread seems located at one end of the large red living room. When she has died, the bed appears to be in a smaller room with a door to the living room. The dreamlike change indicates that the room of life has now been separated from the room of death. Anna is significantly the only one who moves freely between the two rooms, the only one who accepts both.

In his 1973 staging of *The Ghost Sonata*, Bergman replaced Strindberg's hope for divine grace with a belief in human love. The same idea is expressed in *Cries and Whispers*, where Anna, not God, dries the tears of the dead woman and where the fact that Agnes' crying does not cease when she dies seems to contradict the words of the Revelation concerning the solace awaiting the blessed after death.

However, after the paradisaic flashback of the four women in the swing, the film ends with the assurance: "*Then the cries and the whispers cease,*" an assurance pointing to the following passage from Revelation (21.4):

> And God shall wipe away all tears from their eyes; and there shall be no more death, neither sorrow, nor crying, neither shall there be any more pain: for the former things are passed away.[12]

Unlike the situation in *The Ghost Sonata*, the final vision in *Cries and Whispers* is only implicitly a flashforward of a heavenly paradise; explicitly it is a flashback of an earthly one. Through Agnes' diary, we witness the happy communion between the three sisters. Anna is also present, rocking the sisters as a mother would her children. Unlike the diary-writer, Agnes, we realize that the togetherness of the sisters is purely momentary and that the only lasting communion is the one between Agnes and Anna.

As the diary-writing Agnes had done earlier, Anna now recalls the happy moment of communion in the park. Significantly, her reading of the diary takes place in her own room. Again, we see the flowers and the apples. Anna is sitting on her bed, looking down at her daughter's empty bed, thinking of Agnes. She lights the candle we earlier saw her blow out and then starts to read from the diary which she has kept in her drawer. The white burning candle, slowly dissolving into Agnes, dressed in white, expresses Anna's hopeful faith that Agnes now lives in a blessed hereafter. Agnes at this point resembles her dead mother, whom we saw earlier in the same environment, she, too, in white. The Chopin mazurka, which earlier formed a bridge between Anna's intercession for her dead daughter and Agnes' memory of her dead mother, now returns. Suggestively, the music combines the two 'memorial' sequences. When Bergman first has Anna read aloud from Agnes' diary and then, when the flashback begins, change to Agnes' voice, it is an expression of how Anna at this moment experiences Agnes as very alive, very close to her. The whole sound-image arrangement indicates that the dead Agnes in Anna's imagination merges with her dead daughter. Agnes' words in the diary about her moment of absolute happiness are applicable also to Anna – but for her, the feeling of happiness concerns a communion not with the living but with the dead.

For the believing Anna, the final words can only mean that Agnes has found rest in God. Some spectators will share her hope. Others will prefer to see the final silence simply as a sign that Agnes has found rest in the earth.

Autumn Sonata (1978)

As the title indicates, there is a connection between Bergman's chamber film[1] *Autumn Sonata* and Strindberg's chamber play *The Ghost Sonata*. Bergman's film, which opens with a sonata by Händel, comes in fact even closer to chamber music than Strindberg's drama. The unities of time and place are more strictly adhered to than in the play. There are four central characters corresponding to the four instruments in a string quartet.[2] Music plays a dominant role. One of the chief characters is an internationally famous pianist. Also structurally we may, in analogy with the sonata form, speak of an exposition, a realization, and a short, concluding repeat.

More important than this rather general description of the structure[3] is the fact that the film medium itself favors the connection with music. In Bergman's words: "I would say that there is no art form that has so much in common with film as music. Both affect our emotions directly, not via the intellect."[4] One might add that the visual rhythm of film is akin to the aural one of music. Both in film and in music we deal with a dynamic flow that is much more emotionally determined than what we find in fiction.

The script of *Autumn Sonata* is divided into a Prologue, followed by 18 scenes and an Epilogue. On the level of the present, the action takes place within one revolution of the sun – as recommended by classical dramaturgy. Charlotte (Ingrid Bergman) arrives to the vicarage at 11 a.m. and leaves in the morning the next day – after a nocturnal confrontation with her daughter Eva (Liv Ullmann). Spatially, the action takes place in the vicarage, apart from a couple of sequences at the end: Eva in the churchyard, Charlotte in the train. The spatial unity emphasizes Eva's static existence – as opposed to Charlotte's restless travelling.

The construction of the plot is akin to that of analytical drama. As with Ibsen, it is mainly based on revelations of past events, revelations which lead to turbulent psychological interaction. Such disclosures are frequently motivated by the sudden appearance of an outsider. Through their legitimate ignorance, Mrs. Linde in *A Doll's House* and Gregers Werle in *The Wild Duck* help to inform the spectators about circumstances known to the other characters. While in these plays, we are confronted with a reunion between old friends, in *Autumn Sonata* the reunion is between mother and daughter – after seven years. As this indicates, the two have a problematic relationship. Why then does the meeting come about? The outward reason is that Charlotte's lover, Leonardo, has just died. This causes Eva to write a letter of condolence, in which she invites the mother to come and stay with her and her husband, Viktor (Halvar Björk). What causes her to do this? Compassion for her mother – despite everything? A need to be seen at last by the mother, now left alone? A wish to rebuke the mother, to do justice?[5] Or a desire for revenge, albeit unconscious, when the mother, an ageing widow soon to conclude a career as an internationally acclaimed concert pianist, for the first time finds herself in a weak position?

As with Ibsen and Strindberg, the question of guilt is fundamental. By linking the guilt through several generations, Bergman can gradually push it back in time. The arrangement is very similar to that in Strindberg's chamber play *The Pelican*, staged twice by Bergman, where the selfish mother, Elise, appears exceedingly guilt-laden until the end of the play. There she defends herself against her daughter Gerda's accusations by referring to the fact that her situation has been no better than the daughter's:

> Do you know about *my* childhood? Do you have any idea of what a bad home I had, what wickedness I learned there? ... So don't blame me; then I won't blame my parents, who could blame theirs, and so on!

When Eva reproaches her mother for her egoism, Charlotte defends herself in much the same way as Elise:

> They [the parents] regarded us children with surprised benevolence, but without any warmth or real interest. I can't remember either of them ever having touched me or my brothers.... Actually I was completely ignorant of everything to do with love: tenderness, contact, intimacy, warmth.

Charlotte finds that she cannot be blamed for her lack of love. For how can you expect warmth from a mother who has never received any herself? However, the children will eventually become parents and in turn be confronted with a child generation. Like a boomerang, the criticism they as children have delivered against their parents will then hit themselves.

In the confrontation between the two generations, one may feel inclined to side with the children and see the parents – or one of them – as mainly responsible for the defects of the children. Or one may side with the parents and see the criticism of the children as a sign of lacking self-knowledge and need of projections. In *Autumn Sonata*, we see both sides and realize that we are dealing, as it says in the film, with different realities. At the same time, there is something that unites the generations, "since the grown-ups are still children who have to live disguised as grown-ups."

Contrasting with the physically handicapped but spiritually healthy Helena, called Lena (Lena Nyman), are her physically healthy but spiritually handicapped mother and sister. Eva has lived a life in the shadow of her parents. She worships her authoritarian mother. She has abstained from the great love of her youth, Stefan, and chosen a husband, Viktor, who is an obvious father substitute. She has given up her writing and now devotes herself to piano playing – in imitation of her mother. Being a clergyman, Viktor is a man of the word. The same is true of Eva-the-author. Charlotte, on the other hand, has devoted her life to music, the wordless art. The fourth character in this family drama, Helena, is lacking in words as a result of her illness.

The distrust of verbal communication is a frequent theme with Bergman. Here, too, Strindberg has been an inspiration. "In silence you can't hide anything ... as you can in words," says the Old Man in *The Ghost Sonata*; and a little later, the same idea returns in the Colonel's remark to his wife: "What's the point of talking, when we can't fool each other?" The same idea is expressed in *Autumn Sonata*. To speak often means to put on a mask, to perform a socially acceptable role. Charlotte devotes herself to this kind of verbal cheating. But as an artist, in her music, she is genuine. As one could expect from an artist, she is a divided person. Her antithesis in this respect is the wordless Helena, the distinctly positive character in the film. Between these two, we find Eva and Viktor. Significantly, Eva has changed from writing to piano playing, from the art of words to that of music. It indicates her increasing distrust of language as a means of communication. But her writing-desk is still very close to the grand piano.

Viktor seems to undergo a similar development. In the Prologue, he still has faith in language: "I'd like to tell her just for once that she is loved wholeheartedly, but I can't say it in such a way that she'd believe me. I can't find the right words." In the Epilogue, this naive fixation on words is undermined: "If only I could talk to her, but it's all just a lot of dusty words and empty phrases."

Already as a child Eva experienced the discrepancy between words and the reality they are supposed to describe. "I knew instinctively that you hardly ever meant what you said," she reproaches the mother. The words, she points out, did not fit the mother's glances or intonation. This is clearly demonstrated when Charlotte, against her will, is confronted with Lena. Her declarations of love are here contradicted by her artificial intonation and facial expression. Even more than Eva, Lena distrusts verbal communication. Her illness bears witness to this. Faced with the false words, she has in protest practically lost the power of speech. Unlike the others, Lena constantly expresses her true feelings, and she does it through glances, gestures, movements, inarticulate sounds.

In contrast to animals, human beings have a richly differentiated language. Usually this is taken as a proof that man is a more highly developed creature. To

Bergman, this is a doubtful truth. Language is for him, as for Strindberg, just as much a sign of degeneration. Along with the words, dividedness entered into the world. Having eaten from the Tree of Knowledge, man, no longer naked, learnt to use words, behind which he could hide his true self. He began to play roles. The Girl in *The Seventh Seal*, Anna in *Cries and Whispers*, and Lena in *Autumn Sonata* – all women! – are characters who, in their combination of muteness and goodness, are close to the dumb animals, and like them unable to play roles.

Opposed to them are the verbal characters, in *Autumn Sonata* Charlotte, Eva and Viktor. These are all subject to the 'Original Sin' of language. Eva accuses Viktor of using "words that have no real sense," of suffering from "a kind of occupational disease." But the discrepancy between the words and the reality they are supposed to express also concerns Eva. Even in her initial letter, the phrase "dearest Mother," used three times, expresses tender feelings which Eva does not at all have.

The first meeting between mother and daughter after seven years is marked by mutual nervousness and the appurtenant verbal smoke-screens. In the script, only Eva's reaction is recorded, a cascade of enthusiasm hiding a need to suppress: "Oh, you do look tired." The power struggle has begun. In the film, we instead hear a dialogue, in which mother and daughter demonstrate their master/slave relationship. Charlotte's artificial enthusiasm does not concern Eva but the house and the view.

Like *Through a Glass Darkly*, *Autumn Sonata* is about a parent who is also a practising artist and who has had a fatal influence on his/her family. In *Through a Glass Darkly*, the play Minus has written is at once a protest against his father's way of writing, a strange attempt to reach out to him (strange since the father cannot possibly appreciate Minus' play), perhaps even a form of self-punishment. In *Autumn Sonata*, Eva's piano playing, similarly, may be seen both as a pathetic expression of her need to establish contact with the mother and as an aggressive form of masochism, aggressive since she "places her mother in a situation in which she [the mother] cannot possibly please her."[6]

Since language is a writer's working material, an artist who distrusts this material would rather deal with pictures or tones than with words. In *Autumn Sonata*, artistry is connected with music. When Charlotte boastfully speaks of her successes as a pianist, there is no reason to doubt that she is right. She *has* been very successful. In her music, she can be generous to large audiences, while in her life she cannot reach out even to those closest to her. She constantly falsifies her relations to her own family. Neither the marriage to Josef nor her relationship with Leonardo has been the way she wants to see it. Characteristically, the latter asks her to leave him shortly before he dies. She has deserted her children. She has constantly placed her artistic career above care for her own

Autumn Sonata: The internationally renowned pianist Charlotte demonstrates to her frustrated daughter Eva how Chopin should be played.

family. An egocentric escape from responsibility and human kindness has mingled with a need to get away from the false words to the truthful music.

A central scene in the film is the one when first Eva, then Charlotte play the same Chopin prelude. Eva's manner of playing, Charlotte tells her, was defective not so much because she is technically inexperienced but because her performance was sentimental rather than emotional:

> The prelude you played tells of suppressed pain, not of reveries. You must be calm, clear, and harsh. The temperature is feverishly high, but the expression is manly and controlled. ... This second prelude must be made to sound almost *ugly*. It must never become ingratiating. *It should sound wrong.* You must battle your way through it and emerge triumphant.

This severe indirect criticism contrasts with Charlotte's evaluation immediately after Eva has finished playing:

EVA. I want to know what I did wrong.
CHARLOTTE. You didn't do anything wrong.

This should be compared to the following lines at the end of the nocturnal confrontation between the two, appearing only in the script:

CHARLOTTE. ... What did I do wrong?
EVA. You did nothing wrong.

In this latter case, question and answer concern Charlotte's relationship to her family, especially to her daughters. The phrasing in the two passages is similar. Both mother and daughter maintain that the other has done nothing wrong. Yet Charlotte dislikes Eva's manner of playing, and Eva dislikes Charlotte's manner of living. The mother finds her daughter "sentimental," the daughter considers her mother "emotionally crippled."

When Eva is playing, Charlotte is sitting in the background. Her face reveals that she is at once moved by Eva and tormented at her manner of playing. When Charlotte is playing, Eva keeps looking at her mother's face, not at her hands. In both cases Bergman focusses on the listener rather than the player. It is the reaction of the listener that matters, not least because it is the receiver with whom the spectator most naturally identifies.

The relationship between art and life seems in Charlotte's case to be antithetic. She has succeeded in music but failed in life. Eva entertains this view. To her, the mother's ability to enter into music markedly contrasts with her inability to enter into the souls of other people. Art has become a substitute for life. To Charlotte, by contrast, art and life are analogous. Her description of how the Chopin prelude should be played – and how she herself plays it – is a disguised description of how life should be lived. At the end of the film, she points out that the warmth and generosity she demonstrates as a pianist indicate that she possesses these qualities as a human being. Who is right?

As always with Bergman, the characters in *Autumn Sonata* play different psychological roles. But the roles are not fixed. In the beginning of the film, Charlotte is the teaching mother, Eva the learning child. Later, during the nocturnal confrontation, the roles are reversed. Eva here sits in judgement on Charlotte; her implacable face returns time and again in low angle, Charlotte's perspective. The mother has been reduced to a helpless child.

Here and there in the film, there are short flashbacks providing glimpses of the mother-daughter relationship in the past. The long shots chosen for these flashbacks suggest not only that the spatial distance corresponds to a temporal one: the people in the background are hazy – as is our remembrance of things past. It also signifies a psycho-logical distance between the child in the foreground and the grown-ups in the back-ground. Along with Eva, we look into her past. The camera is on the eye level of a child.

A question to be posed is: How do the biological roles relate to the psychologi-cal roles? Eva maintains that "there is no difference between children and grown-ups, since the grown-ups are still children who have to live disguised as grown-ups." Nevertheless, she later blames the mother for what she has done to her as a child: "A child is always vulnerable...." Charlotte, on the other hand, self-defensively sticks to the psychological aspect: "*I've never grown up....*" A weighty exchange of words amounts to the same:

> EVA. I was a child.
> CHARLOTTE. Does that matter?

Lena incarnates the combination. Biologically grown up, she is treated like a child be-cause of her illness. In her bed, she is surrounded by teddy bears. Just as Agnes in *Cries and Whispers* to Anna is a substitute for her dead daughter, so Lena is to Eva a substitute for her dead son. She is mothering her younger sister in front of Charlotte – as though she wants to remind Charlotte of her negligence as a mother. Lena's essential part in the film is to incarnate, make visible, both Eva's and Charlotte's feelings of helplessness, of long-ing for safety and consolation. In the beginning, we sense especially the connection be-tween the sisters, Lena's love for Leonardo corresponding to Eva's for Stefan. In both cases, Charlotte has been an obstacle.

Charlotte's nightmare is illuminating in this connection. In the script, it says:

> *The door opens.* CHARLOTTE *is very frightened. Suddenly* HELENA *rushes into the room and throws herself over her mother. She is heavy and strong. After a short struggle* CHARLOTTE *wakes up.*

Charlotte is here haunted by guilt feelings toward Lena. In the film, the nightmare is given another, more suggestive expression. It begins with a close-up of Charlotte's face and hand in the twilight. Suddenly a woman's hand caressingly creeps into hers. For a moment, we experience the situation realistically – the way Charlotte does in her dream. The caressing hand remains unidentified, since figuratively speaking it is both Lena's and Eva's hand. The hand caresses Charlotte's cheek, then moves behind her head. Sud-denly, it seems to tear at her hair. Charlotte wakes up screaming. The nightmare has recreated her experience of her daughters' ambivalent attitude to her, their longing for contact and their need for revenge.

At the end of the culminating confrontation scene, Bergman intercuts between Charlotte in a low child's position and Lena, tormented, rolling across the floor. Charlotte's appeal to Eva – "Eva dear, help me!" – corresponds to Lena's desperate "Help! Mother, come!" (not in script) – significantly, the only words by her which are clearly distinguishable. Lena incarnates at this moment both Eva's and Charlotte's longing for communion and understanding.

The film opens with Viktor, in close-up, telling about how he and Eva, visible in the far background, first met. Plainly expository, the situation serves to provide the spectator with basic information. It may be compared to the opening of *Scenes from a Marriage*, where a reporter from a ladies' journal is interviewing Johan and Marianne. The polished façade shown to the world will soon crumble, and the hierarchic man-wife relationship, quite appropriate to the readers of the ladies' journal, will soon appear untenable.

In *Autumn Sonata*, the purpose is quite different. Viktor turns directly to the spectator, facing him/her squarely – as though we had asked him, just before the film

Autumn Sonata opens with Viktor providing exposition *ad spectatores* in the dark foreground, while his wife Eva in the light background is writing a letter to her mother Charlotte.

began, to tell us about his private life. Bergman here combines two old dramaturgic devices: the Prologue of classical drama and the conversation between a stage figure and his confidant. If the situation nevertheless seems new, it is because the confidant is not a figure on the screen but the spectator in the auditorium. Viktor is significantly placed between Eva, who cannot hear what he is saying, and the spectator. The barrier between screen and auditorium is demolished.

Viktor at this point is standing in a door opening, in dark clothes against a dark wall. To the left of him, we look into the light living room where Eva is sitting by the window next to the photo of her dead son Erik. The striking spatial contrast – reminiscent of the one opening the breakfast scene in *Wild Strawberries* – turns Viktor into an outsider, placed by the frame of the 'proscenium' outside the 'stage area' proper. Proxemically, he is separated from both mother and child, who are bathing in light. (Behind little Erik's blond hair one divines a halo of light, visualizing the parents' glorification of the dead child.)

In *Autumn Sonata*, Bergman abstains from using straight voice-over in connection with soliloquies. (Eva's final soliloquy is, as we shall see, a border case.) The characters utter their soliloquies aloud – as they would on the stage. This means a retheatricalization of the film medium – quite in line with Bergman's striving for stylization of a recognizable reality. Presumably, he finds the voice-over technique artificial and defeating its own purpose. For is it not precisely when the words are born spontaneously on our lips, when our thoughts are immediately verbalized, that the adequate facial expression appears?[7]

Having failed in their attempt at reconciliation, mother and daughter separate. Instead of staying "for a long time" in the vicarage, Charlotte departs early next morning. At the end of the film, Bergman effectively crosscuts between Charlotte's talking to her agent Paul (Gunnar Björnstrand) in an elegant first class compartment and Eva talking to her dead son Erik in the churchyard.

In the script, this passage (Scene 18) covers two pages. The corresponding sequence in the film is done as follows:

> CHARLOTTE, *in an elegant beige dress, is sitting in a first class compartment, smoking. Opposite her, her agent* PAUL, *in black suit, is reading a paper. Outside the compartment window a beautiful landscape – forest and still waters – is gliding past. Evening sun. Train rattle.*
> CHARLOTTE *in English.* Paul, it was good of you to come with me. I don't think I could have taken it alone. I don't know, I had a slight shock, I think. My daughter Helena was there – quite unexpectedly. And sicker than ever.

Why can't she die? *Looks out through the window. Pause. Looks again at* PAUL. Do you think it's cruel of me to talk like that?

A churchyard high above a fjord with still water. In the foreground grave-stones, in the background EVA, in gray coat and black boots, is seen walking. Daylight.

EVA. Poor little Mother, rushing off like that. She looked so frightened, and suddenly so old and tired. Her face had shrunk, and her nose was red with weeping. Now I'll never see her again.

Close-up of PAUL, *who has fallen asleep. Train rattle.*

CHARLOTTE *in English.* Paul! PAUL *wakes up.* Listen, don't go to sleep now. *Pan to* CHARLOTTE. The critics always say that I'm a generous musi-cian. No one plays Schumann's piano concerto with a warmer tone. Nor the big Brahms sonata. I'm not stingy with myself. Or am I?

EVA *is sitting on the wall of the churchyard next to a big birch. She is looking at* ERIK'S *white gravestone in the foreground.*

EVA. It will soon be dark, and it's getting cold. I must go home and get dinner for Viktor and Helena. *Dissolve to extreme long shot of* EVA, *the birch and the gravestone.* I can't die now. I'm afraid to commit suicide. Maybe God will want to use me one day, and then he'll set me free from my prison.

Red-toned, frontal close-up of CHARLOTTE. *Train rattle.*

CHARLOTTE *in English.* Paul, see that little village. The lights are on al-ready in the houses. People are going about doing their evening duties, some-body is preparing dinner, *Close-up of* PAUL *who takes off his spectacles.* the children are doing their homework. *Red-toned close-up of* CHARLOTTE, *minute in-zoom.*

CHARLOTTE *in Swedish.* I feel so shut out. I'm always homesick, but when I get home I realize it must be something else I long for.

Extreme long shot of EVA *in the background, gravestones in the foreground.*

EVA. Erik, are you stroking my cheek? Are you whispering in my ear? Are you with me now? We'll never leave each other, you and I.

Two-shot PAUL *and* CHARLOTTE *in profile, next to each other. Train rattle.*

CHARLOTTE *in English.* What would I do without you? *Kisses his nose.*

And what would you do without me? PAUL *kisses her hand.* Think what a trying time you have with your violinists. And what the hell of a noise they make when they practice. *They laugh. He shyly caresses her hand, looks out of the window. She withdraws her hand, turns towards the window, sees her own reflection in the black window which is partly hidden behind the lamp in the compartment. Loud train rattle.*

In the background the vicarage with illuminated windows in the twilight. EVA, *hardly visible in the foreground, is walking up to the house.*
EVA. There's a light in Helena's room. Viktor's there, talking to her. That's good. He's kind. He's telling her that Mother has gone away.

Is the silent Paul, whose name means 'humble,' a counterpart of Lena? Is he a man who has discovered the emptiness of words and who prefers to communicate through glances and caresses? Or is he an absent-minded gentleman who merely pretends to listen when it is in his interest to do so? Is he perhaps another Viktor, an indication that mother and daughter are attracted to the same type of man? In the script, Charlotte's statement that Paul "is kind" is followed by Eva's statement that Viktor "is kind." Is he of flesh-and-blood at all or, as his silence may suggest, merely a figment, an incarnation of Charlotte's needs at this moment?[8] Does he ultimately represent her wishful thinking of death?[9]

In the script, we never learn *where* Eva is soliloquizing. In the film, her environment at this point must be established. Bergman selects the churchyard. The silent realm of the dead becomes an effective contrast to the noisy train, and Eva's calm walking along the wall of the churchyard, with the magnificent fjord in the background forms a parallel-by-contrast to Charlotte's journey through the low-lying landscape rushing by outside the compartment window. Although the two events seem to take place simultaneously, it is considerably lighter in the churchyard than outside the train. Presumably, Bergman was less interested in the factual light than in light as an indication of two stages on the journey of life. Clearly, the setting sun and the approaching darkness are especially relevant to the ageing woman. When she looks into the darkness, she meets her own mirrored self on the window pane – a complex metaphor suggesting man's imprisonment in himself, his loneliness before death and his sense of self-confrontation when facing death.[10]

As already indicated, Charlotte's conversation with Paul comes close to a soliloquy, a thinking aloud. This is especially true when she switches from English to Swedish, a language which Paul cannot understand. The transition to the mother tongue characteristically takes place in a passage expressing homesickness.

While Charlotte seeks consolation from a seemingly living person, Eva – like Anna in *Cries and Whispers* – is in her imagination together with her dead child. The crosscutting at this point reverses the situation early in the film, when we saw Eva seeking consolation from Viktor, while Charlotte was speaking to the photo of her dead lover. Here, too, the crosscutting indicates that the difference between dialogue and soliloquy is negligible, that the dead Leonardo is in fact a better 'listener' than the living Viktor, that communication with the dead functions better than with the living.

The extreme long shots in the churchyard sequence have a neutralizing effect, diminishing the pathos of the situation. The discrepancy that hereby arises between camera distance and vocal proximity corresponds to Eva's sense of contact with her dead child.

The letter which shapes the foundation for a happy end has a long tradition on the stage. Bergman relates to this tradition in the spectacular *deus ex machina* resolution at the end of *The Magician* and, more quietly, at the end of *Autumn Sonata*. The two letters in the latter film – one in the Prologue, the other in the Epilogue – serve to frame the action. Both are written by Eva, both are directed to her mother Charlotte, and both are kept in a friendly tone. But there the resemblance ceases. Let us look more closely at the context of the two letters.

The first is a letter of invitation, kept in a humble, almost ingratiating tone. We learn that mother and daughter have not met in seven years and that Eva is now anxious to have the mother visit her. The spectator wonders why. As soon as the letter is finished, Eva enters her husband's study to read the letter to him before mailing it. With paternalistic benevolence, Viktor approves of the letter. The dialogue between husband and wife is realistic.

Instead of the idyllic reunion both women have been hoping for now that one has lost a son and the other a lover, Charlotte's visit leads to a confrontation. The mother, held responsible for her behavior in the past, proves defenceless against the daughter's accusations. When she leaves, both she and Eva have a feeling that they will never meet again. The break is a fact.

Then comes the reversal in the Epilogue. Again Eva is sitting by the window writing a letter to her mother. This time she intends to mail it directly, without having Viktor look at it. As it happens, Eva meets him in the hall. As it happens, he is on his way to the post office. She asks him to mail the letter. And she adds: "You may read it if you like." She does not try to keep the content of the letter secret. She does not ask for his approval. Compared with the Eva of the Prologue, the Eva of the Epilogue acts like a grown-up person.

The coincidences which, of course, dramaturgically are not coincidences at all mean that the spectator via Viktor is informed about the content of the letter:

Long shot of VIKTOR *reading the letter. He approaches the hall – and the camera.* "I have realized that I wronged you. I met you with demands instead of with affection. I tormented you with an old soured hatred which is no longer real. *Close-up of* VIKTOR. *Dark background.* Everything I did was wrong and I want to ask your forgiveness. *Frontal close-up of* EVA, *with glasses, open face, tender voice. Light background.* I've no idea whether this letter will reach you, I don't even know if you will read it. Perhaps everything is already too late. But I hope all the same that my discovery will not be in vain. There is a kind of mercy after all. I mean the enormous chance of looking after each other, of helping each other, of showing affection. I want you to know that I will never let you go again or let you vanish out of my life. I'm going to persist! I won't give up, even if it should be too late. *Frontal close-up of* CHARLOTTE, *without glasses, looking down – as though she were reading* EVA'S *letter. Light background.* I don't think it is too late. CHARLOTTE *raises her face, opens her lips as though she is whispering something and closes them again. Tender, open, helpless face – like that of a child.* It must not be too late." *Close-up of* VIKTOR, *looking down at the letter. Tilt down to his hands, which put the letter in its envelope. Fade-out.*

It can be seen that compared with the first letter, the second one is presented indirectly and subjectively. It is in Viktor's imagination that the faces of the two women are evoked, and the way in which it is done reveals his hope that a final reconciliation between mother and daughter will be possible. By itself, the letter is hardly unambiguous. Eva's assurance that she will never let the mother "go again" may sound rather authoritarian. But this is toned down by the way in which it is said – *in Viktor's imagination.*

More striking than the face of the wife is that of the mother. Here we deal with a subjective flashforward. Viktor not only imagines that Charlotte receives and reads the letter, something that is questioned by Eva herself; he also envisages how she reacts to it. While Charlotte earlier needed her glasses to be able to read, she can now do without. She has taken off the protective mask. By contrast, Eva keeps her glasses – while in the earlier confrontation scene she took them off. To Viktor, she apparently seems less conciliatory than the mother.

It should also be noticed that the camera gradually approaches the faces. We get a little closer to Eva than to Viktor, and yet a little closer to Charlotte – after which we return to the somewhat greater distance to Viktor. The distances here contribute to the emotional loading which culminates in the words accompanying the Charlotte frames. But the differences are small, and the main impression is that the two women (the sender and receiver of the letter) now try to reach out to one another with greater honesty than they have shown before. Viktor's hope that a reconciliation is possible is transmitted emotionally, via the close-ups of the women, to the spectator.[11]

Fanny and Alexander (1982)

Fanny and Alexander exists in two versions, a shorter one released for cinema transmission and a longer one meant for television. It is the latter, which agrees better with the published script and is regarded as the proper one by Bergman,[1] that will be considered here.

Intended in the first place as a television series, the script of *Fanny and Alexander* is divided into five "acts," to which are added, in classical theater idiom, a Prologue and an Epilogue.

In the Prologue, which figures only in the script, we are introduced to the town in which the drama unfolds. The town, which boasts a castle, a cathedral, a university, and a theater, is never named; that would diminish its universality. The year is 1907.

Act I describes the Christmas celebrations, first in the theater, then in the Ekdahl home. In Act II, the managing director of the theater, Oscar Ekdahl (Allan Edwall), suffers a stroke during a rehearsal of *Hamlet*, is driven home, dies, and is buried. In Act III his young widow Emilie (Ewa Fröhling) is remarried to Bishop Edvard Vergérus (Jan Malmsjö), breaks with the theater, and moves with her children Alexander (Bertil Guve) and Fanny (Pernilla Allwin) to the Bishop's residence. Act IV charts the "events of the summer" of 1909; scenes from idyllic Eknäs, the Ekdahls' summer place in the archipelago, are intertwined with scenes demonstrating the strict routine in the Bishop's house, where Emilie and her children are 'imprisoned.' Act V begins with a description of how the children are rescued from the Bishop's residence and taken to Isak Jacobi's (Erland Josephson) mysterious antique shop and apartment, after which these two contrasting environments are intertwined. In the final scene of this act, omitted from the series, Emilie returns to the theater after the Bishop's death.

In the Epilogue we are back among the Ekdahls, now happier than ever. It is May (Sw. 'maj'), the lilacs are in bloom. Emilie and the nanny Maj (Pernilla Wallgren) have each given birth to a daughter, and it is the day of the joint christening. We have some fragmentary impression of what the future holds for Maj, Gustav Adolf's (Jarl Kulle) daughter, and Emilie. In the closing images, lacking in the script, we see Alexander in the lap of his grandmother Helena (Gunn Wållgren) who reads Strindberg's Explanatory Note to *A Dream Play* aloud to him.

The title of *Fanny and Alexander* may appear trivial and slightly confusing, since Fanny's part in the film is rather small compared with Alexander's. Actually, the title is quite meaningful. Referring to the names of two children, brother and sister, it indicates that it is the child's perspective – and the artistic Ekdahls have by and large retained this perspective – that predominates in the film. In Bergman's view, there is no fundamental difference between the perspective of children and grown-ups since, in the words of Eva in *Autumn Sonata*, "the grown-ups are still children who have to live disguised as grown-ups." Like the author of *A Dream Play*, Bergman sees human beings as children (Sw. 'människobarn').

That Fanny's name is mentioned first, despite her being the younger, scarcely springs from conventional etiquette. It is a discreet indication of the women's prominent role in the TV series – in contrast to male society's 'Adam and Eve.'

The blonde, eight-year-old Fanny, who was already *"healthy and plump"* when she was born, stands for earthiness and affirmation, while her darker brother Alexander, the elder by two years, *"small and weakly"* from the cradle, is an introvert brooder and seeker, a day-dreaming misanthrope with his gaze directed towards a reality beyond the visible one. It is significantly he who remains in contact with the dead father.

The light and the dark, woman and man, anima and animus, yin and yang – in the final analysis, Fanny and Alexander give shape to the conflicting tendencies in man, dramatically split up into two individuals, as we know it from Bergman's earlier films: Antonius Block and Jöns in *The Seventh Seal*, Ester and Anna in *The Silence*, Elisabet and Alma in *Persona*. However, this time it is not gender but age that links the names.

The family to which Fanny and Alexander belong is called Ekdahl, a name that ever since Ibsen's *The Wild Duck* has become synonymous with people consoling themselves with illusions about life. Like Ibsen's Ekdals, Bergman's socially superior Ekdahls – note the inserted 'h' – have a need to embellish reality in order to endure it. "If you deprive an average man of his illusions you simultaneously steal his happiness," says Relling in Ibsen's play. "Rob a man of his subterfuges and he goes mad and begins hitting out," declares Gustav Adolf Ekdahl in Bergman's film.

Ibsen contrasts the uncompromising childhood world of Hedvig and Gregers with the adult "life lie" existence of the Ekdals. In the same way, Bergman sets the childhood purity of Fanny and Alexander against the "subterfuges" of the grown-ups, their façade mentality and role-playing.

At the same time, there is an undercurrent connecting the children with the grown-ups. As we have seen, Alexander, too, feels the need to escape from harsh reality. Contrary to his younger sister, who has the strength to accept existence on its own terms, he is already on his way to the adult world. Seen from this standpoint, their difference in age is significant: Fanny and Alexander are incarnations of stages on life's way.

Correspondingly, the elderly grandmother, Helena Ekdahl, represents another phase of existence, the experience of old age. The frankness of the children and the old lady's ability to see things in perspective gives all three of them a sense of those essentials of existence that are lacking during the chaotic "middle period" – adult life.

Fanny and Alexander also have their theatrical counterparts – as do the cheerful Gustav Adolf and his tragic brother Carl – in the happy mask of Comedy and the melancholy mask of Tragedy. Significantly, the opening shot of the series, showing the Acropolis as the backdrop in Alexander's toy theatre, includes these two masks.

The series shows predominantly two contrasting environments: the cozy Ekdahl household, with its close attachment to the theater (illusion), and the ascetic Bishop's residence, with its ties to the church (religion). The tension between these two milieux, these alternative ways of life, is one that may be traced through Bergman's entire film career, even aesthetically. Alongside a series of multifaceted films, rich in setting and characters, he has also created his pared-down chamber films. These two kinds correspond, if you will, to the over-decorated, dazzlingly colored Ekdahl milieu and the austere Vergérus one with its restricted color scheme reminiscent of black-and-white film.

The question about the meaning of life that features so strongly in Strindberg's *Dream Play*, and the answer to which one expects to find behind the mysterious door with its four-leaf clover hole, is also posed in *Fanny and Alexander*. Like Strindberg, Bergman emphasizes the unreality of life itself. What became of "the whole long interval," Helena asks herself, rather like the aged Nina Leeds in O'Neill's *Strange Interlude*. She is referring to the adult period between childhood and old age, but in the context – she addresses the question to her dead son – her speculation also refers to life as such, that brief journey from something unknown to something unknown.

It is true that most of the Ekdahls do not ponder over life's larger issues. "We Ekdahls have not come into the world to see through it," Gustav Adolf declares in his Epilogue speech. But in this respect, they contrast with the brooding Hamlet figure of Alexander, with Edvard Vergérus, who attempts to solve the mystery of life with the aid of a harsh and punitive God, and with Isak Jacobi's animistic monism.

The door with the four-leaf clover has its Bergman equivalent in the invisible jib-door that separates Helena's apartment from Oscar and Emilie's. Psychologically, this door symbolizes the undercurrent relationships that exist despite the impression people give of being separated from one another, incapable of 'entering' one another. Metaphysically, the jib-door raises the question whether or not there is an exit from life, a 'room' beyond earthly existence.

The metaphysical aspect becomes dominant when Alexander is confronted in Jacobi's apartment with "*a black-painted jib-door*," from which a screaming god emerges. On closer inspection, this god turns out to be merely a huge marionette that flops to the floor when the man who pulls the strings, the atheist Aron, releases it. This god, identical to the one worshipped by Edvard Vergérus, is unveiled as a man-made construction. The unmasking of the marionette-god anticipates that of the Bishop, whose domineering posture finally degenerates into an abject crawling about the floor.

The Christian dualism of grace and punishment, heaven and hell, gives way to a Jewish, pantheistic monism, a belief that "everything is alive, everything is God and the thought of God, not only the good but also the cruellest things." This belief plays the same cathartic role in *Fanny and Alexander* as the Brahmin myth of the Fall of Man in *A Dream Play*. Isak's perception of God may also be compared with the psychological monism that is contained in the names Fanny and Alexander.

Although Alexander, who is haunted by the ghost of his dead father, should be susceptible to the pantheistic belief in demons, he adheres rather to a personal god, be it a "piss-and-shit-god." Characteristically, the Bishop's sacrorhetorical image of God is repeatedly contrasted with Alexander's blasphemous catalogue of expletives, expressive of his sexual inferiority complex vis-à-vis his stepfather.

Freud chose to locate the reason for Hamlet's not immediately taking revenge on his stepfather in the Prince's own repressed childhood desire: the yearning to get his father out of the way so that he himself might enjoy his mother's favors. Because the stepfather has already performed both actions, Hamlet's energies are numbed and re-placed by self-reproach, since "he himself is literally no better than the sinner whom he is to punish."[2]

This model can also be applied to the triangle formed by Edvard, Emilie, and Alexander.[3] Their correspondence to the leading characters in *Hamlet* is blatantly underlined when Emilie tells her son: "Don't act Hamlet, my son. I'm not Queen Gertrude, your kind stepfather is no king of Denmark, and this is not Elsinore castle, even if it does look gloomy." What for Emilie are fantasies or pure lies are realities for Alexander.

In Bergman's script, Gertrude's 'infidelity' has its equivalent in the insinua-tions that Alexander and Fanny are not Oscar's children – compare his role as Joseph in the Nativity play – but this allusion to Emilie's amorous escapades does not figure in the screen version.

Alexander's erotic attraction to his mother and concomitant hatred of his stepfather has an obvious Oedipal tinge. Already in the prelude to the film, we see Alex-ander snuggle down into his granny's ample bed and pull the cover over himself. A little later Helena fusses over him. The vague impression that the contact between mother and son may not be what it should be is reinforced when Maj, the children's nanny, is shown to function as a substitute mother – like so many servants of former times.

During the pillow fight in the nursery, Maj plays out a sexual situation with Alexander. And when, not long afterwards, he is lying in bed, she comes to him and whispers:

> Tonight you can't sleep in Maj's bed because Maj will have a visitor, you see, and Maj can't have any number of men in her bed, can she now? All the same, you're Maj's sweetheart, you know that, don't you?

At which point Alexander turns abruptly away from her.

Here the mother's 'treachery' toward her son, in favor of another 'man,' is clearly anticipated. As opposed to the young Hamlet (whose age is indeterminate), Alexander is still a child and so cannot compete on sexual terms with the adult Edvard. His constant chattering to himself about sexual matters testifies to his problem in this area.

The contrast between child and grown-up and the linking of the religious and sexual spheres are manifested most significantly when the marionette-god asks Alexander in Edvard's abstract, rhetorical tones: "Is there anything greater than love?" and in Alexander's concrete, blasphemous response: "Well, if there is it would be His Grace the bishop's cockstand. I can't think of anything else as I'm only ten years old and haven't much experience." The (archetypal) loathing of the boy for the adult has, in other words, a double cause, and it is precisely in his combination of virile ladies' man and punitive clergyman that Vergérus appears so menacing an opponent in Alexander's eyes.

Appears. For it is clear that the film accommodates elements of strong subjectivity. They include Oscar's numerous returns after his death; through differences in costume and lighting it is made clear that we are dealing here with a subjective reality. They also include Alexander's story about Edvard's "murder" of his first wife and their two children, a fantasy engineered by his hatred for the Bishop and at the same time a harbinger of the fate that will soon befall Edvard's second wife and *her* children.

But often it is tantalizingly vague as to where the demarcation line runs between objective and subjective reality. Is one, for example, to accept the enormous Ekdahl apartment as an authentic replica of a patrician home? One certainly can. But one may also see it as absurdly large by virtue of its being viewed through the eyes of a child. Bergman seems to choose to imply this later on, when at the start of the film he places Alexander beneath a table and lets him peep out at the room from this low position; this is a pictorial indication that what follows is dominated by the child's point of view.

In the script, the Prologue consists, we recall, of a panoramic description of the town in which the action unfolds. "*A river with a fairly swift current and several small cataracts and waterfalls flows through the town*," it says here. The Prologue of the film is quite different. It contains no description of the town. And although the swift river is visible in the opening shots, it is no longer realistic but mythic; streaming towards a foaming waterfall, marked by an obvious border, it represents life's inevitable movement towards death. Synchronized with the images of streaming water, as though in appraisal of this transient life, are the light, exuberant bars from the second movement of Schumann's piano quintet op. 44. Alternatively, the nondiegetic romantic music replacing the diegetic sound we would expect – the roar of the waterfall – may be seen as an expression of man's need to exorcise death by means of art (music). A similar combination of music and image – with marked seasonal changes, indicating the phases of life – is repeated in the beginning of each act/part of the film as a reminder of life's inconstancy and brevity.

As soon as the Prologue proper begins, Bergman cuts from this wide perspective of the stream of life to the small one of Alexander and his world. Significantly, we first see him via his puppet theater. The sequence begins with a close-up of the theater, causing us to believe that we are confronted with the Royal Theater in Copenhagen. Already here Bergman attunes us to Alexander's mingling of reality and fantasy. And the key word in this process is "theater." The red curtain is lifted, and we witness a romantic setting. When the backdrop is lifted, we see Alexander's huge face behind the tiny paper figures on the stage.

What we witness here is an inward movement which is at the same time a movement from illusion to reality. What is presented is the child living in a self-created fantasy world, a world that can be surveyed and controlled. But it is also the director as creator of illusion, as magician. Eventually, Alexander is to meet a kinsman in Aron (Mats Bergman), who also rules over a self-created world of puppets. Behind the boards representing the world, there is a hidden manipulator who controls everything happening on these boards. The same may be true of the world mirrored on the stage. Also behind the world in which we live there is – perhaps – a hidden Director.

From the world of the theater, we move to the affluent Ekdahl interior, seen from the child's low optical point of view, this, too, a theatrical world filled with lots of properties. Along with Alexander, we explore the gigantic apartment. Moving from one room to another he keeps shouting: "Fanny! Mother! ... Siri! ... Maj! ... Granny!" It is as though only women can fill the emptiness around him. Eventually, he lies down on his back under a table and clasps his hands as though he were praying. In a long, low-angle shot we see, with him, two large rooms in a suite. The spectator has taken his position in front of a deep 'stage.'[4]

Suddenly, the lighting changes miraculously. The half-naked woman sculpture by the window is strongly lit by the sun,[5] and the room behind it turns intensely red.

The glass prisms of the crystal chandelier, in close-up, begin to move. The woman sculpture raises one arm. A dull sound appears to emanate from a scythe drawn through the carpet, and soon we see a grinning skull in a black, hooded cloak stealing towards the woman behind the leaves of a potted palm.[6] Alternating with these visions, we see Alexander's bewildered or thoughtful face in close-up. In the child's imagination, the apartment has turned into a world where the white woman and the black-clad skeleton represent not only life and death or – as in the opening shots of the river – the transformation from the one to the other, but also point forward to the struggle between the white Oscar and the black Edvard, between him who is a living dead and him who is dead in life.

The brittle, childish, music-box music accompanying the miraculous visions is suddenly replaced by an unpleasant clash which returns Alexander, and us, to reality. The visionary light fades. The 'theater performance' is finished and is replaced by gray, everyday reality. A servant is putting coals into the iron stove in the corridor. Then grandmother Helena enters and takes care of Alexander.

A child experiences reality differently from an adult. For the child, it frequently appears startling, secretive, terrifying. This is connected not least with the behavior of grown-ups. He who wants to present a child's experience of life to an adult audience is therefore compelled to make it differ, in one way or another, from the reality familiar to that audience. Bergman achieves this by means of stylization and a touch of the grotesque. What strikes us as dreamlike, unrealistic may be seen as manifestations of a reality we left behind when we grew up. Bergman's tendency to blur the border between objective and subjective reality is apparent in the Ekdahl interior. By and large, it looks perfectly realistic. An opulent bourgeois home at the turn of the century might have appeared like this.[7] Confirmation of this may be found in the following description of the living conditions of the Swedish bourgeoisie around this time:

> When one examines pictures of these overloaded interiors, it is the theatrical element that is most conspicuous. As never before, families were investing time and money into the *shaping* of their living quarters, building up an entire landscape and atmosphere in room after room ... The home became the stage on which the family displayed its opulence and its social status. ... This conscious or unconscious theatrical way of thinking corresponded well to the new image of man as a refined actor. ... The warm colors, the generous curves, and the soft material, all radiated sensuality. The home became a theater box from which the family gazed out at the world.[8]

As appears from this description, the graceful feminine and theatrical features in the scarlet interiors of the Ekdahl home are not of Bergman's fabrication. On the contrary, they constitute a social and ideological sign-language that is to be found in the turn of the century environment mirrored in the film.

However, the connection between theater and home is much stronger in Bergman's version. We cut directly from the theater to the Ekdahl house opposite it, so splendidly lit up and decorated for Christmas that it assumes a theatrical character. This impression is kept up also in the interior. The Ekdahl living room "is framed by heavy velvet curtains, reminiscent of the curtain in a theater – which, moreover, have the same color as the curtain of Alexander's puppet theater."[9] Similarly, we cut from the theater's *Play about the Joyful Birth of Christ* to the reading aloud about this same event in Helena's living room. Already at the theater, we participate in the material good cheer when Gustav Adolf Ekdahl storms in at the head of his restaurant staff, thereby anticipating the long dance to the Ekdahl kitchen that we are soon to witness.

By blending the two settings in this way, Bergman illustrates one of the series' basic premises: that life and theater are intimately related to each other. But while the actors on the stage consciously perform their roles, in ordinary life we constantly devote ourselves to role-playing without being aware of it.

Helena, like Elisabet in *Persona* before her, brings the two areas together when she speaks by turns of her roles on stage and in life; the one kind seems as real to her as the other. Even the funeral of her son, Oscar, becomes a performance in her eyes. When it is said of him that he is a poor actor, it is metaphorically a positive assessment. Oscar does not play any roles in life. His love is pure and unequivocal, like a child's. In his way, he corresponds to Ibsen's Hedvig.

Part of the social role-playing consists in appearing more remarkable than one really is. This is noticeable in the royalist aspirations of the Ekdahls. Oscar Ekdahl Sr. and Oscar Ekdahl Jr. correspond to King Oscar I and King Oscar II. Oscar Ekdahl Jr.'s brothers are called Gustav Adolf and Carl, just like the crown prince and prince at the time. The series begins at Christmas, 1907. A couple of weeks later Oscar dies and is succeeded as director of the theater by his wife. It is an 'accession' that rhymes not only with that of Hamlet I and Claudius but also with Gustav V's succession to the throne following the death of Oscar II in December 1907. The amorous adventures of Gustav Adolf and Carl are on a regal level. "Have you ever seen such a crown prince?" cries the former in an intimate scene with his mistress Maj. Carl's wife Lydia is German just as the then Queen Viktoria, and the daughter of Gustav Adolf and Maj is christened Helena Viktoria in the Epilogue. Helena wears royal decorations. Oscar lies on his bier like a monarch, and the cortege from the cathedral has the look of a state funeral.

As already suggested, all these allusions dovetail with the conservatism of the Ekdahl family, their need to embellish existence by embellishing themselves. The same mentality may be discerned in their Ibsenite forebears. But the references also form a historical and ideological framework around the story. We find ourselves in the Oscarian realm of Sweden, with its bourgeois standards and values. At the same time, we are reminded of another monarchy with a dubious double morality, "the rotten state of Denmark," encountered in *Hamlet*. The combination of a 20th century Swedish reality and a fictional Danish one some 400 years earlier implies that then and now, theater and life, are interwoven, and that human nature remains remarkably stable in its instability.

But kings, princes, and princesses are creations we also associate with the world of fairy tales, and thus with childhood. As children we identify with such figures. Life still lies before us, tempting and promising. Carl (Börje Ahlstedt) refers to this when he laconically sums up life in these terms: "First I'm a prince, the heir to the kingdom. Suddenly, before I know it, I'm deposed. Death taps me on the shoulder."

The Ekdahls cling to the ideals of a vanished era. The Divine Right of Kings was already an anachronism in 1907. The foundations of a male-governed, conservative society were beginning to totter. There is an amusing comment to this development in the Prologue: "God, finally, holds his hand over the king, and the waltz from *The Merry Widow* is played as a duet in almost every family that owns a piano."[10] The combination of the King and the Merry Widow is naturally an allusion to Claudius and Gertrude. But the waltz also refers to the dawn of female emancipation: The widow Helena takes over the running of the theater in the wake of her husband, and the widow Emilie follows in her footsteps. When Emilie moves to the Bishop's residence, Gustav Adolf takes over the business but he cannot manage it, and not until Emilie returns to the theater is there any sign of a renaissance. "Prince" Carl and "second-rate Napoleon" Gustav Adolf will never inherit the kingdom. Instead, it will be the latter's illegitimate daughter who is proclaimed "empress."

Fanny and Alexander, it has been said, deals with "the downfall of the patriarchy, its degeneration, disintegration and eventual collapse."[11] There is a certain truth in this. It is no mere coincidence that it is two *girls* who are honored at the christening in the Epilogue and that they are named Helena Viktoria and Aurora. But the future belongs to the women not so much because now, almost a century later, we know that history has developed in this direction. The reason is rather that women in Bergman's eyes are stronger than men by virtue of being "close to life" – to quote one of his film titles. As is usually the case in Bergman's films, the women cherish tender and loving contacts, while the men tend to be stiff, lonely, alienated.

The erotic relationships also illustrate the power struggle between men and women, not least during the sexual act. Gustav Adolf fails when he assumes the traditional male position atop his mistress; a satisfying intercourse takes place only when she straddles him. Gustav Adolf's problems in this area are again demonstrated in the sex scene with his wife Alma; once more he ends up in the supine position. Similarly, Carl sinks down exhausted on the marital bed, even more pitiful than his not particularly powerful wife. As for the third brother, Oscar, it is suggested in the script that he is impotent.

A central theme in the series is the contrast between the big and the small world. In Oscar's speech to the performers – yet another *Hamlet* reference – the small world, tantamount to that of the theater, is defended. We need theater (illusion) as a consolation and protection against "the hard world out there." The theater is referred to as "a small room of orderliness, routine, conscientiousness, and love." The implication is that it possesses everything that the big world lacks.

When Emilie is about to exchange the illusory world of the theater for, as she believes, the more truthful one of religion, she gives a speech – not included in the screen version – to the company which directly contradicts Oscar's. The theater's capacity for creating illusion is equated now with life's falsehoods. Actors deceive themselves into identifying with the roles they play instead of discovering their own identity. They also try to imagine that their own small world is more important than the big one outside. That is the easy way out.

When Gustav Adolf returns to this theme in the Epilogue, he declares:

We might just as well ignore the big things. We must live in the little, the little world. We shall be content with that and cultivate it and make the best of it. Suddenly death strikes, suddenly the abyss opens, the storm howls and disaster is upon us – all that we *know*. But let us not think of all that unpleasantness.

During this speech, all the Ekdahls and their closest friends are gathered around a huge table, the circular shape of which emphasizes the sense of harmonious togetherness. (At the Christmas dinner they were sitting at a large square table; at the funeral dinner, the table was in cruciform shape, with the Bishop in the middle.) Emilie has realized that her escape from the theater to the church was an error, and she is once again happily restored to the illusory existence of the Ekdahls.

By the small world, Gustav Adolf is referring not merely to the world of the theater but also to everything that human beings have around them and that can make them happy: "good food, gentle smiles, fruit-trees in bloom, waltzes." It is an epicurean *carpe diem* concept that the restaurateur enunciates here, a defence of the idyll close at hand that one can trace back through Bergman's films to Jof and Mia's wild strawberry meal in *The Seventh Seal*. But it amounts to more than this.

The theme is expanded upon in Gustav Adolf's speech in two important respects. Firstly, the small world, the private happiness, is now not just in contrast to the larger world without, the global world of suffering, but also to the unknown world that lies beyond life. The small world is equated with *this* world, *this* life, the only one we know. Gustav Adolf's pleading for the small world amounts to a repudiation of all transcendent endeavors. His worldly outlook agrees to a considerable extent with what Bergman, ever since *The Silence* – originally called *God's Silence* – has been a spokesman for.

When Gustav Adolf voices his love for the small world, he is standing behind Fanny, Alexander, and his own daughter, Jenny. His position strengthens the impression that the small world is related to the world of the children, while the big world by inference is associated with that of the grown-ups. To "cultivate, make the best of" the small world is to create a hopeful future for mankind. But living in a children's world also

The baptismal meal in the Epilogue of *Fanny and Alexander* takes place at a 'democratic' circular table, to the accompaniment of life-affirming waltz music. In his speech, Gustav Adolf, here facing the children in the background, pays homage to "the little world."

implies that one retains the childlike mind, its spontaneity and sense of being close to life. This is what children, women, and artists have in common.

Gustav Adolf's cheerful, earthbound gospel does not apply to Bergman's alter ego, Alexander. Like Isak, he dwells in a world of demons. His thoughts and feelings are dominated by his white-clad father and his black-clad stepfather, the representatives of good and evil. Gradually, the white ghost disappears from his consciousness, first visually, then acoustically when the three high notes Oscar plays on the family's piano finally die away. The stepfather perishes, through Alexander's telepathic wish, energized by Ismael, in the hellfire he himself unleashes, 'murdered' by his own inner cancer, embodied in the bloated, scrofulous, bestial figure of the aunt (played by a man), as repulsive as Vergérus is attractive.

The character of Ismael, whose wailing lament resounds through the final segment of the film, is one of the more enigmatic features of *Fanny and Alexander*. According to Bergman, he is not so much "the son of a servant" as the prototype for the rebellious avenger, the titan, the Prometheus bound. "His hand will be against every man, and every man's hand against him," says Ismael, describing himself in the relevant biblical terms. In Ismael, Bergman has drawn the picture of a hybrid personality; even in speech – he speaks Finno-Swedish – Ismael's androgynous nature is brought out (the part is played by a woman, Stina Ekblad). Ismael unites the male and the female, Fanny and Alexander, and precisely because of this, he appears deviant and supernatural. Like Alexander, Ismael is a Hamlet figure. He is dressed in "*a black suit much too small for him and a scarf*", gifted, learned, misanthropic, mad or pretending to be so, with "awkward talents," "dangerous," and therefore "introvert."

When Alexander, of whom it is said that he "*ought to have been a girl*," has to write down his name, he writes that of Ismael. "Perhaps we are the same person. Perhaps we have no limits; perhaps we flow into each other, stream through each other, boundlessly and magnificently," Ismael comments. This line of thought, which is linked to Isak's monistic image of the world, is visually emphasized when the two boys stand close to each other, cheek to cheek. This situation, reminiscent of the double face of *Persona*, marks the culmination of that longing for togetherness that has in various ways been present throughout the film. Alternatively, Alexander and Ismael may be seen as two distinct voices within the same self and their dialogue as a soliloquy, one voice representing a passive tendency, the other an active one. "It's not I talking. It is yourself," says Ismael to Alexander.

While in the script the stepfather is conspicuously absent at the end and thus seems to have been defeated by Alexander, he pops up at the close of the screen version, as he appeared in life, in a most telling situation. Alexander has secretly been helping himself to biscuits, when suddenly the black-clad Bishop looms up behind him. Alexander falls down beside the stove, stunned. The Bishop's golden cross dangles above his head, and he hears a voice hissing, "You won't escape me!" Alexander gets up, rushes to his granny Helena, and puts his head in her lap, just as he did in the beginning when he was frightened by Death. His flight is one from the masculine god to the female lap, from the transcendent to the immanent, from coldness to warmth, from death to life.

Fanny and Alexander: Grandmother Helena reads to Alexander from Strindberg's Note to *A Dream Play*: "Anything can happen, everything is possible and probable."

Thus, *Fanny and Alexander* concludes with a picture of Helena and Alexander, the old and the young, in loving union. His desolate calling out to the women and lonely meandering through the empty apartment in the opening has found a response in the form of maternal consolation. The gray crocheted shawl worn by the grandmother at the end is significantly a combination of the star-covered coverlet being knitted by the maternal Doorkeeper in *A Dream Play*, and the warm and comforting shawl she wears and that is later handed over to Indra's Daughter. At the end, Emilie suggests that she and Helena should act in Strindberg's recently published drama.[12] The shawl indicates that Helena is to play the part of the Doorkeeper, while Emilie undoubtedly intends to keep the part of

Indra's Daughter for herself. The relationship between the two is indicated in their costumes: Helena in dark, brownish red and Emilie in a lighter, warm red, indicating that life has returned to her.[13] These references remind us that while Strindberg's play is about a divine daughter who descends to the Earth only to return to her celestial origin at the end, in Bergman's series the opposite movement occurs. Here an actress 'ascends' from the sensual world (the theater) to the spiritual world (the church) only to return to the world of the senses at the end. A transcendental perspective has been replaced by an immanent one.

In the final lines – not appearing in the script – the grandmother promises, with Strindberg, that "anything can happen, everything is possible and probable. Time and space do not exist. Against an insignificant background the imagination spins and weaves new designs." Her quotation offers a key to the pattern of *Fanny and Alexander* – the interweaving of dream and reality – and gives voice, moreover, to an approach to life that recognizes the indispensability of the imagination.

That Strindberg is given the final word in *Fanny and Alexander* is a clear indication of the dreamplay character of the series. It is also a tribute to the writer who has meant the most to Bergman, both ideologically and aesthetically.

PART 3

THE RADIO DIRECTOR

Strindberg, *Easter* (1952)

One of the central idea's in *A Dream Play* is the recurrent discovery that our imagination far exceeds reality. This tenet explains the attraction theater and film exercise. But it is perhaps especially relevant with regard to radio drama. For "as imagined pictures may be more beautiful and powerful than actual ones, the absence of the visual component in this form of drama may well be a considerable asset." Listening to a radio play is "more akin to the experience one undergoes when *dreaming* than to that of the reader of a novel: the mind is turned to a field of internal vision." Radio drama "approximates musical form – which is not surprising as both have sounds in time as their raw material."[1]

In view of these circumstances, so close to Bergman's central concerns, it is not surprising that he has taken a lifelong interest in radio drama. Starting in 1942, he sent a manuscript entitled *The Travel Companion*, based on a tale by Hans Christian Andersen, to the Swedish radio; the play was refused. A few years later, he tried to get other plays of his own broadcast: *Rakel and the Cinema Doorman, Jack Among the Actors, To My Terror.* "Unsuitable for radio," was the harsh comment he received, by which was meant that these plays were too coarse for a mass audience.[2]

Bergman's debut as a director of radio drama came in 1946, when he turned his own stage version of a contemporary Swedish play, Björn-Erik Höijer's *Requiem*, into a radio play. To date he is responsible for 39 radio productions, including eight Strindberg, three Hjalmar Bergman and three Ingmar Bergman. In the following, we shall examine two of these productions, beginning with his pioneering adaptation of Strindberg's *Easter*, eventually regarded as one of his most successful radio performances.

As the title indicates, Strindberg's *Easter* (1901) is patterned on the Passion of Christ. The first act plays on Maundy Thursday, the second on Good Friday, the third and last on Easter Eve. Each act has its own lighting – opening with a last ray of sun and ending with sunshine streaming into the Heyst living room, where all the acts are set. Each act is preceded by a part from Haydn's *The Seven Last Words of Our Saviour on the Cross*, Act I by the introductory maestoso adagio, Act II by "Father, forgive them, for they know not what they do" (Luke 23.34) as largo, and Act III with "I thirst" (John 19.31) as adagio.

The daughter in the family, Eleonora, is the Christ figure of the play, and her *satisfactio vicaria* represents one of the play's basic themes. Another is what has been called the benevolent nemesis, that is, the idea that good deeds are rewarded.[3] The plot revolves around Elis' (and his mother's) change from implacability to conciliation.

Bergman's production of *Easter* was a radical departure from earlier radio versions of the play. Although *Easter* is not unduly long even for radio, more than one-fourth of the text was cut. Deviations from what Bergman considered the main plot were mercilessly omitted. Seeing Elis as the central character, Bergman excluded many of Eleonora's speeches, especially her occultist lines. He also reduced the schoolboy Benjamin's part.

When his version was first broadcast, in 1952, several critics were opposed to the reduction of Eleonora's part, seeing *her* as the central figure. But Bergman felt that although she may be so ideologically and thematically, dramaturgically she is not. Being a Christ figure, she is not, like Elis, a divided character who undergoes an inner change. This may be true, but Elis is a problematic protagonist for another reason: his rather vague conversion takes place exceedingly late in the play. More personal reasons – his own affinity with the male figure – no doubt contributed to Bergman's decision to make Elis the focal character.

Haydn's *Die sieben Worte des Erlösers am Kreuze* (1785) exists in four different versions: instrumental, string quartet, piano, and oratorio. Strindberg does not specify which of these versions he has in mind. Since *Easter* has all the characteristics of a chamber play, Bergman logically settled for the string quartet version. He also expanded on Strindberg's scheme and had Haydn's music intoned not three but seven (!) times.

The first time it is heard, it 'embraces' the narrator's announcement "Maundy Thursday." Later in Act I, the chiming of church bells, that forms the background for Elis' (Anders Ek) and his wife Kristina's (Barbro Hiort af Ornäs) somber dialogue, 'dissolves' into Haydn's more harmonious music when the young Eleonora (Maj-Britt Nilsson) and Benjamin (Birger Malmsten) 'enter the stage.' Haydn's music is heard, softly, as Eleonora voices her pantheistic universalism – "For me there is no time and no space," etc. – and it concludes Act I when Eleonora – referring to the concert Kristina is going to with Petrus and where precisely Haydn's *Seven Last Words* will be performed – says "Mother, see thy son!" (John 19.26) and starts to cry.

There is another 'dissolve' from Haydn's music to the ticking of a clock opening Act II, soon followed by the narrator's announcement: "Good Friday." The striking of the clock tells us that it is 6 p.m.; presumably it is also an allusion to the darkness of "the sixth hour ... unto the ninth hour" (Mat. 27.45) surrounding the death of Jesus. The chiming of church bells, that is heard as Kristina leaves Elis for the concert, 'dissolves' again into Haydn's music as Eleonora quotes: "But I have prayed for thee" (Luke 22.32). A fragment from *Seven Last Words* concludes Act II and 'embraces' the narrator's "Easter Eve" opening the last act. At the end of the play Eleonora and Benjamin are left alone 'on the stage':

> ELEONORA. We'll get to the country, Benjamin! In two months! If they'd only go fast! Now I tear the sheets from the calendar and strew them! See how the days go! April! May! June! And the sun is shining on all of them! See! ... Now you're to thank God, who helped us to get to the country!
> BENJAMIN *shyly*. Mayn't I say it silently?
> ELEONORA. Yes, you may say it silently! For now the clouds are gone and then it can be heard up there!

Accompanying these hopeful, final speeches is the seventh and last joyous fragment from Haydn's opus with which the performance is concluded. The wonderfully naive way in which Maj-Britt Nilsson phrases Eleonora's faith in her final speech is, as it were, carried over into Haydn's serene strings.

As appears from this description, sound effects are used very selectively by Bergman in this performance to emphasize the two conflicting moods of the play. The somber, monotonous chiming of the church bells contrasts with Haydn's melodious, graceful music, just as suffering and a sense of punishment, associated mostly with Elis, contrast with joy and a sense of reconciliation, associated with Eleonora.

Focussing on these two sounds, Bergman, one critic wrote,

> abstained from all the usual sound effects. No steps, no doors which opened and closed, no swish-swish from Lindkvist's galoshes.... People never came or left, they were just suddenly present or suddenly absent. It lent a mood of unreality and dream to the piece....[4]

The benevolent nemesis in the play is incarnated by Lindkvist, the creditor, whose announced visit, the Heysts fear, will ruin them. Strindberg skilfully prepares for his arrival by having Elis, standing by the window, discover him outside in the street already in Act I; the end of his speech, with its frequent use of onomatopoeia, reads:

> ELIS. ...those overshoes! "Swish, swish" like the Easter switch ... listen to those overshoes ... "wolves, wolves, mad, madder, maddest, swish, swish!" Watch it! He sees me! He sees me!... *Bows toward the street.* ... He greeted me first! He's smiling! He's waving his hand...and... *Sinks down by the desk weeping.* He went by!

A stage director may stick to Strindberg's piece of teichoscopy, and have Elis report what he sees to the other characters – and to the audience – who do not share his vision. But many directors prefer to make Lindkvist partly visible in the form of a shadow appearing outside the drawn curtains. As the man approaches, the shadow grows bigger. When the shadow has become gigantic, it adequately corresponds to the fear of the unknown that the Heyst family nourishes at this moment.

In Bergman's radio version, lacking the visual code, their fear is expressed solely by verbal and paralinguistic means on the part of the actor playing Elis. Anders Ek gradually raises his voice and increases his tempo until Lindkvist's (Gunnar Olsson) friendly greeting of him makes him break down in happiness from a feeling of undeserved grace. "As he is telling," one critic wrote, "he makes the shadow grow."[5] The speech is rendered with many subtle verbal and paralinguistic nuances, difficult to pinpoint in a performance analysis, yet of utmost importance in radio drama, which generally speaking is a more actor- and less director-oriented type of theater than the one seen on stage or screen.

A Matter of the Soul (1990)

Bergman's *A Matter of the Soul* was first broadcast, under his own direction, on January 14, 1990.[1] In September of the same year, it won the jury's special Prix Italia. Virtually a monodrama – only toward the end is a second voice heard briefly – the play has a formal affinity with Strindberg's *The Stronger*, O'Neill's *Before Breakfast* and Cocteau's *La Voix humaine*; Bergman directed Cocteau's drama for the radio in 1956.

The play is divided into 11 short scenes. It opens on a winter morning at half past ten with a gloomy Viktoria (Jane Friedmann) still in bed. As a reminder of her age – she is 43 – one of her teeth is coming loose, a situation similar to that in Strindberg's one-act *The First Warning* (originally entitled *The First Tooth*), which Bergman directed for the radio in 1960. In an authoritarian tone, Viktoria asks Anna to help her with various household matters; it is unclear whether Anna is a servant, a temporary nurse, or a grown-up daughter. She then reproaches her husband Alfred, who is a professor, for his indifference to her sexual needs. Scene II takes place at the opening of an art exhibition, where Viktoria addresses several people. In the following scene, she visits the house of her parents and addresses first her father, then, in another room, her mother. In Scene IV, she reports a dream she has just had about a mysterious woman. In the next scene, she is opening a bazaar in the presence of her husband; she publicly accuses him of adultery, after which she discovers that he has suddenly died; it seems likely that he has committed suicide – as does the unfaithful husband in *Before Breakfast*, also called Alfred. At the end of Scene VI, featuring Alfred's funeral, Viktoria tries to unmask her husband by pulling him out of his coffin by the ears. Accompanied by Anna, she is in the following scene on her way to a mental hospital in Switzerland. Having escaped from the hospital, she next finds herself in a hotel room together with a worker, whom she alternately seduces and abuses – sharing Miss Julie's attitude to Jean. In Scene IX, she is moved to a ward for the disturbed, after an attempt to kill a professor (!) at the hospital. In Scene X, she addresses a girl "aged eleven or twelve" dressed "in institutional clothes" – obviously her own youthful self. Recognizing in the final scene that Viktoria is no longer a suitable name for her (for reasons indicated in *A Dream Play*, from whence Bergman has obviously borrowed the name), she discovers that this girl – her alter ego – is nameless and "deaf and dumb." Toward the end of the scene another voice is heard, that of an Old Woman.

Early in the play, Viktoria complains: "I just speak all the time and people don't answer or they just walk away from me." This is verified in the monodrama form

Bergman has chosen for his play, a form half-way between dialogue (since someone is being addressed) and monologue (since the addressee remains mute).

If *A Matter of the Soul* had been a stage play, we would have been able to tell whether the addressees are real or imagined. But since we are dealing with a radio drama, this cannot be ascertained. And this is precisely the point. As readers of the published script, we are inclined to assume that the characters Viktoria addresses are physically present. But if that is the case, the time references are confusing. We learn that Viktoria as a student contacted Eugène Carrière shortly before he died in 1906. If we assume that she was about 20 at the time, it follows that the action is set around 1929. Since Caruso, who is singing at the bazaar (Scene V), died in 1921, this scene must describe a situation preceding the one in Scene I and must consequently be a memory that Viktoria recalls. The question is then: How do the scenes temporally relate to one another? Is the development on the whole linear, or does the initial scene represent the latest stage in Viktoria's life? There is no clear answer to this question. We are free to see the play either as a study of Viktoria's development from sanity to insanity or as a description of memories and fantasies in the head of a woman who contemplates taking her own life. It is hardly a coincidence that the play ends with the word "poisoning."

It should be noted that whereas the first scene in the published script contains such acting directions as "*A knock at the door.*" and "ALFRED *leaves the room.*", such directions are later lacking. This *could* be taken as an indication that Anna and Alfred are physically present only in Scene I, and that in the following scenes both they and the rest of the addressed characters are merely imagined. Viewed in this way, the play moves from dialogue to monologue, from realism to fantasy.

As listeners to the performance, we are more inclined to let the fantasy aspect prevail. Abstaining from the sound of doors or footsteps, even in the beginning, to indicate the appearance and disappearance of the characters, Bergman suggests that Viktoria is totally alone and that even Anna and Alfred are present only in her imagination. Similarly, the performance supports the idea that in the scenes following the initial one, Viktoria is vividly reminiscing about past events in her life and even wishfully inventing some of them, like the meeting with Richard Strauss.

Viewed as a monologue, the people Viktoria addresses *are unwilling* to answer her. Viewed as an interior monologue, they *cannot* answer her, since in this case they are only present in her mind. What Bergman is attempting in *A Matter of the Soul*, I would suggest, is to make the characters surrounding Viktoria as real to the listener as they are to her. Here again, he tries to break down the barrier between performer and recipient. And precisely because we are dealing with a monodrama, the radio medium assists him in this endeavor.

"When life comes close to its end," the Poet in *A Dream Play* says, "every-thing and everyone rushes by in a single procession." Bergman's monodrama may be seen as a description of what passes through Viktoria's mind as her life is coming close to its end. Already in the first scene, she voices her suicidal inclinations. The mysterious lady, who keeps her face half-veiled and who suddenly begins to cry and then disappears; the dark, swift-moving river which turns into "a pond with deep black water"; and Viktoria's own discovery that she is "getting cold," yet cannot leave "this terminus" – all these dream elements are rather transparent references to death. In the final scene, these references, now with biblical connotations, become explicit: "There is a storm on the way. Such a strange light, my heart beats fast, can you feel? Maybe this is the day of judgement."

Throughout the play, Viktoria has been addressing numerous people. No one answers her. In the mental hospital, she is confronted with her own self, a little girl lacking a name and completely unable to communicate with the world around her, more truthful in her 'nothingness' than the role-playing grown-up Viktoria. When finally her monologue turns into a dialogue, her speaking partner is an Old Woman, who is at once a nurse at the hospital and an incarnation of death related to the veiled mysterious lady but now a benevolent mother figure, handing her a precious red stone, "no bigger than a drop of blood," that "makes your hand warm." Viktoria's longing at the end of Scene III – "There you are at last! Mummy! My dearest darling mummy!" – has been fulfilled.[2]

In the performance, the feeling that Viktoria is gradually being drained of life is strengthened by the strategic use of music. Contrasting with the orchestral waltz in the art exhibition scene and the piano music ("The Maiden's Prayer") in the bazaar scene, Arvo Pärt's 'celestial' *Fratres* for 12 cello's is heard four times, softly as though from a great distance, the last time after Viktoria has been quoting from the Revelation 6.12-14 and told the girl – herself – to go to sleep. Like the Young Lady at the end of *The Ghost Sonata*, Viktoria seems to be on her way to another shore.

Bergman at times resorts to acting directions in the script which cannot be realized in the finished product. When Viktoria moves from her father's to her mother's room, this is indicated by an acting direction – "*She walks through twilit rooms.*" – that cannot be communicated to the listener. This is complemented by an acoustic indication: "*Opens a door.*" In the performance, the sound of the door is replaced by another and more meaningful sound. While Viktoria is still in her father's room, we hear the ticking of a clock. When she moves into the mother's room, the ticking stops. Since the ceasing of the sound is also synchronized with the father's falling asleep, the impression is com-municated that Viktoria's moving from one room to another is tantamount to her moving from life to death.

Bergman also employs suggestive aural 'dissolves,' as when the train whistle at the end of Scene VI, representing the anguish experienced by Viktoria as she tries to unmask her husband, grows louder and turns into a real train whistle when, in Scene VII, we find her in a train compartment. Similarly, the worrying tolling at a railway crossing in Scene VII 'dissolves' into the tolling of a church bell in Scene VIII.

Viktoria's many-faceted part is a challenge for any actress, and Jane Friedmann manages the paralinguistic recreation of her abrupt alternating between the public and the private, 'mask' and 'face,' aural 'long shots' and 'close-ups,' superbly. This is especially noticeable in Scene III, where her way of addressing four different people reveals four different attitudes, and in Scene VIII where, in a matter of seconds, she declares herself to be – and plays the roles of – actress, mental patient, and whore, indicative of her disintegrating ego.

The mere fact that Bergman, after a number of TV productions, has chosen to write a play for the 'old-fashioned' radio medium is an indication that to him, this is a medium in its own right, with special possibilities. With its obvious limitations, it is, or can be, both more intimate and more poetical than visual theater. Having not only a sharp eye but also an exceedingly sensitive ear,[3] Bergman must feel a natural attraction to what has aptly been called the theater of the ear.

EPILOGUE

Between Stage and Screen

To call a film theatrical is still for many the same as rejecting it. For a long time, directors have tried to set film off against theater by accentuating that which theater could not express easily: realistic exteriors, mass scenes, swift changes in time and space, dynamic visual transitions, close-ups. The arrival of television has created a new situation. Theater no longer appears a threat to film. The threat comes from television, which favors many of the techniques traditionally associated with film and which, like film, is regarded as a mainly realistic medium. Just as photography a century ago caused artists to paint in a different, less realistic mode, so one would expect that television might work a similar reorientation on the part of filmmakers, away from realism and in favor of a retheatricalization of film.

It is here that Bergman's directorial profile comes in. His extensive work as a stage director has saved him from the deadly realism characterizing the products of many 'pure' filmmakers. Characteristic of Bergman as a film director is precisely the alloy between what we traditionally regard as distinctively theatrical (concentration on the characters, stylization) and what we see as typical for the film (realism in the description of the characters and their environment). For Bergman, these distinctions are exceedingly relative. In his films, 'authoritarian' cinematic close-ups mingle with 'democratic' theatrical long shots in a meaningful way. In his artistic universe, there are few waterproof bulkheads between theater and film. Both in his stage and in his screen productions, he knows how to mediate expressively between what we conventionally regard as inherent to the two media.

Naturally, each medium has its own characteristics that to a great extent affects the shape of the performance. The temporal and spatial flexibility of film, its power to make instant use of flashbacks and flashforwards, to approach characters and objects from various distances and angles, and to get closer to the human face than we ever do in real life – all these things make film very different from theater. Yet it is worth considering, that at about the time when the film was born, Strindberg demonstrated in his *Dream Play* that "time and space do not exist" and that "the characters split, double, redouble, evaporate, condense, fragment, cohere." In other words, the boundaries between theater and film are not as fixed as we often imagine. As we have seen, Bergman's directorial vision frequently surpasses, or at least diminishes, media differences. Besides, the fact that he has constantly alternated between productions for stage, radio and screen increases the possibility of a certain spill-over from one production to another, irrespective of the medium.

In the preceding examination of some of his outstanding stage, screen, and radio performances, the cohesion of Bergman's work as a director has frequently been indicated. It is now time to consider to what extent he has been a film director in his stage productions and a stage director in his screen productions; and the possible impact on his work in both these media from radio where only sound counts. In short, it is time to look for a coherent directorial vision behind the media Bergman has chosen and the techniques he has employed.

A far-reaching 'cinematic' element in Bergman's stage performances is the tendency to reduce the dialogue considerably and replace words with suggestive groupings, gestures, and mimicry, that is, visual instead of verbal signifiers. Another step in the direction of film is the tendency to replace the traditional division of plays into acts with a looser structure – a series of scenes or tableaux. This restructuring leads to a more dynamic flow of the stage performances, which is increased even further when they are presented without an interval.

The wealth of audiovisual signifiers that in a stage performance is communicated to an audience more or less simultaneously is a problem for any director. How much of this multitude can the spectators cope with? Characteristic of Bergman's direction is the careful distribution of signifiers, so that the audience has time to notice and experience them. This kind of distribution, which involves suppressing simultaneity in favor of consecutiveness, may well owe something to the filmmaker's concern for shot succession, the consecutive distribution of signifiers within each film sequence.

In a stage performance, we can never get as close to the characters as in a film. Bergman nevertheless approaches the screen media by having the major characters appear as much as possible within the area where they "are strongest," most visible, usually a rectangle at center downstage.[1]

Lighting has, due to the fast technical development, become an exceedingly important element in stage performances. Bergman's experience as a film director, working closely with outstanding film photographers like Gunnar Fischer and Sven Nykvist, has certainly helped to make him aware of the potentials of light, also in the theater. Referring to Nykvist, he once told an interviewer: "Our common passion – and I feel this even on the stage – is to create light: light and faces surrounded by shadows. This is what fascinates me!"[2] In another interview, he gave an illuminating example:

> The actors' relation to the stage is also a part of the rhythm of the performance, and if you change the angle at which the light strikes the stage, you achieve a completely new rhythm.[3]

If Bergman's varied lighting by itself contributes highly to the visual suggestiveness of his stage performances, the relative lack of stage properties further aids the audience in paying attention to the lighting. Of primary importance is the strong frontal lighting. This is not *per se* a cinematic device. Rather, it testifies to Bergman's 'cinematic' concern with the human face, his anxiety to make it fully visible to the audience. The preference for strong frontal lighting is thus subordinated to the director's central concern: the character on the stage – in whom the audience are mirroring themselves.

To the most obvious cinematic effects in Bergman's stage performances belong the back projections, which can instantly appear and disappear. If frequently resorted to, back projections create an environment on the stage which is, in fact, more cinematic than theatrical. This is never the case with Bergman, who either makes incidental use of such effects (*The Ghost Sonata, Long Day's Journey*) or employs them as a modest background (*To Damascus, A Doll's House*). Since a stage performance is necessarily three-dimensional and 'in color,' the two-dimensional, usually black-and-white projections indicate that we are dealing here with a different, inner reality. By annexing cinematic projections to the theatrical event, Bergman transcends the inability of theater to enter the souls of the characters.

Choreographically, Bergman at times chooses to freeze the movements of the characters, a cinematic device resorted to in the initial circling of *The Dream Play* and, intermittently, in the commentatory dancing of *The Winter's Tale*. The instant stasis that is hereby effectuated punctuates the fluidity of the performance and paradoxically makes us at the same time more involved in it – since the sudden change activates us mentally – and detached from it, since the artificiality of the action makes us more aware that we are witnessing a performance.

Films from the last decades usually contain a pre-title sequence. This can have an expository function, showing briefly some events leading to the situation in the film proper, as in Joseph Losey's *A Doll's House*. Or it can emblematically present the theme of the film, as in Alf Sjöberg's *Miss Julie*. While Bergman has rarely made use of pre-title sequences in his films – *Wild Strawberries* and *Persona* being exceptions – he has frequently offered what we may call a play-before-the-play in his stage performances. This was the case in his 1955 production of Molière's *Don Juan*, where, in the initial pantomime, an unromantic Don Juan in nightshirt was seen being dressed in his seductive costume by a matter-of-fact Sganarelle. From the very beginning, this Don Juan was unmasked. By placing him in front of a mirror,[4] Bergman could at once point to his fundamental weakness: his narcissism, his inability to love anyone but himself. Both the pantomime and the mirror appeared again in the opening of Bergman's *Hedda Gabler* productions, where the director, unlike Ibsen, immediately revealed not only that Hedda was pregnant but that she hated being 'misformed.' Scrutinizing herself before the mirror, she violently pressed her hands against her abdomen, suggesting her desire to have the expected child aborted.[5] As we have seen, an additional pantomimic and emblematic play-before-the-play occurred also in *Long Day's Journey* and – with but a few words spoken – in *A Doll's House*. Whether or not inspired by the convention, in cinema, of beginning with a pre-title sequence, establishing the real or symbolic situation, Bergman in all these cases chose to open his production with an enigmatic, suspense-creating piece of 'silent film.'

Turning now to the opposite situation, let us see to what extent theatrical elements can be found in the films. The first thing that strikes one is that most of the early films are, in fact, qua structure disguised plays. Characteristically, several of them are divided into acts or scenes. Gradually, however, the script-writer freed himself from the yoke of intrigue drama and his later films have a looser shape; they are theme-oriented rather than plot-oriented. In this respect Bergman's development, in fact, runs parallel with Strindberg's.

Bergman, it has been said, is more interested in pictorial composition than in camera movement.[6] (There are, significantly, more spectacular camera angles in *Torment*, directed by Alf Sjöberg, than in the Bergman films directed by Bergman himself.) As in the case of Orson Welles – another director who has divided his time between stage and screen – Bergman's relatively fixed, calm or slow camera reflects not so much a national temperament as "a desire to show an image that is uniformly understandable and that compels the spectator to make his own choice."[7]

Other characteristics that may owe something to Bergman's work in the theater are his adherence, on the whole, to continuity editing, his preference for panning above cutting, and his interest in long takes, Märta's reading of her letter to Tomas in *Winter Light*, lasting for several minutes, being an extreme example. The film trilogy, one critic asserts, "possesses several affinities with the theatrical," for example "the deemphasis of cinematic framing in favor of stage settings, and the elimination of high and low angle photography in favor of straight-on angles."[8] In the TV play *After the Rehearsal*, which is set on a stage, Bergman suggestively oscillates between cinematic close-ups, showing the naked, vulnerable faces, and theatrical long shots, suggesting that although the characters are dealing with very personal problems, they are nevertheless frequently performing, playing parts, to one another.

Just as Bergman in some of his stage productions has resorted to a play-within-the-play technique – we have seen examples of this in connection with *The Dream Play* and, notably, *The Winter's Tale* – so he has frequently included some sort of performance in his films.[9] Apart from the examples provided earlier in our discussion of *The Seventh Seal*, *Persona*, and *Fanny and Alexander*, many others could be mentioned.

Thus, in *Illicit Interlude*, the 'made-up' world of the ballet contrasts with the purity of nature in the Stockholm archipelago. In *The Naked Night*, the life of the roving circus artists is contrasted with that of the settled burghers, and the world of the theater with that of the circus. In *The Magician*, the itinerant mesmerist Albert Emanuel Vogler and his troupe offer hypnotic seances – read: stage and screen performances – to the bourgeoisie. In *Through a Glass Darkly*, David, a novelist, is treated to a Chekhovian stage performance by his children Karin and Minus. Anna, in *The Silence*, visits a music-hall, where she witnesses a sexual performance both on stage and in the auditorium. *The Ritual* deals with the relationship between three actors and their censor. *After the Rehearsal* focusses on a director who is planning his fifth *Dream Play* production, and the whole play is acted out on a stage among the properties belonging to some of his earlier productions – as well to those of his originator. In the preface to *The Best Intentions*, Bergman says that he has shaped the series in a "cinematographic, dramatic" form; at the same time, he remarks that in his imagination the main characters "in this considerable mise-en-scène" appear "on an intensely lit stage."

As these examples suggest, the thematic constellation 'performance versus life' is central to Bergman's work. The antithesis that is implied in this constellation is that between role-playing and authenticity, mask and face. Rather than claim that the artists devote themselves to role-playing, whereas the non-artists are authentic, we might say that the former wear many masks, while the latter – Edvard in *Fanny and Alexander* being a lucid example – wear only one. Moreover, while the artists are conscious of their role-playing in life – the actresses Elisabet in *Persona* and Helena in *Fanny and Alexander* are very explicit about this – the non-artists are naively unaware of it. By mixing real-life situations with performance situations, Bergman can effectively demonstrate how role-playing is as common in life as in art. Moreover, he can organize suggestive reversals and show how role-playing on the stage can actually signify authenticity while seeming authenticity in life can actually be a form of role-playing.

As is generally the case concerning directors, Bergman's work for stage and screen has hitherto been examined primarily with regard to the visual and verbal components, while the aural ones have been largely neglected. This is a pity since the latter – whether sound effects or music – form an important integral part of the total stage or screen production. Although Bergman is by nature exceedingly sensitive to sounds, it is reasonable to assume that his work for the radio has increased his awareness of what sound can do also in other media.

As we all know, music is usually used much more sparsely on the stage than on the screen, where it figures more frequently on the big than on the small screen. In his early films, Bergman adjusts to the tradition and makes ample use of music. In his later films – when he was living with the brilliant pianist Käbi Laretei – music is used much more sparsely. As a result, it becomes a vital part of the thematic 'message,' an universal 'language' of community as opposed to ordinary, verbal languages which promote separateness, isolation. Music used in this thematic sense is prominent, because occasional, in *The Silence* and, as we have seen, in *Cries and Whispers* and *Autumn Sonata*. The universal power of music is emblematically emphasized in the ouverture of the TV opera *The Magic Flute*, significantly set in a theater. Here the camera picks out male and female faces of different age and color, all attentively listening to Mozart's music. Within this collective, one recurrent face is singled out: that of a little girl. Comparable to the face of the very young Mozart, shown once, she becomes the mediator between the composer and the audience. Being a child, she is the ideal, open-minded recipient.

It is often said that theater focusses on characters, film on their environment. This is a doubtful truth, since the possibilities in film to use close-ups makes it even more character-centred in a sense than theater. In Bergman's case the difference is in any case not very marked. In some of his films, notably the chamber films, he has proven almost as ascetic in his environmental description as in the theater, and although most of his filmic environments, in obedience to the medium, are reasonably realistic, this does not mean that the frames are cluttered with paraphernalia. Since Bergman's camera is usually close to the characters, we normally see very little of the background per shot and what we see is carefully chosen. In other words, the medium helps to provide the selectivity that secures concentration on the human beings.

Conversely, Bergman has rarely offered his audience a play on an empty stage, as he did in *Hamlet*. In *King Lear*, the bare stage was furnished – apart from two emblematic props on the forestage: the crown and the map of Lear's kingdom – by the servants, who were reduced to chairs for the royalty to sit on. One reason why Bergman usually does not relish an empty stage is that he wants to show his audience a stage that in the course of the performance *becomes* empty, in conformance with the human unmasking taking place. When Bergman on the stage prefers a sparse environment with few props, he distils, so that the spectator can concentrate on what is essential – the human figures – and find time to take in what is around them. The high amount of selectivity leads to a heightened, stylized realism.

As for the temporal environment, it is obvious that the non-specificity he frequently subscribes to on the stage is more difficult to retain in the films, although in many of the later films, shot in the existential landscape of his beloved island, Fårö, he deliberately seems to avoid temporal signifiers. If any period is preferred by him, both on stage and screen, it is the early part of this century, perhaps because it is a period that an audience today can relate to, perhaps for more personal nostalgic reasons.

More striking than Bergman's environmental concern is his interest in the characters inhabiting the various environments, especially their faces. The significant groupings of characters and faces function as metaphors of human relations. We deal with a number of pregnant, carefully composed images, a kind of *tableaux vivants*. The 'holy' trinity at the end of *The Ghost Sonata*, the 'mirror scene' toward the end of *Miss Julie*, the 'bridal gown scene' concluding *Long Day's Journey*, the dance of death at the end of *The Seventh Seal*, the paradisaic vision concluding *Wild Strawberries*, the divided double face in *Persona*, the pietà scene in *Cries and Whispers* – these are but some of the visual emblems that remain imprinted in our memory long after the show is over. It is no coincidence that these images frequently appear toward the end of the performances. Not until we have been emotionally involved in the characters and their destinies will such 'still lives' be truly engaging. At the same time they will, at this late stage, be metaphorically pregnant.

The varying relations between the characters is registered through symbolic changes in their grouping. In the films, it may also be indicated by varying camera distances and angles. The shot transitions in the settlements between Isak and Alman, Elisabet and Alma, Eva and Charlotte, Edvard and Alexander offer rich examples in expressive imagery. There is in all these cases a suggestive uncertainty of whether we are dealing with two individual egos or two parts of the same ego. Here the ability, inherent in moving images, to visualize and metaphorize both inner events and inner relations is vividly demonstrated.

For all their importance, media aspects are in Bergman's case always subordinated to thematic concerns. These concerns can be summarized in a simplifying way as 'mask versus face,' 'life versus art' and 'dream versus reality.' Yet since film to Bergman, unlike theater, is 'hypnotization,' it follows that the last opposition can be presented more effectively on the big screen than on the stage. This has partly to do with the different situations of reception. When watching a film, you sit "in the dark, very silent, very far from other people."[10]

This brings us to a question that has always been of primary importance to Bergman: the relationship between performer and recipient. The true performance, he never tires of reminding us, takes place neither on the stage nor on the screen but in the mind and heart, especially the heart, of the recipient. The spectator or listener is invited to take part in the performance via his or her own imagination. To increase this cooperative possibility emotionally, Bergman has constantly tried to bring the characters as close as possible to the audience. In the theater, this can be done quite resolutely by adding an apron stage to the ordinary one, as Bergman did at the City Theater in Malmö, or by having the audience surround the characters, as he did in his production of *Woyzeck*.[11]

More often he has turned the stage into a mirror of the auditorium. In *Hedda Gabler*, the red living room was a continuation of the classically red room in which the audience was seated. In *The Wild Duck*, the attic – created here merely by light and shadow – was placed on the forestage and, by implication, in the auditorium, "its exact shape and dimensions left to the imagination,"[12] so that the characters did not turn away from the audience when looking at the invisible duck but faced it, enabling the spectators to see their reactions. The example illustrates how Bergman, like the directors of art cinema generally, is "concerned less with action than reaction."[13] For the same reason, the house in *The Ghost Sonata* was placed in the auditorium *and* on the stage, where its horseshoe form mirrored the shape of the auditorium. Again, in *King Lear*, the red color of the huge concave 'wall' that closed in the acting space corresponded to the traditional theater-red horseshoe of the auditorium. The same shape was given to the *art nouveau* salon in *The Winter's Tale* – a synthesis between the auditorium and the quadrangular foyer of Dramaten. In all these cases, Bergman was breaking down the barrier between stage and auditorium, performers and recipients, and, ultimately, between theater and life, in the attempt to create a sense of communion, a feeling that "all the world's a stage" and that we are all 'actors' in this *theatrum mundi*.

This sense of communion has been further emphasized by Bergman's habit in later performances of having the actors remain on the stage even when they are 'off-stage,' so that they form an 'audience' mediating between the on-stage characters and the real audience. This was done not only in *The Misanthrope*,[14] where it could be justified historically,[15] but also in *The Dream Play*, *King Lear*, and, as we have seen, *A Doll's House* and *The Winter's Tale*. When Bergman, in *The Dream Play*, at times placed the Poet at his desk, center downstage, with his back to the audience, which so to speak witnessed the play from behind his shoulder, he was providing 'a point of view shot,' indicating that if the Poet was the dreamer of the play, so was the audience.

In the many films in which a performance of some sort takes place – one of the most striking features of Bergman's cinema – we have by definition a second audience. This diegetic screen audience serves to mediate between the characters and/or events observed both by them and the real audience. The screen audience can be heterogeneous, as in *The Seventh Seal* or *The Magician*, where reactions to the performers are divided.[16] It can be an audience that, being less informed than the real one, is unable to distinguish between 'art' and reality – as when the circus performance in *The Naked Night* turns into a ferocious fight, believed to be part of the program. The communion between the screen audience and the real one, which is here ironically detached, is at other times strongly suggested, especially when the optical point of view of the two audiences is more or less identical. Thus, the most worrying aspect of the rape in *The*

Virgin Spring is not the brutality of the rapists but the passivity of the eyewitness, Ingeri (Gunnel Lindblom), since it is she who, as spectator of this 'performance,' is a stand-in for the real spectator.

But communion with the audience can also be established by having the characters look straight at the audience. As we noted earlier, Bergman made this possible in *The Wild Duck* and *The Ghost Sonata* by placing the attic and the house respectively not backstage, as the text has it, but in the auditorium, so that the characters could face the audience. In the same way, the Stockholm production of *Hedda Gabler*, one critic noted, opened with Hedda staring "into the darkness, where we sat."[17] A similar position, breaking with the illusion of the fourth wall, was given to Mary Tyrone, when she was soliloquizing at the end of *Long Day's Journey*. However, in both cases the frontal positions of the characters suggested not so much their communion with the audience as their desire to escape from their stage environment.

Much more surprising than the characters' facing of the audience in these realistic plays is the corresponding situation in a realistic film context. When Monika in *Summer with Monika*, in close-up, suddenly looks straight at the audience, it is a shock effect not least because Bergman here violates an unwritten law in cinema. A similar effect is attained when Elisabet in *Persona*, also in close-up, raises her camera and takes a snapshot of the audience. In either case, we may speak of a face-to-face situation or mirror effect serving to attack the audience and thereby engage it directly in the screened events.

Drama, it is often said, is an objective art form. Lacking an external narrator who can freely enter the characters' interiors, the recipient of a play, unlike the reader of a novel or the spectator of a film, can only infer from what the characters say and do what they are thinking and feeling – as we do in real life. However, it is questionable to what extent drama after Strindberg can still be called objective.[18] As we have seen, several of Strindberg's protagonists appear as observers of the action we see unfolding on the stage. Mediating between the audience and the characters, their function is to bridge the distance between stage and auditorium – much as the classical Greek chorus even spatially bridged the distance between the three individual characters and the spectators. Relating to this at once old and new tradition, Bergman in some of his stage productions at times isolates one character from the rest – Agnes in *The Dream Play*, the Student in *The Ghost Sonata*, Cordelia (Lena Olin) in *King Lear*, Ophelia (Pernilla Östergren) in *Hamlet*, Edmund in *Long Day's Journey* – allotting him or her the role of observer of the other characters, in this activity comparable to the watching audience or even to the film camera. Do such mediators make the performances more or less subjective? There can be no clear answer to this question. Insofar as they are individuals, appearing as internal 'narrators,' they will increase the subjectivity of the performances. We are asked to experience the play not directly but via one of these figural narrators – as though what is enacted on the stage, although it may seem to represent reality, actually represents his or her experience of reality. The characters function as filters.[19] On the other hand, these characters, precisely because of their mediating function, help to 'objectify' the staged events. For how can we experience as subjective what we ourselves share in? It is hardly a coincidence that the mediators tend to be young. Remaining outside or at the periphery of the sinful world in which the other characters dwell, they may be compared to children set off from their guilt-laden parents, the adults, by virtue of their innocence. Insofar as they serve as reminders to the recipients of their own past, they have a universalizing function.

With his deep concern for the relation between dream and reality, Bergman pursues, in all the media, a tradition launched in drama by Strindberg and in theater by Olof Molander. The key term within this tradition is Strindberg's "half-reality," used by the author to characterize his own *To Damascus* and meaning "reality seen from a point of view reminiscent of that found in dreams."[20] Not only in his productions of Strindberg's so-called dream plays, where it is called for, but also in many of his other stage productions, Bergman has emphasized this aspect. Thus, in his 1989 version of *A Doll's House*, Nora "acted out a dream of life from which she was struggling to awake" and "scenes of almost blatant reality" alternated with "a mood of dreamlike detachment."[21] In agreement with the quotations from Shakespeare and Dowson, *Long Day's Journey* was set in a dreamlike mood. "Bergman has transformed *Peer Gynt* into a dream play," wrote a critic after the opening in 1991.[22]

This tendency is even more marked in Bergman's films, where we are often confronted with an oscillation between realistic (objective) and dreamlike (subjective) sequences. Such an oscillation lends itself to film which, unlike theater, can express swift transitions from an outer to an inner reality and vice versa. This is also saying that the film medium lends itself to expressing conflicts between an outer reality and an inner one, visualized in the form of dreams and visions.

Bergman's concern for an inner reality is demonstrated not least in his predilection for mental point of view shots, shots in which we share not only a character's optical or perceptual point of view – this happens in virtually every film – but also his or her experience of it. Jof's, Isak's, Anna's, Maria's, Viktor's, Charlotte's, and Alexander's visions or fantasies are examples of mental point of view shots which call for an unrealistic approach (soft focus, slow motion, extreme camera angles, etc.). What is remarkable here is that Bergman usually abstains from such spectacular effects and prefers almost imperceptible transitions. By this means, he creates the impression that the dream does not essentially differ from what we call reality. When in *Wild Strawberries*, old Isak is standing in the dark hall, experiencing the light dining room of his childhood in the background, there is nothing in this shot that is visually unrealistic. Even so, it demonstrates how the Isak of the present reminisces about a situation in the past which he has, strictly speaking, not experienced himself. Similarly, Karin's self-mutilation in *Cries and Whispers* is presented in a completely realistic way; yet retrospectively, we are inclined to see it as a self-destructive and revengeful fantasy.[23] The most extreme case of oscillation between dream and reality we find in *Persona*, where the spectator often does not know whether (s)he is witnessing an outer or an inner reality or whether these shots express Alma's or Elisabet's experience. The borders are blotted out.

Even in such a gray-realistic film as *Winter Light*, there are two sequences in which we witness Tomas' inner struggle. In one case this occurs explicitly. As Tomas is reading Märta's letter to him, the extremely long take showing her face straight-on, in close-up, forces us to see Märta the way Tomas at this moment experiences her. Bergman in this way creates the maximal identification between the addressee of the letter and the spectator. The second case is more implicit. When Tomas is visited by Jonas, we first experience the situation as realistic. Not until later do we realize that the visit has taken place only in Tomas' imagination. Like Tomas, we initially take for reality what turns out to have been a fantasy. Again, the device serves to increase our identification with the tormented parson. The border between objective and subjective reality is blotted out. In all these cases, Bergman subtly applies the Strindbergian principle of half-reality.

As we have seen, *The Seventh Seal*, *Wild Strawberries*, *Cries and Whispers* and *Autumn Sonata* all end with mental point of view shots. Jof envisages how Death guides six human beings to "the dark lands" and how "the rain washes their faces and cleans the salt of the tears from their cheeks." Isak has a vision of his parents, long dead. Agnes comes alive in Anna's memory. Viktor imagines how Charlotte will react to her daughter's letter. These are endings which can be relatively harmonious precisely because they are highly subjective. Objectively speaking, they are much darker. As a result, our impressions are mingled, and we are left with unresolved, ambiguous endings. The same is true of the ending of *Fanny and Alexander*. In a subjective shot we see, along with Alexander, the dead Bishop, now incarnating the guilt feelings that will continue to haunt the boy. Then follows the objective series of shots showing how Alexander seeks protection and consolation at the bosom of his grandmother.

In the beginning of *Fanny and Alexander*, Bergman takes us from Alexander busying himself with his puppet theater to his experience of the Ekdahl living room as a 'theater,' and from there to his experience of the nursery with its magic lantern as a 'cinema.'[24] We move, so to speak, from the director for the stage to the one for the screen. As a conjurer of moving images in both rooms Alexander is the ideal recipient, since he is so involved in his self-invented performance that it becomes a second reality to him.[25] Alexander is obviously the kindred spirit of his creator, who in his youth experienced the magic of theater when he saw how the Lawyer in *A Dream Play* handled a hairpin. *"There was no hairpin, but I saw it."*[26]

As these emblematic situations indicate, Bergman's primary concern has always been how to stimulate the imagination of the audience, so that they become emotionally involved in what he and his actors offer them. No one has described this basic problem of communication as communicatively as Bergman himself in the parable of the magic chair:

> You are an actor and you take up this terrible chair ... and you put it up here on the table, and then you tell the audience: "My dear friends, you may think this chair looks terrible but you are mistaken. This is the most expensive and most beautiful diamond-encrusted gold chair ever created. It was made for a small Chinese empress six thousand years ago; she died sitting on it, and it was buried with her. Now it's here – and it is very, very fragile. But now take care of it, for I must leave you for a few moments." Then you come back as a scoundrel, and you begin to knock the chair around – and the entire audience will hate that scoundrel. They will become anxious because they have accepted the suggestion and have developed feelings about the chair. And *that* is theater.[27]

Since the situation described here is dramatized in the nursery scene of *Fanny and Alexander*, the parable applies not only to theater but also to film and, in fact, to any performance, since in a performance everything has a representative function and is dependent on our suspension of disbelief. What matters is the director's, the actors' and not least the audience's own ability to let the performance take place in the imagination – the hearts – of the receivers, the only 'medium' that ultimately counts. Few directors, if any, have taken this fundamental communicative task as seriously as Bergman – and managed it as well.

Notes

The Stage and the Screen

[1] Béranger in Steene (1972), p. 14.

[2] Cowie (1992), p. 18.

[3] For a discussion of Bergman's work with his actors while preparing a stage or film production, see Sjöman, Sjögren (1969), and Törnqvist (1973a and b).

[4] Sjöman, p. 102.

[5] Bergman (1973), p. 99.

[6] Bergman (1973), p. 163.

[7] Steene (1972), p. 43.

[8] See especially Young, passim.

[9] Koskinen (1984), p. 11.

[10] In his Erasmus speech (1965) Bergman stated that "people today can reject the theater," since in the TV age they "live in the midst of a drama which is constantly exploding in local tragedy." See Bergman (1972), p. 14.

[11] Zern, p. 59.

[12] Bergman (1994b), p. 11.

[13] Bergman (1973), p. 24.

[14] Törnqvist (1973), p. 111.

[15] Assayas/Björkman, p. 19.

[16] Bergman (1989), p. 73.

[17] Steene (1972), p. 44.

[18] Donner, p. 81.

[19] Sjöman, p. 13.

[20] Strindberg (1959), p. 19.

[21] Strindberg (1959), p. 19.

[22] Bergman (1973), p. 168.

[23] Sjöman, p. 24.

[24] Cowie (1992), p. 141.

[25] Quoted from Marker (1992), p. 60. Bergman claims (1989, p. 33) that he was merely 12 when he saw *A Dream Play* for the first time, but this is hardly possible since the play was not performed in Stockholm around that time. Molander's brilliant first production of *A Dream Play* opened at Dramaten in 1935, when Bergman was 17.

[26] Sjögren, pp. 91-3, 130, 177.

[27] A detailed account of the relationship between Bergman's scripts and films is found in Steene (1987).

[28] Sjöman, p. 25.

[29] Bergman (1975), p. 92.

[30] Bergman (1973), p. 166.

[31] Bergman (1976), p. 8.

[32] Bergman (1989), p. 73.

[33] Bergman (1994b), p. 14.

[34] Mosley, p. 18.

[35] Esslin, p. 172.

Strindberg, *The Dream Play* (1970)

[1] Originally entitled *Drömspelet (The Dream Play)*, Strindberg changed the title into *Ett drömspel (A Dream Play)* in the second, 1904, edition.

[2] *Röster i Radio*, No. 17, 1963.

[3] Bergman (1989), p. 36.

[4] Ollén, p. 34.

[5] For a discussion of this question, see Lunin, p. 182ff.

[6] In his introduction, the translator, Michael Meyer, remarks (p. xvi) that *A Dream Play* "in its original form, scarcely any longer seemed theatrically valid" to Bergman in 1970. However, in his fourth production, in 1986, Bergman (1989, p. 36) "wanted to play the text with no changes or deletions, just as the writer had written it." Ironically, this faithful version turned out to be the least successful of his four attempts at the play.

[7] For Strindberg's scene division, see Törnqvist (1982), p. 149.

[8] Åke Janzon in *Svenska Dagbladet*, March 15, 1970.

[9] Marker (1992), pp. 117-18.

[10] See Törnqvist (1988), p. 284.

[11] Bark, p. 153.

[12] Per Erik Wahlund in *Kvällsposten*, March 15, 1970.

[13] Marker (1992), p. 111.

[14] Marker (1992), p. 119.

[15] The affinity with Pirandello's *Six Characters in Search of an Author*, which Bergman had staged in 1953 and again in 1967, is evident.

Strindberg, *The Ghost Sonata* (1973)

[1]   Falck, p. 53.

[2]   Bryant-Bertail, p. 307.

[3]   Rokem, pp. 66-8.

[4]   This is a mirror, found in many old Swedish houses, enabling people indoors to see what is happening in the street without being seen themselves.

[5]   I use the term 'sequence,' in relation to drama texts and stage performances, for a section whose beginning and end are determined by a change of character constellation, of place and/or of time. As a film term, 'sequence,' of course, has the different and looser meaning of being a segment "involving one complete stretch of action" (Bordwell/Thompson, p. 496).

[6]   In his pioneering study of the play, Northam (pp. 41, 48) draws attention to this.

[7]   Törnqvist (1973a), p. 3.

[8]   Bergman in Törnqvist (1973b), p. 192.

[9]   Törnqvist (1973a), p. 8.

[10]   Cf. Northam, p. 41.

[11]   Törnqvist (1973a), p. 10.

[12]   Törnqvist (1973b), p. 108.

Strindberg, *Miss Julie* (1985)

[1]   Marker (1983).

[2]   Bergman in Marker (1983), p. 32.

[3]   Marker (1983), p. 17.

[4]   Bergman in Marker (1983), p. 17.

[5]   Gunilla Palmstierna-Weiss in a taped interview with E.T., Oct., 1987.

[6]   Bergman in *Svenska Dagbladet*, Dec. 3, 1985.

[7]   Bergman in Marker (1983), p. 15.

[8]   Sprinchorn (pp. 22-3) was the first to draw attention to this significant parallel.

[9]   For a transcription, see Törnqvist/Jacobs, pp. 173-5.

[10]   The theater program only lists the actors/actresses, not their parts. I have here given them individual names in conformance with the practice in the Munich production. Cf. Marker (1983), p. 37.

[11]   Bergman in Marker (1983), p. 15.

[12]   Bergman in Marker (1983), p. 14.

[13]   Bergman in *Svenska Dagbladet*, Dec. 3, 1985.

O'Neill, *Long Day's Journey into Night* (1988)

1 Statement by O'Neill quoted from Krutch, p. xvii.

2 Olsson, p. 103.

3 *Svenska Dagbladet*, Feb. 16, 1972.

4 Eldridge, p. 287.

5 Gunilla Palmstierna-Weiss in a taped interview with E.T., May, 1988.

6 A photo of the veranda with the young Eugene, his brother Jamie, and his father James was reproduced in the theater program.

7 Bergman apparently expected the spectators to identify the projected house with the O'Neill summer house, although there was no photo of it in the program.

8 Cf. the mask-like, neo-classical New England columns prescribed by O'Neill for the mansion in *Mourning Becomes Electra*.

9 Törnqvist (1969), p. 101.

10 In a deeper sense, Bergman's Edmund was less akin to Trigorin than to Konstantin, the young writer who kills first the seagull, then himself. Compare Edmund's longing for death and his wish that he had been born a seagull.

11 See Törnqvist (1969), pp. 239-40.

12 Frenz, p. 3.

Ibsen, *A Doll's House* (1989)

1 The German script has been published in English translation in Marker (1983), pp. 47-99. The book also contains a lengthy discussion of the production, pp. 19-31.

2 The impact of Ibsen's play on Bergman's screen works, notably *Scenes from a Marriage*, is examined in Törnqvist (1995), pp. 163-8.

3 For an analysis of the drama text, see Törnqvist (1995), pp. 11-49.

4 Marker (1983), p. 23.

5 Marker (1983), p. 20.

6 Leif Zern in *Expressen*, Nov. 18, 1989.

7 The new technique used to create this background is known as Scanaprint.

8 Bergman was not the first director who set the ending of the play in the marital bedroom. In his 1953 London production, Peter Ashmore did just that.

9 Tove Ellefsen in *Dagens Nyheter*, Nov. 18, 1989.

10 It is noteworthy that another Swedish director, Bo Widerberg, in recent TV productions of Strindberg's *The Father* and Ibsen's *The Wild Duck*, has focussed on the victimized single children, both daughters, in the two plays.

[11]   Cf. Bergman's *Wild Strawberries*, where three generations, born out of cold wombs, are fatefully linked to each other.

Shakespeare, *The Winter's Tale* (1994)

[1]   "När lägger du av, Ingmar? Anna Salander samtalar med Ingmar Bergman" *Dramat*, No. 3, 1994, p. 38. Although the interview is no doubt a fake and Anna Salander none other but the director himself, the references to Bergman's childhood should be heeded.

[2]   Libretto by the LP recording of Bergman's *Magic Flute,* Sveriges Radio, Stockholm, 1975, p. 34.

[3]   *Dramat*, No. 3, 1994, p. 38.

[4]   Libretto of *The Magic Flute*, pp. 21-22.

[5]   "Förord till en översättning," in *Kung Lear*, *Program*, No. 9, Stockholm, 1984, p. 6.

[6]   This will appear in the following, where quotations from the dialogue of the play do not render the original Shakesperean text but are fairly literal translations of the Swedish text used by Bergman.

[7]   Theater program of *Vintersagan*, pp. 11-12.

[8]   Leif Zern in *Dagens Nyheter* April 30, 1994.

[9]   Ingamaj Beck in *Dramat*, No. 3, 1994, p. 30.

[10]   Cf., for accessibility, the original, where the corresponding passage reads:
    Th'offences we have made you do, we'll answer,
    If you first sinn'd with us, and that with us
    You did continue fault, and that you slipp'd not
    With any but with us. (Act I.2)

[11]   Christina Lundberg in *Sundsvalls Tidning*, May 3, 1994.

[12]   John Lahr in *The New Yorker*, Oct. 3, 1994, p. 106. Lahr rightly points out the similarity between the dance at this point and Edvard Munch's *The Dance of Life*, noting that the exclusion motif appears in both. It might be added that both with Munch and Bergman, the bright red dress of the young woman, who seems enamoured with her dancing partner, strongly contrasts with the mat costumes of the other dancers.

[13]   Lahr, p. 106.

[14]   Lennart Mörk in *Dramat*, No. 2, 1994, p. 26.

[15]   Pafford in Shakespeare (1993a), p. lxxxii.

[16]   Compare, for example, little Ingmar and Mamillius witnessing a row between their parents; the father's and Leontes' momentary inclination to kill themselves; the dead mother as seemingly alive and the 'resurrection' of Hermione. See Bergman (1989), pp. 7, 17.

[17]   Olle Grönstedt in *NU*, May 19, 1994, p. 9.

The Seventh Seal (1957)

[1] The American translation of the film is published in Bergman (1960).

[2] Sjögren (1968), p. 119.

[3] Bergman in Steene (1972), pp. 70-71.

[4] Bergman in Donner, p. 138.

[5] Cf. Sarris, p. 87. Bergman's *Peer Gynt*, with Max von Sydow in the lead, opened at Malmö City Theater three weeks after *The Seventh Seal* had its premiere.

[6] Bergman (1973), p. 117. The nuclear threat later figures in *Winter Light* and *Shame*.

[7] Steene (1983), p. 594.

[8] In 1974, Bergman staged *To Damascus I-II* at Dramaten.

[9] Bergman (1973), p. 117. In Bergman's staging of *Ur-Faust* at the City Theater in Malmö in 1958, Faust (Max von Sydow) and Mephistopheles (Toivo Pawlo) were "masked like a couple of twins" (Sjögren, 1968, p. 221).

[10] This reading is not in the script.

[11] Steene (1968), p. 62.

[12] Cowie (1992), p. 142.

[13] Cf. Bergman (1994a), p. 236: "Bengt Ekerot and I agreed that Death should have the features of a white clown. An amalgamation of a clown mask and a skull."

[14] Wood, p. 82.

[15] Sarris, p. 84.

[16] Cf. Cowie (1992), p. 144.

[17] The exuberant description in this scene may well have been inspired by Pieter Brueghel Jr.'s famous painting of a village market and theater performance. See Gascoigne, Pl. XIV.

[18] As has often been pointed out, *The Seventh Seal* is inspired by Strindberg's historical drama *The Saga of the Folkungs*, which Bergman saw in Olof Molander's production at Dramaten in 1937. The resemblances concern especially the flagellant scene.

[19] The description of the flagellant procession and of the Monk may well owe something to J.P. Jacobsen's short story "The Plague in Bergamo" (1881).

[20] The scene could be compared to the near-authentic Communion with which *Winter Light* opens.

[21] In the script, she exchanges a few lines with Jöns when she first meets him. By omitting these speeches, Bergman could give added emphasis to the Girl's "*Consummatum est.*"

[22] Ironically, the best known of all Bergman's images has always been wrongly reproduced. Unlike the situation in the reproductions, the dance of death in the film goes uphill, from right to left.

[23] Silhouette effects were frequently resorted to in Bergman's 1958 production of *Ur-Faust*.

[24] Wood, p. 89.

[25] Sarris, p. 89.

Wild Strawberries (1957)

[1] It is significant that at a conference devoted to the relationship film/dream, the films of Bergman were selected as objects of study. See Petrič.

[2] Bergman (1973), p. 44.

[3] Bergman (1960), p. xvii.

[4] Bergman (1994a), p. 48.

[5] As has often been pointed out, the initials correspond to those of his creator: Ernst Ingmar Bergman. In Bergman (1994a), p. 20, it states: "Isak Borg equals me. *I B* equals *Ice* and *Borg* (the Swedish word for *fortress*). ... I had created a figure who, on the outside looked like my father but *was me, through and through*." The first time the surname is mentioned in the script, it is "Berg" rather than "Borg." We may also note the autobiographical endings of such names as Al*man* and Åker*man*, the latter an amalgamation of Åkerblom, the maiden name of Bergman's mother, and Bergman.

[6] According to Swedish academic tradition, you become a jubilee doctor – not to be confused with an honorary doctor – 50 years after you have received your doctorate.

[7] Cf. the statement in Bergman (1994a), p. 22: "Actually I am living permanently in my dream, from which I make brief forays into reality."

[8] For a more detailed description of the narrative levels, see Branigan, pp. 104-5.

[9] The hearse sequence may be seen as a homage to Victor Sjöström's famous silent film *The Phantom Carriage* (1921), a film which according to Bergman (1994a, p. 24) "has influenced [his] own work, right down to minute details."

[10] Steene (1968), p. 71.

[11] In the script, the parallel is even more striking. When Alman tries to get his car started again, it states that "the car had gone a few feet when one of the front wheels rolled off and slid down into the ditch."

[12] The relationship Isak-Evald comes very close to that between Werle and his son Gregers in Ibsen's *The Wild Duck*, staged by Bergman in 1971.

[13] Cf. the marionette god in *Fanny and Alexander*.

[14] Just as in Strindberg's *To Damascus I*, the protagonist is confronted with a "*funeral procession*," and just as there the corpse functions as the protagonist's alter ego. See Törnqvist (1982), pp. 79-80.

[15] By giving the same Christian name to Isak's fiancée in the past and the hitchhiking girl in the present and moreover letting the same actress play both parts, Bergman could emphasize Isak's inability or unwillingness to keep the two women, the past and the present, apart.

[16] As we have seen, Bergman staged *Peer Gynt* in the spring of 1957, shortly before he wrote the script for *Wild Strawberries*.

[17] Wood, p. 76.

[18] Gado (p. 223) has made an attempt to interpret the text on the blackboard. This is love's labor lost, since the point is precisely that we should *not* understand it.

[19] The scene seems inspired by the rape in Kurosawa's *Rashomon*, a film which Bergman viewed "dozens of times" (Gado, p. 241).

[20] About the final scene, Bergman has said (1994a), p. 20: "I was looking for my father and my mother, but I could not find them. In the final scene of *Wild Strawberries*, there is a strong element of nostalgia and desire...."

Strindberg, *Storm* (1960)

[1] Anglo-American translators have suggested no fewer than five different English titles for Strindberg's first chamber play: *The Storm, The Thunderstorm, Storm, Stormy Weather* and *Thunder in the Air*.

[2] The transmission, throughout Scandinavia (Nordvision), took place on January 22 (Strindberg's birthday), 1960.

[3] Carl Johan Elmquist of *Politiken* in Ollén, p. 20.

[4] But see Johns, pp. 292-303.

[5] Strindberg's stage directions in *Storm* are closely examined in relation to 1907 Östermalm reality in Hanes Harvey, pp. 185-245.

[6] Cf. Åke Perlström's remark in *Göteborgs-Posten* (Jan. 23, 1960): "the austerely closed nature of Birgitta Morales' scenery interestingly reflected Strindberg's [suggestion of] constraint and cramped space around the characters of the play." It is, however, Bergman rather than Strindberg who suggests these things.

[7] Cf. *A Dream Play*, where the Mother, who is soon to die, keeps trimming the burning candle in front of her and where quickly alternating light (day) and darkness (night) represent the passing of time.

[8] This was actually the original title of the play.

[9] *Sight and Sound*, Vol. 29, No. 2, 1960, p. 98.

Persona (1966)

1   For a further comparison, see Blackwell (1986), pp. 100-102.

2   This sequence, sometimes referred to as the film's prologue corresponding with its meta-filmic epilogue, has been extensively but not exhaustively dealt with by Simon (pp. 225-52, 308-10), Kawin (pp. 106-19), Blackwell (1986, pp. 11-38), and Gado (pp. 324-27).

3   Kawin, p. 110.

4   Bergman (1973), p. 202.

5   Kawin, p. 107.

6   Bergman (1973), p. 202.

7   Cf. Sontag, p. 263: "The surface he touches suggests a movie screen, but also a portrait and a mirror."

8   In the list of characters appearing in *Svensk filmografi*, 6, p. 288, it explicitly says: "Jörgen Lindström *The boy, Elisabet's son.*"

9   Björkman (p. 82) rightly points out that the boy's gesture can be seen both as one of rapprochement and one of rejection.

10 Cowie (1970), pp. 193-4.

11 Bergom-Larsson, p. 63.

12 Simon, pp. 243, 309. The former expression is Bergman's.

13 Livingston, p. 181.

14 Blackwell (1986) , p. 19.

15 Bergman staged Pirandello's play in April 1967, shortly after he had finished *Persona*.

16 Bergman (1973), pp. 198-9.

17 Bergman (1973), p. 199.

18 Bergman (1989), p. 202.

19 Cf. the director's telling Liv that she should "gather all her feeling into her lips" when listening to Alma's narration. See Bergman (1973), p. 208.

20 Simon, p. 309.

Cries and Whispers (1973)

1   Bergman is said to have been inspired concerning this title by the description of Mozart's 21st piano concerto given by a Swedish music critic. The slow movement of this concerto formed the leitmotif of Bo Widerberg's film *Elvira Madigan* (1967), ending in *Liebestod*.

[2] The situation resembles that in Edvard Munch's painting *Death in the Sickroom.*

[3] Gado, p. 408.

[4] Cf. the distant voices in the pre-credit morgue sequence of *Persona.*

[5] Cf. "the death-watch" in *The Ghost Sonata*, the clock that is stopped by the Mummy when she condemns the Old Man to death.

[6] Mellen, p. 302.

[7] The name may also be combined with Agnès de Jésus, who published her sister's, St. Theresa's (1873-97), autobiography, *Histoire d'une âme* (1898). In *Cries and Whispers*, Karin regards a painting of *"St. Theresa in the sacred third stage of prayer."*

[8] However, Bergman complicates the situation by having Maria read from the same red book that the mother had been reading in the early garden flashback. Via *The Pickwick Papers*, Agnes is reminded of the dead mother. Cf. the significance of the red book in *To Damascus.*

[9] This shot is very reminiscent of Edvard Munch's *Death Struggle.*

[10] Cf. Marty, p. 160: "l'étrange similitude entre la Vierge tenant son enfant mort et la Vierge berçant son nouveau-né."

[11] Mosley (p. 159) somewhat vaguely speaks of the sequence as "a vehicle for the expression of collective guilt." At the same time he sees it as an expression of Anna's "dream of Agnes resurrected."

[12] Strindberg originally planned to have these words inserted "in fiery writing above *Toten-Insel*" at the end of his *Ghost Sonata*. Letter to Emil Schering April 7, 1907. The idea was, however, abandoned.

Autumn Sonata (1978)

[1] This is what Bergman himself has called the film. Cf. Gado, p. 481.

[2] Cf. Gado, p. 482: "the film is a kind of sonata da camera played by four instruments."

[3] What Bergman originally had in mind was something more poetical and 'musical' than was finally realized: "Three acts in three kinds of lighting: one evening light, one night light, and one morning light. No cumbersome sets, two faces ...." (Bergman, 1994a, p. 335). In another statement the connection with music is made even clearer. The film, Bergman says, was originally meant as "un mouvement, ou plutôt trois mouvements comme dans une sonate" (Assayas, p. 22).

[4] Bergman (1960), p. xvii.

[5] Gado, p. 483.

[6] Livingston, p. 247.

[7] It should be observed, however, that Bergman resorts to voice-over in *Wild Strawberries* and in the beginning and end of his teleplay *After the Rehearsal.*

[8] Cf. Hedda Gabler's desire to travel by train with a male companion, not her husband. Bergman has staged Ibsen's play three times.

[9] Cf. Bergman's view that Miss Julie in the end "takes death for her companion" (Marker, 1983, p. 17).

[10] The death connotation is obvious whether we experience the darkness outside the compartment window as a sign that night has suddenly fallen or, like Cowie (1992, p. 325) and Gado (p. 485), as an indication that the train is entering a tunnel. Already in 1956, Bergman directed Pär Lagerkvist's *The Difficult Hour I*, in his version called *The Tunnel*, for the radio.

[11] Bergman's view (1994a, p. 328) that the two women's "hate becomes cemented. The daughter can never forgive the mother. The mother can never forgive the daughter" implies that we must wholly reject Viktor's wishful thinking. But can we really? And how does this view agree with Bergman's statement that the film "peut paraître pessimiste, mais si je l'ai réussi, ce sera mon film le plus optimiste" (quoted from Marty, p. 181)?

Fanny and Alexander (1982)

[1] Bergman (1994a), p. 377.

[2] Freud, p. 367.

[3] Bergman staged *Hamlet* at Dramaten in 1986. It is hard to tell whether *Fanny and Alexander* inspired him to produce Shakespeare's play or an early plan to do the play inspired him to make the film.

[4] Bergman's own childhood home, which has partly been a model for the Ekdahl apartment, also inspired him in the stage design for his fourth (1986) production of *A Dream Play*. Cf. Bergman (1989), p. 37.

[5] Cf. the sun-lit woman sculpture in Act I of *The Ghost Sonata*.

[6] For the autobiographical background of this passage, see Bergman (1989), p. 21.

[7] The exterior of the house in fact bears a close resemblance to the so-called Red House in Stockholm, where Strindberg lived from 1901 to 1908. This house was pulled down some years ago, and a new apartment house, where Bergman chose to live for some time, was erected in its place.

[8] Frykman/Löfgren, pp. 105, 110.

[9] Koskinen (1983), p. 260.

[10] Bergman staged Franz Lehár's operetta with great success at the Malmö City Theater in 1954.

[11] Camilla Jordan Daasnes in *Vinduet*, No. 1, 1983.

[12] Bergman here deviates from authenticity. As we have seen, *A Dream Play* was al-

ready published in 1902 together with two other plays and was first produced in 1907. The play did not exist as a separate publication in May 1909, when the film ends.

[13] Vos, pp. 70, 72.

Strindberg, *Easter* (1952)

[1] Esslin, pp. 172, 177, 181.
[2] Lars Ring in *Svenska Dagbladet*, July 14, 1988.
[3] Lamm, 2, p. 205.
[4] Urban Stenström in *Svenska Dagbladet*, April 15, 1952.
[5] Ole Hessler in *Dagens Nyheter*, March 22, 1989.

A Matter of the Soul (1990)

[1] An English version was broadcast on BBC's Radio 3 in March 1990 with Anna Massey in the main part.
[2] The situation is strikingly similar to the dream sequence in Bergman's early film *Prison*, where Birgitta Carolina meets a girl in mourning – her alter ego – whose black-gloved hand offers Birgitta Carolina a radiant stone, "the most beautiful stone I've ever seen." Later when Birgitta Carolina has knifed herself and is about to die, this dreamy woman appears again, hands her the shining stone, and consolingly tells her: "Don't be afraid. Carry on. I shall stay with you all the time. It's me, your mother."
[3] The singular forms are literally the appropriate ones. For a long time, one of the world's outstanding directors has had to manage with one good eye and one good ear. See Bergman (1994b), p. 13.

Between Stage and Screen

[1] Bergman in Marker (1992), p. 17.
[2] Bergman (1975), pp. 129-30.
[3] Bergman in Marker (1992), p. 17.
[4] Mirrors abound in Bergman's stage and, particularly, in his screen productions. For a penetrating examination of the filmic mirrors, see Koskinen (1993), pp. 61-153.
[5] Cf. Sjögren (1968), pp. 255-6 and Marker (1992), pp. 201-2.
[6] Höök, p. 165.

[7] Bazin, p. 92.

[8] Blackwell (1981), p. 61.

[9] For a discussion of the film-aesthetic aspects of the play-within-the-film with regard to Bergman, see Koskinen (1993), pp. 155-262.

[10] Bergman in Marker (1992), p. 32.

[11] Sjögren (1969), p. 12.

[12] O'Reilly, p. 84.

[13] Bordwell, p. 208.

[14] An extensive semiotic analysis of the Copenhagen production of this play is found in Wiingaard.

[15] Marker (1992), p. 162.

[16] Livingston, pp. 23, 79-80.

[17] Siegfried Melchinger as quoted in Marker (1992), p. 200.

[18] See Szondi, pp. 28-9, 46-7.

[19] For the narratological significance of the term, see Chatman, p. 143.

[20] Brandell, p. 266.

[21] Marker (1992), pp. 233, 243.

[22] Lars Ring in *Svenska Dagbladet*, April 28, 1991.

[23] Cf. Long, p. 136.

[24] Koskinen (1983), p. 260.

[25] Interestingly, Alexander perfectly fits Bordwell's definition (p. 62) of the implied author, "the invisible puppeteer, not a speaker or visible presence but the omnipotent artistic figure behind the work."

[26] Bergman (1989), p. 33.

[27] Marker (1992), pp. 20-21.

Selected Bibliography

References to reviews are found only in the Notes.

Assayas, Olivier and Stig Björkman, "Conversation avec Ingmar Bergman," *Cahiers du cinéma*, No. 436, Oct. 1990

Bazin, André, *What is Cinema?*, Vol. 1, trans. Hugh Gray, Berkeley: University of California Press, 1967

Bergman, Ingmar, *Four Screenplays: Smiles of a Summer Night, The Seventh Seal, Wild Strawberries, The Magician*, trans. Lars Malmström and David Kushner, London and New York: Simon & Schuster, 1960

    Wood Painting, trans. Randolph Goodman and Leif Sjöberg, *Tulane Drama Review*, Vol. 6, Winter, 1961

    Persona and *Shame*, trans. Keith Bradfield, London and New York: Marion Boyars, 1972

    Bergman on Bergman, ed. by Stig Björkman, Torsten Manns and Jonas Sima, trans. Paul Britten Austin, New York: Simon & Schuster, 1973

    "Each Film is my Last" (1966) and "Ingmar Bergman: An Interview" (by Charles Thomas Samuels, 1972), reprinted in Stuart M. Kaminsky (ed.), *Ingmar Bergman: Essays in Criticism*, London-Oxford-New York: Oxford University Press, 1975

    Four Stories by Ingmar Bergman: The Touch, Cries and Whispers, The Hour of the Wolf, A Passion, trans. Alan Blair, London: Marion Boyars, 1976

    Autumn Sonata, trans. Alan Blair, New York: Pantheon, 1978

    Fanny and Alexander, trans. Alan Blair, New York: Pantheon, 1982

    The Magic Lantern: An Autobiography, trans. Joan Tate, Harmondsworth: Penguin, 1989

    A Matter of the Soul, trans. Eivor Martinus, in *New Swedish Plays*, ed. by Gunilla Anderman, Norwich: Norvik Press, 1992

    The Best Intentions, trans. Joan Tate, New York: Arcade, 1993

    Images: My Life in Film, trans. Marianne Ruuth, London: Bloomsbury, 1994a

    Femte akten, Stockholm: Norstedts, 1994b

Bergom-Larsson, Maria, *Ingmar Bergman och den borgerliga ideologin*, Stockholm: Norstedts, 1976

Billquist, Fritiof, *Ingmar Bergman – teatermannen och filmskaparen*, Stockholm: Natur och Kultur, 1960

Björkman, Stig, "Det oåtkomliga," *Chaplin*, Vol. 30, Nos. 2-3, 1988

Blackwell, Marilyn Johns, "The Chamber Plays and the Trilogy: A Revaluation of the Case of Strindberg and Bergman," in Marilyn Johns Blackwell (ed.), *Structures of Influence: A Comparative Approach to August Strindberg*, Chapel Hill: University of North Carolina Press, 1981

Persona: The Transcendent Image, Urbana, Ill. and Chicago: University of Illinois Press, 1986

Bordwell, David, *Narration in the Fiction Film*, London: Routledge, 1988

Bordwell, David and Kristin Thompson, *Film Art: An Introduction*, 4th ed., New York: McGraw-Hill, 1993

Brandell, Gunnar, *Strindberg in Inferno*, trans. Barry Jacobs, Cambridge, Mass.: Harvard University Press, 1974

Branigan, Edward, *Narrative Comprehension and Film*, London and New York: Routledge, 1992

Bryant-Bertail, Sara, "The Tower of Babel: Space and Movement in *The Ghost Sonata*," in Göran Stockenström (ed.), *Strindberg's Dramaturgy*, Minneapolis: University of Minnesota Press, 1988

Chatman, Seymour, *Coming to Terms: The Rhetoric of Narrative in Fiction and Film*, Ithaca and London: Cornell University Press, 1990

Cowie, Peter, *Sweden 2*, Screen Series, London: A. Zwemmer Ltd, and New York: A.S. Barnes & Co., 1970

Ingmar Bergman: A Critical Biography, London: Andre Deutsch, 1992

Donner, Jörn, *The Personal Vision of Ingmar Bergman*, Bloomington: Indiana University Press, 1972

Eldridge, Florence, "Reflections on *Long Day's Journey into Night*: First Curtain Call for Mary Tyrone," in Virginia Floyd (ed.), *O'Neill: A World View*, New York: Frederick Ungar, 1979

Esslin, Martin, *Mediations: Essays on Brecht, Beckett and the Media*, London: Methuen, 1980

Falck, August, *Fem år med Strindberg*, Stockholm: Wahlström & Widstrand, 1935

Frenz, Horst (ed.), *American Playwrights on Drama*, New York: Hill & Wang, 1965

Freud, Sigmund, *The Interpretation of Dreams*, trans. James Strachey, Harmondsworth: Penguin, 1991

Frykman, Jonas and Orvar Löfgren, *Den kultiverade människan*, Malmö: Liber, 1979

Gado, Frank, *The Passion of Ingmar Bergman*, Durham: Duke University Press, 1986

Gascoigne, Bamber, *World Theatre*, Boston and Toronto: Little Brown, 1968

Hanes Harvey, Anne-Charlotte, *Strindberg's Symbolic Room: Commanding Form for Set Design in Selected Strindberg Scripts, 1887-1907*, diss., University of Minnesota, 1984

Höök, Marianne, *Ingmar Bergman*, Stockholm: Wahlström & Widstrand, 1962

Johns, Marilyn E., "Journey into Autumn: *Oväder* and *Smultronstället*," *Scandinavian Studies*, Vol. 50, No. 3, 1978

Kawin, Bruce, *Mindscreen: Bergman, Godard, and First-Person Film*, Princeton, N.J.: Princeton University Press, 1978

Koskinen, Maaret, "Teatern som metafor: En analys av Bergmans *Fanny och Alexander*," *Chaplin*, Vol. 25, No. 6, 1983

"The Typically Swedish in Ingmar Bergman," *Chaplin*, 25th Anniversary Issue, 1984

Spel och speglingar: En studie i Ingmar Bergmans filmiska estetik, Stockholm: Department of Theatre and Cinema Arts, 1993

Krutch, Joseph Wood, Introduction to *Nine Plays by Eugene O'Neill*, New York, 1932

Lamm, Martin, *Strindbergs dramer*, Vol. 1-2, Stockholm: Bonniers, 1924-26

Livingston, Paisley, *Ingmar Bergman and the Rituals of Art*, Ithaca and London: Cornell University Press, 1982

Long, Robert Emmet, *Ingmar Bergman: Film and Stage*, New York: Abrahams, 1994

Lunin, *Strindbergs Dramen*, Emsdetten: Lechte, 1962

Marker, Lise-Lone and Frederick J., *Ingmar Bergman: A Project for the Theatre*, New York: Frederick Ungar, 1983

Ingmar Bergman: A Life in the Theater, Cambridge: Cambridge University Press, 1992

Marty, Joseph, *Ingmar Bergman: Une poétique du désir*, Paris: Les Éditions du Cerf, 1991

Mellen, Joan, "*Cries and Whispers*: Bergman and Women," in Stuart M. Kaminsky (ed.), *Ingmar Bergman: Essays in Criticism*, London-Oxford-New York: Oxford University Press, 1975

Mosley, Philip, *Ingmar Bergman: The Cinema as Mistress*, London and Boston: Marion Boyars, 1981

Northam, J.R., "Strindberg's Spook Sonata," in Carl Reinhold Smedmark (ed.), *Essays on Strindberg*, Stockholm: The Strindberg Society, 1966

Ollén, Gunnar, *Strindberg i TV*, Stockholm: Sveriges Radio, 1971

Olsson, Tom J.A., *O'Neill och Dramaten*, Stockholm: Akademilitteratur, 1977

O'Reilly, Willem Thomas, *Ingmar Bergman's Theatre Direction, 1952-1974*, diss., University of California, 1980

Petrič, Vlada (ed.), *Film and Dreams: An Approach to Ingmar Bergman*, South Salem, N. Y.: Redgrave, 1981

Rokem, Freddie, *Theatrical Space in Ibsen, Chekhov and Strindberg: Public Forms of Privacy*, Ann Arbor, Mich.: Umi Research Press, 1986

Sarris, Andrew, "*The Seventh Seal*," in Birgitta Steene (ed.), *Focus on The Seventh Seal*, Englewoord Cliffs, N.J.: Prentice-Hall, 1972

Shakespeare, William, *Kung Lear*, trans. Britt Hallqvist, Stockholm: Dramaten, 1984

The Winter's Tale, The Arden Shakespeare, ed. by J.H.P. Pafford, London and New York: Routledge, 1993a

En vintersaga, trans. Britt G. Hallqvist and Claes Schaar, Stockholm: Ordfront, 1993b

Simons, John, *Ingmar Bergman Directs*, New York: Harcourt Brace, 1972

Sjögren, Henrik, *Ingmar Bergman på teatern*, Stockholm: Almqvist & Wiksell, 1968

Regi: Ingmar Bergman: Dagbok från Dramaten 1969, Stockholm: Gebers, 1969

Sjöman, Vilgot, *L 136: Diary with Ingmar Bergman*, trans. Alan Blair, Ann Arbor, Mich.: Karoma, 1978

Sontag, Susan, "*Persona*: The Film in Depth," in Stuart M. Kaminsky (ed.), *Ingmar Bergman: Essays in Criticism*, London-Oxford-New York: Oxford University Press, 1975

Sprinchorn, Evert, "Julie's End," in Carl Reinhold Smedmark (ed.), *Essays on Strindberg*, Stockholm: The Strindberg Society, 1966

Steene, Birgitta, *Ingmar Bergman*, Boston: Twayne, 1968

(ed.) *Focus on The Seventh Seal*, Englewood Cliffs, N.J.: Prentice-Hall, 1972

"*Det sjunde inseglet*: Filmen som ångestens och nådens metafor," *Svensk filmografi*, Vol. 5, Stockholm: Svenska Filminstitutet, 1983

Ingmar Bergman: A Guide to References and Resources, Boston: G.K. Hall & Co., 1987

Strindberg, August, *Open Letters to the Intimate Theater*, trans. and introd. Walter Johnson, Seattle and London: University of Washington Press, 1959

A Dream Play, adapted by Ingmar Bergman, introd. and trans. Michael Meyer, London: Secker & Warburg, 1973

Szondi, Peter, *Theory of the Modern Drama*, trans. Michael Hays, Cambridge: Polity Press, 1987

Törnqvist, Egil, *A Drama of Souls: Studies in O'Neill's Super-naturalistic Technique*, New Haven and London: Yale University Press, 1969

"Ingmar Bergman Directs Strindberg's *Ghost Sonata*," *Theatre Quarterly*, Vol. 3, No. 11, July-Sept. 1973a

Bergman och Strindberg: Spöksonaten – *drama och iscensättning, Dramaten 1973*, Stockholm: Prisma, 1973b

Strindbergian Drama: Themes and Structure, Stockholm: Almqvist and Wiksell, Int., and Atlantic Highlands, N.J.: Humanities Press, 1982

"Staging *A Dream Play*," in Göran Stockenström (ed.), *Strindberg's Dramaturgy*, Minneapolis: University of Minnesota Press, 1988

Transposing Drama: Studies in Representation, London: Macmillan, 1991

Ibsen: A Doll's House, Cambridge: Cambridge University Press, 1995

Törnqvist, Egil and Barry Jacobs, *Strindberg's* Miss Julie: *A Play and its Transpositions*, Norwich: Norvik Press, 1988

Vos, Marik, *Dräkterna i dramat: Mitt år med* Fanny och Alexander, Stockholm: Norstedts, 1984

Wingaard, Jytte, *Teatersemiologi*, Copenhagen: Berlingske, 1976

Wood, Robin, *Ingmar Bergman*, London: Studio Vista, 1969

Young, Vernon, *Cinema Borealis: Ingmar Bergman and the Swedish Ethos*, New York: David Lewis, 1971

Zern, Leif, *Se Bergman*, Stockholm: Norstedts, 1993

Åhlander, Lars (ed.), *Svensk filmografi*, Vols. 4-7, Stockholm: Svenska Filminstitutet, 1980-88

Note: Extensive filmographies are found in Bergman (1973 and 1994a), Cowie (1992), Gado, Livingston, Marty, Steene (1987) and Åhlander. Lists of Bergman's theater productions are found in Cowie (1992), Höök, Marker (1992) and Sjögren (1968).

List of Illustrations

Index

light, 20, 25, 202
   atmospheric, 35-6, 62
   bright, 36, 45, 62, 77, 179
   'celestial', 45, 126
   cold, 36
   cosmic, 144
   diegetic, 131, 135
   dim, 36
   functional, 35-6
   realistic, 35-6
   silhouette, 99, 102, 110, 122-3
   soft, 45
   spotlight, 28
   symbolic, 35-6, 85, 170
   warm, 36
   weather conditions, 14, 61, 99, 151
location, *see* setting
Losey, Joseph, 203

Maeterlinck, Maurice
   Intérieur, 135
Mahler, Gustav, 60
make-up, 51
   hair, 38, 46, 88
March, Fredric, 67
Martinson, Harry
   Aniara, 96
medium
   audiovisual, 18
   Biblia pauperum, 95-6
   'film' on stage, 60, 201-3
   international, 12
   national, 12, 19
   opera, 11
   realistic, 201
   textual, 18, 20
   'theater' on screen, 204-7
   unspecifified, 18
mimicry, 64
Molander, Olof, 16-17, 27, 130, 210
Molière (pseud. for Jean Baptiste Poque-
   lin), 14
   Don Juan, 13, 203

The Misanthrope (Le Misanthrope), 13
motif, *see* theme
movement
   dance, 99, 110
   freezing of, 25, 27, 88, 140, 203
Mozart, Wolfgang Amadeus, 206
   see also Schikaneder, Emanuel
Munch, Edvard
   Jealousy (Sjalusi), 119
   Scream (Skrik), 104
music, 102, 122, 191, 205
   Almqvist, Carl Jonas Love
      "The Flower of the Heart" (Hjär-
         tats blomma), 90
      Songes, 83, 85
   Bach, Johann Sebastian
      Suite for cello, No. 5, C minor, 151
   barrel organ, 25
   chamber, 16, 17, 160
   Chopin, Frédéric
      Funeral March, C minor, op. 72/2,
         27
      Mazurka, A minor, op. 17, No. 4,
         148, 159
      Prelude, No. 2, A minor, 164
   coda, 16
   diegetic, 122
   Dies irae, 99
   harp, 44-5, 111, 126
   Haydn, Joseph
      *The Seven Last Words of Our
         Saviour on the Cross (Die
         sieben Worte des Erlösers am
         Kreuze)*, 191
   Händel, Georg Friedrich
      Sonata, F major, op. 1, 160
   Lehár, Franz
      *The Merry Widow (Die lustige
         Witwe)*, 182
   "The Maiden's Prayer" (Jungfruns
      bön), 73, 197
   music-box, 71
   non-diegetic, 122, 134

40-41, 43, 48-50, 55, 57-8, 74, 86-7, 90-2, 104, 107, 133, 168-70, 172
translation, 17, 69, 81-2, 101
  defective, 19, 110
  deletion in, 124
  dubbing, 19
  simultaneous, 12
Tudor, Antony, 88

Vane, Sutton
  Outward Bound, 11
verisimilitude, 66, 70, 71, 75, 79, 87, 88

Vos, Marik, 42

Wallin, Johan Olof
  "Where is the Friend for whom I'm ever yearning" (Var är den Vän som överallt jag söker), 127
Welles, Orson, 204
Williams, Tennessee
  The Rose Tattoo, 17

Zern, Leif, 27